WE'MOON '03

© Holli Zollinger 2001

Mother Earth

GAIA RHYTHMS FOR WOMYN
GREAT MOTHER

We dedicate WE'MOON '03 TO the healing of Earth and all beings.

published by
Mother Tongue Ink

WE'MOON '03: GAIA RHYTHMS FOR WOMYN AND WE'MOON '03 UNBOUND
© Mother Tongue Ink 2002

P.O. Box 1395-A
Estacada, Oregon 97023 USA
Phone: 503-630-7848 Fax: 503-630-7048
toll free: 877-O WEMOON (877-693-6666)
E-mail: matrix@wemoon.ws
URL: http://www.wemoon.ws

We'Moon Crone Editor/Consultant: musawa
Business/We'Moonager: Beth Freewomon, Sevrance Danforth
Production/Promotion: Meghan Garrity
E-Office (electronic data, e-mail, editing): Amy Schutzer
Co-Chiefs: Cherie Smythe, Eaglehawk, Grace Silvia, and Rachael Wilder
Matrix: All of the above
Creatrix/Editing Team: Beth, Bethroot Gwynn, Meghan, musawa

Mother
© *True 2001*

Front cover art: *Mother of Life* © Frankie Hansbearry 2001
Back cover art: *Mountain Weaving* © Durga Bernhard 2000
(See "Cover Notes" on page 7.)

Order direct from Mother Tongue Ink, Publisher and Distributor
(see page 194), or from our other fine wholesale distributors
USA: Baker & Taylor, Bookpeople, Ingram, Koen, Lady Slipper, New Leaf, Northern Sun, Small Changes, Vision Distributors and Vision Works. Canada: Dempsey (Vancouver). International: Airlift (London), Bookpeople (Oakland, CA). The German edition of **We'Moon '03** is distributed by Neue Erde and Labyrinth Verlag (Braunschweig).
Copyrights of individual works belong to each **We'Moon** contributor. Please honor the copyrights. Permission to reproduce any part of this book must be obtained from the contributors and/or Mother Tongue Ink, with certain exceptions. See page 197 for particulars.

Disclaimer: Mother Tongue Ink does not take responsibility for views expressed by artists or writers in their work in **We'Moon 03** or for the outcome of readers' uses of astrological and herbal information contained herein. Caution: use at your own risk, with common sense and/or expert advise from professionals you trust.

Astro-data and ephemerides reprinted with permission from Astro Communications Services, Inc., P.O. Box 34487, San Diego, CA 92163-4487.

We'Moon '03 is printed with soy-based ink on acid-free, 85% recycled paper (min. 30% post-consumer) that is ECF (elemental chlorine-free). Using this paper instead of non-recycled paper saves about 166 trees, 72,600 gallons of water, 618 pounds of air pollution effluents, 48,000 kwh of electricity and 86 cubic feet of landfill space.

As a moon calendar, this book is recyclable; every nineteen years the moon completes a metatonic cycle, returning to the same phase, sign and degree of the zodiac. If you still have **We'Moon '85** you can use it again this year (**We'Moon '03** will be reusable in 2022)!

ISBN: 1-890931-13-6 **We'Moon '03** (with lay flat binding)
ISBN: 1-890931-14-4 **We'Moon '03** (with spiral binding)
ISBN: 1-890931-15-2 **We'Moon '03 Unbound** (with no binding)   Printed and bound in USA.

TABLE OF CONTENTS

1. INTRODUCTION

11. MOON CALENDAR

111. APPENDIX

FEATURE WRITERS

We'Moon Cycles: musawa, Beth Freewomon; Astrologers: Gretchen Lawlor, Heather Roan Robbins, Mari Susan Selby, Sandra Pastorius, Susan Levitt, Demetra George; Herbs: Colette Gardiner; Holydays: Ginny Salkowski.

2003

JANUARY

S	M	T	W	T	F	S
			1	②	3	4
5	6	7	8	9	10	11
12	13	14	15	16	17	⑱
19	20	21	22	23	24	25
26	27	28	29	30	31	

FEBRUARY

S	M	T	W	T	F	S
						①
2	3	4	5	6	7	8
9	10	11	12	13	14	15
⑯	17	18	19	20	21	22
23	24	25	26	27	28	

MARCH

S	M	T	W	T	F	S
						1
②	3	4	5	6	7	8
9	10	11	12	13	14	15
16	17	⑱	19	20	21	22
23	24	25	26	27	28	29
30	31					

APRIL

S	M	T	W	T	F	S
		①	2	3	4	5
6	7	8	9	10	11	12
13	14	15	⑯	17	18	19
20	21	22	23	24	25	26
27	28	29	30			

MAY

S	M	T	W	T	F	S
				①	2	3
4	5	6	7	8	9	10
11	12	13	14	⑮	16	17
18	19	20	21	22	23	24
25	26	27	28	29	�30	31

JUNE

S	M	T	W	T	F	S
1	2	3	4	5	6	7
8	9	10	11	12	13	⑭
15	16	17	18	19	20	21
22	23	24	25	26	27	28
㉙	30					

JULY

S	M	T	W	T	F	S
		1	2	3	4	5
6	7	8	9	10	11	12
⑬	14	15	16	17	18	19
20	21	22	23	24	25	26
27	㉘	29	30	31		

AUGUST

S	M	T	W	T	F	S
					1	2
3	4	5	6	7	8	9
10	⑪	12	13	14	15	16
17	18	19	20	21	22	23
24	25	26	㉗	28	29	30
31						

SEPTEMBER

S	M	T	W	T	F	S
	1	2	3	4	5	6
7	8	9	⑩	11	12	13
14	15	16	17	18	19	20
21	22	23	24	25	26	㉗
28	29	30				

OCTOBER

S	M	T	W	T	F	S
			1	2	3	4
5	6	7	8	9	⑩	11
12	13	14	15	16	17	18
19	20	21	22	23	24	㉕
26	27	28	29	30	31	

NOVEMBER

S	M	T	W	T	F	S
						1
2	3	4	5	6	7	⑧
9	10	11	12	13	14	15
16	17	18	19	20	21	22
㉓	24	25	26	27	28	29
30						

DECEMBER

S	M	T	W	T	F	S
	1	2	3	4	5	6
7	⑧	9	10	11	12	13
14	15	16	17	18	19	20
21	22	㉓	24	25	26	27
28	29	30	31			

● = NEW MOON, PST

¤ *Charlotte Tall Mountain 2001*

○ = FULL MOON, PST

COVER NOTES

Front Cover Art: *Mother of Life* © **Frankie Hansbearry 2001**
In *Mother of Life*, the woman figure is clothed in plant and animal forms. The tree is firmly rooted in her strong shoulders. Our animal and plant teachers are a part of her being and the vast, moving sky reflects the laws of change inherent in the vitality of our planet. Nature, personified as a life-giving and life-taking force, is the source of my creative inspiration and spiritual reflection.

Back Cover Art: *Mountain Weaving* © **Durga Bernhard 2000**
More than anything, the interweaving of the elements in the living tapestry of nature is the ultimate manifestation of the divine feminine. Human and animal, earth and sky, growth and decay, large and small, living and dying forms of nature intertwine in harmonies that are both simple and intricate. This painting represents the human desire to entwine with these forces, to be both at the center of the web and to "disappear" into it.

WHAT'S NEW THIS YEAR

We'Moon '03 contains some changes from past years:
• The last remnant of **We'Moon's** multilingual heritage is the international signs, symbols and languages on the weekly calendar pages. This year, we are using a new combination of languages for the days of the week: Spanish, Dutch, Quechua and German. See page 12 for more info and page 33 for a Quechuan/Incan look at the seasons through the wheel of the year.
• You will find Colette Gardiner's herbal feature, "Great Mother's Healing Herbs," on pages 30-31, instead of interspersed throughout the book.
• The Month at a Glance calendar now starts on Sunday instead of Monday (Moonday) as in past **We'Moons.** See pp. 216–227.
• We have resurrected our "**We'Moon** Ancestor" page—honoring those who have crossed over. See page 197.
• The Address/Note page section has been shortened from sixteen pages to ten pages, starting on page 228.
• We have expanded the one page "Planetary Dance" article into three pages: "Astro Trends for 2003," co-authored by **We'Moon** astrologers, Gretchen Lawlor and Heather Roan Robbins.
•"World Time Zones" and "Signs and Symbols" are now on the last 2 pages of **We'Moon** for easy reference.

Lunar Mother at Boscawen'un Stones

© Monica Sjöö 2001

WHAT IS *WE'MOON*? A HANDBOOK IN NATURAL CYCLES

We'Moon: Gaia Rhythms for Womyn is more than an appointment book, it's a way of life! **We'Moon** is a lunar calendar, a handbook in natural rhythm and comes out of international womyn's culture. Art and writing by we'moon from many lands give a glimpse of the great diversity and uniqueness of a world we create in our own image. **We'Moon** is about *womyn's spirituality* (spirit reality). We share how we live our truth, what inspires us, how we envision our reality in connection with the whole earth and all our relations.

We'moon **means "women."** Instead of defining ourselves in relation to men (as in *wo*man or *fe*male), we use the word *we'moon* to define ourselves by our primary relation to the natural sources of cosmic flow. Other terms we'moon use are *womyn, wimmin, womon, womb-one*. **We'Moon** is a moon calendar for we'moon. As we'moon, we seek to be whole in ourselves, rather than dividing ourselves in half and hoping that some "other half" will complete the picture. We see the whole range of life's potential embodied and expressed by we'moon and do not divide the universe into sex-role stereotypes according to a heterosexual model. **We'Moon** is sacred space in which to explore and celebrate the diversity of she-ness on earth. The calendar is we'moon's space.

We'moon **means "we of the moon."** The moon, whose cycles run in our blood, is the original womyn's calendar. Like the moon, we'moon circle the earth. We are drawn to one another. We come in different shapes, colors and sizes. We are continually transforming. With all our different hues and points of view, we are one.

We'moon culture exists in the diversity and the oneness of our experience as we'moon. *We honor both.* We come from many different ways of life. At the same time, as we'moon, we share a common mother root. We are glad when we'moon from varied backgrounds contribute art and writing. When material is borrowed from cultures other than our own, we ask that it be acknowledged and something given in return. Being conscious of our sources keeps us from engaging in the divisiveness of either *cultural appropriation* (taking what belongs to others) or *cultural fascism* (controlling creative expression). We invite every we'moon to share how the "Mother Tongue" speaks to her, with respect for both cultural integrity and individual freedom.

Gaia Rhythms: 'Gaia' is the ancient Greek goddess of Earth. We show the natural cycles of the moon, sun, planets and stars as they relate to earth. By recording our own activities side by side with those of other heavenly bodies, we may notice what connection, if any, there is for us. The earth revolves around her axis in one day; the moon orbits around the earth in one month ($29^1/_2$ days); the earth orbits around the sun in one year. We experience each of these cycles in the alternating rhythms of day and night, waxing and waning, summer and winter. The earth/moon/sun are our inner circle of kin in the universe. We know where we are in relation to them at all times by the dance of light and shadow as they circle around one another.

The Eyes of Heaven: As seen from earth, the moon and the sun are equal in size: "the left and right eye of heaven," according to Hindu (Eastern) astrology. Unlike the solar-dominated calendars of Christian (Western) patriarchy, the **We'Moon** looks at our experience through both eyes at once. The **lunar eye** of heaven is seen each day in the phases of the moon as she is both reflector and shadow, traveling her $29^1/_2$-day path through the zodiac. The **solar eye** of heaven is apparent at the turning points in the sun's cycle. The year begins with Winter Solstice (in the Northern Hemisphere), the dark renewal time, and journeys through many

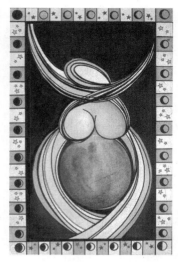

Birthing Gaia
© *Kate Gardner 2001*

seasons and balance points (solstices, equinoxes and the cross-quarter days in between). The **third eye** of heaven may be seen in the stars. Astrology measures the cycles by relating the sun, moon and all other planets in our universe through the star signs (the zodiac), helping us to tell time in the larger cycles of the universe.

Measuring Time and Space: Imagine a clock with many hands. The earth is the center from which we view our universe. The sun, moon and planets are like the hands of the clock. Each one has its own rate of movement through the cycle. The ecliptic, a band of sky around the earth within which all planets have their orbits, is the outer band of the clock where the numbers are. Stars along the ecliptic are grouped into constellations forming the signs of the zodiac—the twelve star signs are like the twelve numbers of the clock. They mark the movements of the planets through the 360° circle of the sky, the clock of time and space.

Whole Earth Perspective: It is important to note that all natural cycles have a mirror image from a whole earth perspective—seasons occur at opposite times in the Northern and Southern Hemispheres and day and night occur at opposite times on opposite sides of the earth as well. Even the moon plays this game—a waxing crescent moon in Australia faces right (e.g., ☾), while in North America it faces left (e.g., ☽). **We'Moon** has a northern hemisphere perspective regarding times, holy days, seasons and lunar phases. See page 33 for a southern hemispere perspective on the seasons.

Whole Sky Perspective: It is also important to note that all over the earth, in varied cultures and times, the dome of the sky has been interacted with in countless ways. The zodiac we speak of is just one of many ways that hu-moons have pictured and related to the stars. In this calendar, we use the tropical zodiac.

⌂ *musawa 1999*

How to Use This Book
Useful Information about the *We'Moon*

Time Zones: All aspects are in Pacific Standard/Daylight Time, with the adjustment for GMT and EDT given at the bottom of each page. To calculate for other areas, see "World Time Zones" (p. 238).

Signs and Symbols at a Glance is an easily accessible handy guide that gives brief definitions for commonly used astrological symbols (p. 239).

Pages are numbered throughout the calendar to facilitate cross referencing. See Table of Contents (p. 5) and Contributor Bylines and Index (pp. 197–206). The names of the days of the week and months are in English with additional foreign language translations included (Spanish, Dutch, Quechua and German).

Moon Pages mark the beginning of each moon cycle with a two-page spread near the new moon. Each Moon page is numbered with Roman numerals (ie., **Moon III**) and contains the dates of that Moon's new and full moon and solar ingress.

Year at a Glance Calendar is on p 6. **Month at a Glance Calendar** can be found on pp. 216–227 and includes daily lunar phases.

Annual Predictions: For your astrological portrait for 2003, turn to Gretchen Lawlor's prediction for your sun sign. See "Astrological Predictions 2003" (p. 23).

Holydays: There is a two-page holy day spread for all 2003 equinoxes, solstices and cross quarter days. These include feature writings by Ginny Salkowski, with descriptive art and writing.

Planetary Ephemeris: Exact planetary positions for every day are given on pp. 210–215. These ephemerides show where each planet is in a zodiac sign at noon GMT, measured by degree in longitude.

Asteroid Ephemeris: Exact positions of asteroids for every ten days are given for sixteen asteroids in the zodiac at midnight GMT on p. 209. See "Asteroids" (p. 207) for more information.

Astrology Basics

Planets: Planets are like chakras in our solar system, allowing for different frequencies or types of energies to be expressed.

Signs: The twelve signs of the zodiac are a mandala in the sky, marking off 30° segments in the 360° circle around the earth. Signs show major shifts in planetary energy through the cycles.

Glyphs: Glyphs are the symbols used to represent planets and signs. (see 239 for Signs and Symbols at a Glance)

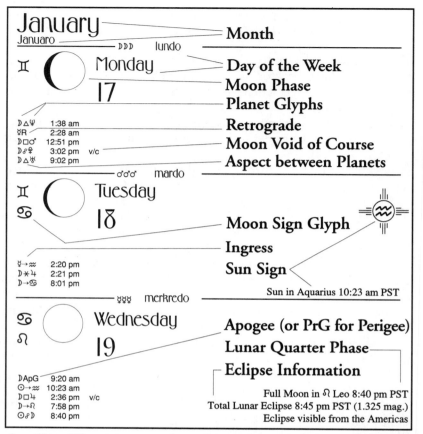

January

Januaro))) lundo

♊ Monday — Month

Day of the Week

Moon Phase

17 — Planet Glyphs

☽△♆   1:38 am — Retrograde
☿R   2:28 am
☽□♂ 12:51 pm — Moon Void of Course
☽☍♀   3:02 pm v/c
☽△♅   9:02 pm — Aspect between Planets

♂♂♂ mardo

♊ Tuesday
♋

18 — Moon Sign Glyph

Ingress

☿→♒ 2:20 pm — Sun Sign
☽✳♃ 2:21 pm
☽→♋ 8:01 pm

Sun in Aquarius 10:23 am PST

☿☿☿ merkredo

♋ Wednesday
♌

19 — Apogee (or PrG for Perigee)

Lunar Quarter Phase

Eclipse Information

☽ApG 9:20 am
☉→♒ 10:23 am
☽□♃ 2:36 pm v/c
☽→♌ 7:58 pm
☉☍☽ 8:40 pm

Full Moon in ♌ Leo 8:40 pm PST
Total Lunar Eclipse 8:45 pm PST (1.325 mag.)
Eclipse visible from the Americas

Sun Sign: The sun enters a new sign once a month (around the 20th or so), completing the whole cycle of the zodiac in one year. The sun sign reflects qualities of your outward shining self. For a description of sign qualities see "Sun Signs" (pp. 14–16).

Moon Sign: The moon changes signs approximately every $2^1/_2$ days, going through all twelve signs of the zodiac every $29^1/_2$ days (the sidereal month). The moon sign reflects qualities of your core inner self. For descriptions see "Moon Signs and Transits" (pp. 17–19).

Moon Phase: Each calendar day is marked with a graphic representation of the phase that the moon is in. Although the moon is not usually visible in the sky during the new or dark moon, we represent her using miniscule crescent moon graphics for the days immediately before and after the *actual* new moon or conjunction. For more information about the moon, see related articles on pp. 21–22.

Lunar Quarter Phase: At the four quarter points of the lunar cycle (new, waxing half, full and waning half) we indicate the phase, sign and exact time for each. These points mark off the "lunar week."

Day of the Week: Each day is associated with a planet whose symbol appears in the line above it (e.g., DDD is for Moon/Monday: lunes, maandag, Montag, Killachaw). The names of the days of the week are displayed prominently in English with translations appearing in the line above them. Four languages (Spanish, Dutch, Quechua and German) rotate weekly in this order throughout the calendar.

Eclipse: The time of greatest eclipse is given, which is not the exact time of the conjunction or opposition. Locations from where eclipses are visible are also given. For lunar and partial solar eclipses, magnitude is given in decimal form (e.g., 0.881 mag.), denoting the fraction of the moon's diameter obscured by the shadow of Earth. For total and annular solar eclipses, the duration of the eclipse in minutes and seconds is given. For more information see "Eclipses" (p. 28).

Aspects ($\square \triangle \mathcal{S} \sigma \times \wedge$): These show the angle of relation between different planets. An aspect is like an astrological weather forecast for the day, indicating which energies are working together easily and which combinations are more challenging. See "Signs and Symbols at a Glance" (p. 239) for a brief explanation of each kind.

Ingresses ($\rightarrow$): Indicate planets moving into new signs.

Moon Void of Course (D v/c): The moon is said to be void of course from the last significant lunar aspect in each sign until the moon enters a new sign. This is a good time to ground and center yourself.

Apogee (ApG): This is the point in the orbit of a planet or the Moon that is farthest from Earth. At this time the effects of transits (when planets pass across the path of another planet) may be less noticeable immediately but may appear later on.

Perigee (PrG): This is the point in the orbit of a planet or the Moon that is nearest to Earth. Transits with the Moon or other planets when they are at perigee will be more intense.

Direct or Retrograde (D or R): These are times when a planet moves forward (D) or backward (R) through the signs of the zodiac (an optical illusion, as when a moving train passes a slower train which appears to be going backward). When a planet is in direct motion, planetary energies are more straightforward; in retrograde, planetary energies turn back in on themselves and are more involuted.

¤ *musawa and Beth Freewomon 2000*

SUN SIGNS

The sun pours out its energy through each sign's filter for one month a year. We feel its pulse in our daily life. The sun's sign influences our energy and colors our conscious world. Each of us holds our sun sign's medicine for the world.

♈ **Aries** (March 20–April 19): While the sun is in Aries we return to our Self, then reach for new beginnings. We have the courage to start over; in the process we may be headstrong and miss the subtleties. Decide what seeds to plant for this turn of the wheel.

Tree Mother
© *Margot Foxfire 1995*

An Aries embodies spring fire; she is erotic and independent, a primal rebel with revolutionary thought. She teaches us to stay centered and listen to our own calling.

♉ **Taurus** (April 19–May 20): The Taurus sun sprouts the seed. Our ideas and creations begin to become solid and durable. This is a time to celebrate your body and the body of the Mother as we garden, sing, touch, make love, strengthen.

The Taurus womon embodies the strength to be soft and the heartbeat of the earth Mother. She makes her beliefs tangible. Comfort is her ritual. The Taurus challenge is to keep the material a sacred vessel, not an end in itself.

♊ **Gemini** (May 20–June 21): While the sun traverses Gemini we learn the magic of communication as we cross-pollinate ideas and crops. Words weave connection. We search for inspiration.

Gemini eyes and nerves sing with electricity. She translates—

from one friend to another or from one culture to another. Gemini challenges are to keep heart and nerves connected and to see through a problem, not just change the subject.

♋ **Cancer** (June 21–July 22): While the sun swims through moon-ruled Cancer we learn the grounding magic of our home, our shell, our temple's hearth. To nourish body and soul we explore work with our chosen family, homeland and what makes us feel safe in the world.

Our moon womon is the guardian of the hearth, heart and culture. Their good minds and unusual memory all work as servant to the heart, their moods a source of wisdom. The Cancer challenge can be to let go, compost, explore.

♌ **Leo** (July 22–Aug. 22): Life is a circus while the sun is at home in Leo—celebrate the ripening of the fruits of your plants and your creativity, passion and plans.

Leo can make a celebration out of any situation—why live a boring life. We gather around her as we gather around a bonfire. In that golden glow, all comes alive. Her challenge is to listen deeply and call people together for good reason.

♍ **Virgo** (Aug. 22–Sept. 22): While the sun works its way through Virgo we bring in the harvest. It is time to sort our life, listen for new patterns and draw blueprints. Our thoughts turn inward and practical as we plan how to manifest the next stage of our dream.

Virgo harvests and sorts the wheat from the chaff. She is a healing force as long as she trains her vision to the harvest. Her challenge is to not get stuck on the chaff.

♎ **Libra** (Sept. 22–Oct. 23): While the sun dances through Libra, meditate on relatedness; bring your life and loves into balance. Infuse beauty into your world. It's time to explore the Libran principle—where there is justice, there is peace.

Libra looks for engagement with equals. She offers kind respect, a steady eye and wants to bring balance to our world and all our relations. Her challenge is to seek internal balance.

♏ **Scorpio** (Oct. 23–Nov. 21): While the sun burrows into Scorpio we prepare for winter's hibernation. It is time to bring our focus inward, concentrate on the mysteries and grow stronger as we face our fears.

A Scorpio is a deep well, a mystery and a detective. She knows nothing is simple. She is more interested in transformation than security. Sexuality is powerful magic to Scorpio. Her challenge is to balance her formidable focus with a broader horizon.

♐ **Sagittarius** (Nov. 21–Dec. 21): While the sun travels through Sagittarius it's time to give thanks for the harvest. Let your restlessness take you anywhere unexplored—new friends, unfamiliar ideas or foreign soil.

Sagittarians live in the big picture. "Don't fence me in" is their theme song. They can speak to anyone. The Sagittarian challenges can be patience with slower mortals and learning to trust connection rather than a geographic cure.

♑ **Capricorn** (Dec. 21–Jan. 20): With the sun in Capricorn, we are renewed by tradition and set our intentions for the year ahead. The Capricorn symbol is a sea-goat: she takes vision from the bottom of the oceanic dreamworld and walks it to the mountaintop.

Capricorns have backbone and help us see structure, form and practicality. She benefits from time alone, but without isolation. She needs goals she believes in—mountain goats aren't comfortable on flat land.

♒ **Aquarius** (Jan. 20–Feb. 18): While the sun moves through Aquarius we dance with our politics and dialogue with our culture. It is time to find like minds and build strange alliances.

The Aquarian understands community. She holds the circle open for us. Innovation is her magic. She can be hypersensitive to the rules—breaking some and unusually bound by others. Her challenge is to build intimacy with herself first and then others.

♓ **Pisces** (Feb.18–March 20): While the sun courses through Pisces we soak it all up, listen to our dreams and ask where compassion will summon our actions in the year ahead.

Pisces feel the web that interconnects all life. Her dreams can hold the vision for all of us and our potential. Pisces are compassionate, intuitive mystics. Her challenge is to build a sound container to hold her dreams and keep her sensitivities intact.

Moon Signs

The moon speaks directly to our spirit. It describes the daily pulse and the emotional matrix we walk through. As the moon changes sign every $2^1/_2$ days, the filters on our inner world change. Let the garden be a metaphor for any project you want to nourish. Our own moon sign indicates our personal, spiritual lineage and our emotional prime directive.

The **Moon in ♈ Aries** asks us to wake up and remember who we truly are, even if it bothers those we love or work for. Tempers, tears and passions run hot. It's a great time for digging new beds, moving boulders, weeding or pest removal, but put a hold on planting. The Moon in Aries womon searches for fire, fierce independence and her own voice. She may need to learn

She Who
Upholds the Stars
© *Nadine Butterfield 2001*

patience and cooperation. She appreciates our fire.

The **Moon in ♉ Taurus** asks us to discover what nurtures us and how to grow deeper roots. We can almost feel the mud oozing between our toes, awakening our senses and sensuality and growing our stubbornness. It is time to cultivate our material resources, our homes and our body. Plant anything you want to grow strong and fertile. The Moon in Taurus womon searches for stability and sensuality. She may need to learn mobility. She offers us comfort, beauty and solid presence.

The **Moon in ♊ Gemini** quickens our nervous system. Build a web of understanding—network, absorb new information. Speak to your plants, trim, but avoid planting. The Moon in Gemini womon wants to understand, she lives and breathes communication. She may need to learn to honor stillness and concentration. She translates for us, questions us.

With the **Moon in ♋ Cancer** our feelings take the lead. Cancer encourages the wisdom rising out of our oceanic unconscious through moods and feelings. Ground in the magic of our home as a temple. Ask what needs protecting and feeding. Plant, fertilize and water your garden. The Moon in Cancer woman searches for what nurtures her soul and the world's. She may need to learn to carry her security with her. She respects our deepest feelings, eases our past fears.

With the **Moon in ♌ Leo** we have the guts to be visible and bring culture to life. In your garden or life, arrange, glorify and weed the extraneous so your star can shine, but don't plant or fertilize. The Moon in Leo woman came here to dramatize and ritualize her world. She may need to learn to find the sacred in the mundane. She offers us celebration and fascination and honors our self-expression.

The **Moon in ♍ Virgo** asks us to consider what needs healing, what needs composting. It's time to study, learn, train, organize and turn our compassion into pragmatic action. Don't get stuck in your head. Weed, prune, amend your garden with nutrients and companion planting. Plant and care for medicinal herbs. The Moon in Virgo woman came here to diagnose and heal her soul and the world's. She needs to learn to celebrate the beauty in each of us. She offers us practical compassion and ancient wisdom.

Moon in ♎ Libra highlights the magic of the dance of inter-relatedness—friendly, romantic and searching for a way to connect. Libra asks us to treat those around us as equals and make sure our politics and art, our lovemaking and our networks integrate. Tend to the beauty of the garden, cultivate, but don't plant. The Moon in Libra woman came here to feel the beauty in cooperation. She may need to learn to hear her own voice under conflict. She offers us bone-deep kindness, mediation and justice.

With the **Moon in ♏ Scorpio**, dig deep. Scorpio weaves the visible and invisible worlds together. We see through and into the roots. Direct this energy away from obsession and towards creation. Sexuality can be potent, musky. Dig in your garden, plant roots, feed the soil and compost. The Moon in Scorpio woman came here to find herself in solitude first and then through transformative action with others. She may need to learn flexibility. She offers us a fearless guide to the inner worlds as she midwifes all transitions.

Moon in ♐ Sagittarius brings out our inner-Artemis; we need to roam, to explore in body and in soul. Our curiosity intensifies. Check out untraveled territory and connect with the organic world. Have a long talk with the animals in your garden. Work the soil but hold off on the planting. The Moon in Sagittarius womon came here to explore. She needs to learn to hold still and work through a challenge. She offers us radical acceptance.

Moon in ♑ Capricorn brings planning magic and takes your ideas, giving them form and hope. We can tap into the inner wisewoman—ask how form, ritual, organization or tradition can serve. Trim, prune, plant slow-growing seedlings and make sure you and your garden have enough water. The Moon in Capricorn womon came here to accomplish and understand compassionate leadership. She may need to learn to respect other rhythms and to love herself, not just what she does. She offers us constructive determination and practical support.

The **Moon in ♒ Aquarius** expands our circles and offers the magic of collaboration; spirit and politics weave together. We can get too farsighted now and need to stay aware of others' feelings. Let go of assumptions and find new, unusual allies. A time to gather plants, mulch, prune and talk to your garden. The Moon in Aquarius womon came here to understand group dynamics. She may need to learn to be comfortable with emotional intimacy. She offers us a global perspective and collaboration.

With the **Moon in ♓ Pisces** we feel the world with compassion, heightened senses and strong imagination. We need quiet time in the temple or back under our covers to deal with sensory overload. A time to vision, listen to inner voices, creative juices and touch each other with new awareness. Plant, transplant, water, fertilize. Moon in Pisces womon came here to feel everything; she may need to filter impressions and find her deep strength. She offers us insight, imagination, and subtle, compassionate medicine while encouraging our vision.

LUNAR RHYTHM

Everything that flows moves in rhythm with the moon. She rules the water element on earth. She pulls on the ocean's tides, the weather, female reproductive cycles, and the life fluids in plants, animals and people. She influences the underground currents in earth energy, the mood swings of mind, body, behavior and emotion. The moon is closer to the earth than any other heavenly body. The earth actually has two primary relationships in the universe: one with the moon who circles around her and one with the sun whom she circles around. Both are equal in her eyes. The phases of the moon reflect the dance of all three: the moon, the sun, and the earth, who together weave the web of light and dark into our lives. No wonder so much of our life on earth is intimately connected with the phases of the moon!

On the following two pages you will find articles about the moon and her cycles that correspond to the chart below.

¤ *musawa 2000*

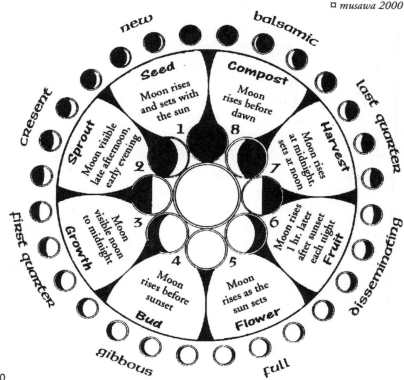

THE EIGHT LUNAR PHASES

As above, so below. Look into the sky and observe which phase the moon is in. Then you will know where you are in the growth cycle of each lunar month. The phase that the moon was in when you were born reflects your purpose, personality and preferences.

The **new moon** is like a SEED planted in the earth. We cannot see her but she is ready to grow, full of potential and energy for her new journey. We'moon born during the new moon are impulsive, passionate and intuitive. They are risk takers and pioneers.

The **crescent moon** is the SPROUT. The seed has broken through the earth and reaches up as she ventures from the dark, moist earth she has known. We'moon born during the crescent moon must break from the past to create their own destiny.

The **first quarter moon** is the GROWTH phase. Roots go deeper, stems shoots up and leaves form as she creates a new strong body. We'moon born during the first quarter moon live a full active life—old structures are cleared away providing room for new development.

The **gibbous moon** is the BUD of the plant, the pulse of life tightly wrapped, wanting to expand. For we'moon born during the gibbous moon, their talents lie in the ability to refine, organize and purify. They are seekers, utilizing spiritual tools as guides on their path.

She opens and blossoms during the **full moon** into the FLOWER, with the desire to share her beauty with others. We'moon born during the full moon enjoy companionship and partnership and desire to merge deeply. Fulfillment and illumination are their goals.

As we go into the darkening phase of the **disseminating moon,** we get the FRUIT of the plant's life cycle—the fruits of wisdom and experience. For we'moon born during the disseminating moon, life must have meaning, purpose. They enjoy sharing their ideas with others.

The **last quarter moon** is the HARVEST phase—the plant gives her life so that others may continue theirs. We'moon born during the last quarter have a powerful internal life of reflection, transformation. They can assume different roles while balancing their internal and external worlds.

The **balsamic moon** is the COMPOST phase, when the nutrients remain in the soil, providing nourishment for the next new seed. We'moon born during the balsamic moon possess the potential to be wise, insightful, understanding and patient. They are prophetic and unique.

¤ *Susan Levitt 2000*

WHERE'S THAT MOON?

Why is the moon sometimes visible during the day? And why does the moon sometimes rise very late at night? The answers lie in what phase the moon is in, which reflects the angle between the sun and moon as seen from Earth. For each of the eight moon phases, the angle between the sun and moon progresses in 45° increments. Each phase lasts approximately 3–4 days of the moon's entire $29^1/_2$ day cycle.

The **new moon** (or dark moon) rises at sunrise and sets at sunset. Astrologically, the sun and the moon are in *conjunction*. Because the sun's light overpowers the nearby moon in the day, and the moon is on the other side of the earth with the sun at night, she is not visible in the sky at all.

The **crescent moon** (or waxing crescent moon) rises midmorning and sets after sunset. She is the first visible sliver of moon seen in the western sky in the late afternoon and early evening.

The **first quarter moon** (or waxing half moon) rises around noon and sets around midnight. Astrologically, the moon is *square* to the sun. She is visible from the time she rises until she sets.

The **gibbous moon** rises midafternoon and sets before dawn. She is the bulging moon getting ready to be full, visible soon after she rises until she sets.

The **full moon** rises at sunset and sets at sunrise. Astrologically, the sun and moon are in *opposition* (ie., opposite each other in the sky and in opposite signs of the zodiac). She is visible all night long from moonrise to moonset.

The **disseminating moon** is the waning full moon getting visibly smaller. She rises midevening and sets midmorning. She is visible from the time she rises almost until she sets.

The **last quarter moon** (or waning half moon) rises around midnight and sets around noon. Astrologically, the moon is *square* to the sun. She is visible from the time she rises until she sets.

The **balsamic moon** (or waning crescent moon) rises before dawn and sets midafternoon. She is the last sliver of moon seen in the eastern sky in the dawn and in the very early morning.

¤ *Susan Levitt, musawa and Beth Freewomon 2000*

Planetary Movements in 2003

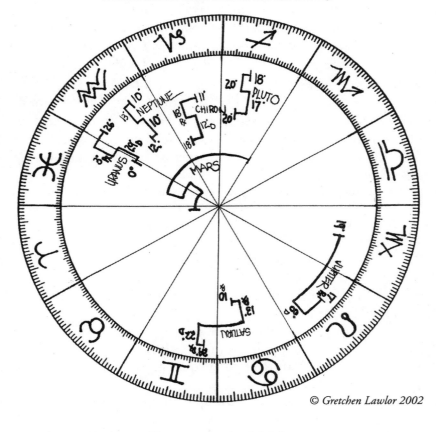

© Gretchen Lawlor 2002

Astrological Predictions 2003

If you know your sun sign, you can find your prediction for this year on the calendar page where the sun enters that sign (see column on right). See page 239 to translate the symbol of your sun sign.

Specific information may be gathered by reading predictions for both your sun sign as well as your rising sign—watch for repeated themes as well as any jangling dissonance. The predictions can provide an excellent navigational map for your own journey through the year.

© Gretchen Lawlor 2002

FLOWER ESSENCES FOR EACH SIGN: 2003

Flower essences* are extremely powerful healing tonics that can restore and rebuild one's energy when rent by emotional, psychic or even collective trauma. The accumulated stress of events put in motion since September 11, 2001 has caused widespread immune hypofunction and exhaustion. Star of Bethlehem is specific for depressed immunity. Combine it with the flower essence form of Echinacea (for energetic assault) and Yerba Santa (for constriction of chest, heart and lung areas) and your own Sun sign essence (see below) to make your own specific healing and empowering 2003 elixier.

*I use the original Bach and FES Essences as they are most broadly available.

♈ **Aries:** Mugwort to wake a slumbering gift for creative innovation.

♉ **Taurus:** California Poppy to go where your flashes of intuition have been leading you.

♊ **Gemini:** Cosmos to speak out your spiritual or political visions of the future.

♋ **Cancer:** Cayenne courage to make a big break from your past towards a new horizon or location.

♌ **Leo:** Bleeding Heart to celebrate diversity and independence in your personal relationships.

♍ **Virgo:** Water Violet to loosen up your approach to others and open to a more diverse social circle.

♎ **Libra:** Morning Glory to make sweeping reforms regarding your mind/body well being.

♏ **Scorpio:** California Wild Rose stimulates will to act in service to Mother Earth.

♐ **Sagittarius:** Hibiscus releases potential for deeper feelings and intimacy held back due to fear or doubt.

♑ **Capricorn:** Hound's Tongue to electrify the brain and shatter mental hangups.

♒ **Aquarius:** Manzanita supports the unearthing and using of lesser-known talents.

♓ **Pisces:** Purple Monkeyflower to become more intuitive about your inner needs.

© Gretchen Lawlor 2002

Uranus, lightning bolt change agent, dances back and forth between Aquarius and Pisces. It finally leaves Aquarius and commits itself to an 8 year journey through Pisces on the last day of 2003. Use Uranus' last electrifying moments in Aquarius (not to return for almost 90 years) to put yourself in settings with the companions who delight most in your wide awake genius self. Seeds of a hopeful future are being inserted under our skins; we become capsule/cocoons of meaningful change.

**Snake Bird
Spiral of Protection**
◻ *Linda Sweatt 2000*

Uranus and Saturn both shift into Water signs, literally and metaphorically breaking the drought (of water and compassion and creative vision) that we suffered in 2002. Uranus' early moments in Pisces are pure vision and spirit. Good dreamers will have dreams, perhaps on behalf of all of us, with glimpses of life in the next 90 years.

In February, expansive Jupiter accentuates the force of Neptune, the oceanic collective unconscious, diving us into the seas of our imaginations, beckons our muse, asks our culture to be more introspective for the next 8 years. Spring 2003 is a great time for gathering, brainstorming. Dive within for a new dream, then bring it back and ground it in action.

Watch for an explosion of fantasy and science fiction into film, music and art. Imagination and technology help us explore our infinitely possible futures or just allow us to escape into make-believe cyberlife for a while. The Internet invasion continues, stay involved and alert to guide the technology as a tool of new vision, nurturing the global village from the grassroots up.

Uranian experimentation shakes down and reorganizes established religion. Small groups of devoted individuals will explore ways of inviting the presence of Spirit without the intercession of clergy. House churches and spiritual companionships flourish as decentralized models of support. Compassionate activists interweave their work and so will groups with wildly diverse visions. This change in vision, the new dream, also has its dangers; our cultural perspective grows more subjective. We'll see new concern for the victims or the dispossessed (Neptunian characters) and notice our own sore places ripe for gentle healing. Watch out for an elevation of the victim-martyr role among ethnic groups, religious factions, relatives and old lovers . . . competing for most victim points and revering their martyrs.

The secret of healthy change through Neptune/Pisces times will be self-responsibility rather than martyrdom, for each of us personally and for our culture. Passivity and delusion are the shadow sides of Neptune and Pisces; we've got to weave our dreams together and be active participants in the new paradigms. The relentless stress of the past few years will take its toll on immune systems. Medicine will become much more eclectic, encompassing subtle body healing methods as it is observed that nothing works better for immune support and nervous exhaustion. An overripe collective psyche will burst open with new maps and signposts of our inner terrain (the last time Uranus entered Pisces, in the 1920s, Carl Jung began publishing his work on the unconscious). Indigenous awareness can lead the way through spiritual practice that incorporates trance and shamanic journey work. Science will take us there with new drugs, but may leave many stranded; we may see a heart-wrenching return to numbing drugs for those who have trouble stretching into the 21st century.

Neptune squares the asteroid Hygeia, symbolic of our mind-body connection, and our boundaries become more permeable, open. While this encourages new interest and ability in intuitive perception, we'll need to watch the boundaries we want and need in our families, in our bodies and in our politics. Be vigilant about water quality, toxins or genetically modified pollen spilling through biological filters.

Repercussions of the immensely challenging Saturn/Pluto opposition of 2001–2002 leave us with the devastated rubble of violently opposing factions slinging their shadows on each other. Personally and politically, the fields have been plowed under, old structures blown away, people left raw and broken open. Who or what is sacrificed in the hunger for power? "Terrorists" and "Anti-Terrorists" alike have to be dealt with—inside and out. How are you retrieving your own authority from those who are addicted to power and manipulation? The failure of popular media to provide the truth (Saturn in Gemini) forces us to step into our own voice of truth, to dispel deep despair (also Saturn in Gemini).

Saturn partners well with Uranus throughout 2003, providing pragmatic structures and good networking to strengthen the voices in local communities. What starts out with talking together will become listening and imagining together, as people use group attunement and prayer to dream up a better future. Saturn shifts into Cancer mid 2003. Practical considerations restrict emotional warmth and the urge to nurture self and others. Initially families may feel stressed, people hunker down in an austere, self-protective way. "Homeland security" as a shadow side of Saturn in Cancer may have us all feeling oppressed. Eventually Saturn in Cancer may actually strengthen family solidarity and draw out in each of us a strong sense of stewardship for the land in a very practical and immediate way. We need to work towards a collective vision of the homeland of Earth and bring out the Demeter in all of us.

© Gretchen Lawlor and Heather Roan Robbins 2002

ECLIPSES

Eclipses demonstrate deep processes of transformation. They crack open doors to our true selves. Eclipses remind us that we are indeed not in control of our lives and that our choices manifest in our response to external stimuli. We can either recognize our fantastic natures and grow like wild flowers, or react to our external world with fear of change. We can use the alignment of the sun, moon and earth as a great ally in our own process of deep transformation. Since ancient times, astrologers have used the eclipse as a means of prediction. To determine the effect of a specific eclipse, check your natal chart and find out in what house the eclipse falls. Each house governs a specific activity or area. The effects of an eclipse are felt whether it's visible or not.

A solar eclipse is a conjunction of the Sun and Moon (new moon) and can be either total, partial or annular (sun visible as a light ring around the moon). A lunar eclipse is an opposition of the Sun and Moon (full moon) and can be either total, partial or appulse (a darkening of the moon's surface). The dates for the 2003 eclipses are May 15, May 30, Nov. 8 and Nov. 23. See particular dates for eclipse types and places from which they are visible.   © *Mari Susan Selby 2002*

RETURN TO SOURCE: MERCURY RETROGRADE ☿R 2003

The cycle of the wing-footed messenger, Mercury, represents our mental and communicative life processes. This companion dancer to the sun (never traveling more than 28° away) inspires mobility and adaptability. Mercury retrogrades three or four times a year, each time in a sign of the same element. During this passage, lasting 20 to 28 days, our attention moves to unfinished business. Since all backward movement symbolizes a return to source, we can use these times to attend to our inner perceptions and reconnect with the spiritual source of our thoughts.

Immediately after the new year begins, Mercury retrogrades in Capricorn, Jan. 2 to 22 (PST), finding us reluctant to move forward. Make resolutions to slow down and tend to any glitches in your systems. When Mercury makes an about face from April 26 to May 20, use Taurus energy to ground yourself—to plant food and eat especially well. Mercury gets us to refocus priorities from Aug. 28 to Sept. 20, while in Virgo. Fall back on good clean habits and health checks. The year ends with Mercury retrograde again in Capricorn from Dec. 17 until Jan. 6, 2004. Are we back where we started from? Give pause, re-think material progress and re-dedicate bottom lines. Flourish in the Now.

© *Sandra Pastorius 2002*

THE YEAR OF THE SHEEP 2003

The year of the Sheep begins on the new moon of February 1, 2003. (Chinese New Year begins the second new moon after Winter Solstice.) Sheep year is a time of peace, calm and contentment. Life's hectic pace is slowed and people are more caring, sensitive and emotional. Family, close friends and intimacy are valued. All the arts flourish and creativity flows. But such refined beauty and elegance is expensive and debts may easily accrue. Sheep "eat paper"—can really spend.

Wemoon born in Sheep years (2003, 1991, 1979, 1967, 1955, 1943, 1931, 1919, 1907) are artistic, kind, inspired, very empathetic and creative. They appreciate beauty and are the connoisseurs of all life has to offer. They find success in artistic fields, especially the healing arts. With a tendency to be introverted, Sheep wemoon require solitary peaceful moments to replenish the soul. Sheep often struggle in youth, but in old age Sheep blossom.

In the wild, Sheep are able to tolerate severe weather conditions and scarcity of food and still survive. A Sheep gal can be strong and persevere when she must. Sheep are calm in appearance yet strong in determination. But they must not let their determination turn into stubbornness nor their independence into isolation.

Some translations refer to Sheep as ram or goat. This is misleading. Ram is a symbol of masculinity and Sheep is essentially feminine. Unlike Aries the Ram, Sheep has little of Aries' fiery combativeness. The translation *goat* evokes Capricorn the Goat. But Sheep rarely possess the drive and ambition to ascend to the mountaintop like Capricorn. In rare instances, Sheep is referred to as deer, due to Sheep's gentle nature. Sheep correlates to the Western sign Cancer.

¤ *Susan Levitt 2002*

Ginko Goddess
© Lisa Robinson 2001

GREAT MOTHER'S HEALING HERBS

To honor the great mother is to honor wholeness, for all things are part of her. On a physical level we can honor the Great Mother in us by connecting with the earth and her cycles and seeing our health as a continuum that we support throughout the year, rather than only when we are sick. Especially in these times, we need each and every one of us strong, active and healthy to support and fight for the kind of world we want to live in.

Winter: Now is the time to support our immunity by including a few extra **roots** in our diets. Roots are generally high in nutrients, they have deep effects and they are ruled by the earth element in many traditions. One of my favorites is Garlic—*Allium sativa*. Garlic is warming and it helps to fight many types of infections. It also prevents problems before they start. Garlic lowers cholesterol, possibly by facilitating liver breakdown of excess fats and cholesterol. It also slows absorption of excess sugar from the intestines and discourages digestive parasites. Eat daily to prevent illness and maintain health. Other roots for winter health include Astragulus, Dandelion, Burdock and Sunchokes.

Spring: Many cultures use spring tonics as cleansers. Supporting our eliminatory systems gives us a good start on the year. Spring is a good time to focus on the fresh **leaves** of medicinal plants. I associate leaves with the element of water. One of my favorites is Nettles—*Urtica dioica*. Often this is used as a kidney tonic to help us remove the body's fluid wastes. It mildly supports the liver and also helps prevent pollen allergies when taken regularly.

It contains large amounts of vitamins and minerals. Due to its high chlorophyll content it can help strengthen the blood as well. Harvest nettles with gloves to avoid getting stung. Cooking destroys their sting so use them in teas, soups, lasagnas as you would spinach. Be sure to harvest early in the year before they flower to avoid kidney irritation. You can also make tea from the dried herb that is available in stores. Other leaves to use at this time are Chickweed, Cleavers, Violets, Dandelion, Watercress and Miner's Lettuce.

Summer: Summer brings unique health challenges. We spend a lot of time outdoors, we are more physically active, and more of our skin is exposed to sun, wind and dirt. While our bodies aren't dealing with the cold of winter is also a good time to work on building immunity. Summer gives us a chance to include **flowers** in our lives. I associate flowers with the element of air, although some traditions associate them with fire. One summer flower is Calendula—*Calendula officinalis*. The petals can be used in salads. Teas and oils made from the flowers can be used on muscle and joints that are strained by summer activity. Calendula combined with St. Joan's/John's Wort is especially nice for this. Use a wash made from the tea of the flowers to help prevent infection in cuts or scrapes. Other summer flowers that can be used medicinally are Lavender, Chamomile, Roses, and Hollyhock.

Fall: Fall is the time of year when we get a chance to evaluate our health and do a little last minute prep work before winter's cold arrives. What body systems are weak and what steps do we need to take to support them? As a general strategy I like to focus on **seeds and fruits.** I like to add extra mushrooms to the diet at this time. Energetically, mushrooms can be considered a fruit or seed and I associate them with the element of fire. There are many types of mushrooms used to promote health. Reishis, Shitakes and Maitakes are probably the most common, however many edible mushrooms have deep immune building properties. They don't work immediately to fight infection, but they work slowly to build overall immunity at a bone deep level to balance health. Use them in soups or stews or simmer them slowly and drink as tea.

THE WHEEL OF THE YEAR: HOLY/HOLIDAYS

The seasonal cycle of the year is created by the tilt of the earth's axis, leaning toward or away from the sun, north to south, as the earth orbits the sun. Solstices are the extreme points all over the world (like new and full moon in the lunar cycle) when days and nights are longest or shortest. On equinoxes, days and nights are equal in all parts of the world (like the light of the half moon). The four cross-quarter days roughly mark the midpoints in between solstices and equinoxes. These natural turning points in the earth's annual cycle are the holidays we commemorate in We'Moon. We use the dates in the ancient Celtic calendar because it most closely approximates the eight spokes of the wheel of the year. As the wheel of this year turns, We'Moon features Ginny Salkowski's interpretation of the Celtic holydays (names and dates in bold as follows). To try to represent the holy/holidays of the world's cultures would fill our pages. Since the seasonal celebrations of most cultures cluster around these same natural turning points, with similar universal themes, we leave it up to you to fill in your own.

Dec. 21: Solstice/Winter: the dwindling and return of the light—Kwanzaa (African-American), Soyal (Hopi), Santa Lucia (Scandanavian), Cassave/Dreaming (Taino), Chanukah (Jewish).

Feb. 2: Imbolc/Mid-Winter: celebrations, prophecy, purification, initiation—Candlemas (Christian), New Years (Tibetan, Chinese, Iroquois), Ground Hog's Day (American), Tu Bi-Shevat (Jewish).

Mar. 19: Equinox/Spring: rebirth, fertility, eggs, resurrection—Passover (Jewish), Easter (Christian), Festivals of the Goddess: Eostare (German), Astarte (Semite), Persephone (Greek).

May 1: Beltane/Mid-Spring: blossoms, planting, fertility, sexuality—May Day (Euro-American), Root Festival (Yakima), Ching Ming (Chinese), Whitsuntide (Dutch).

June 20: Solstice/Summer: sun, fire festivals—Niman Kachina (Hopi), Sundance (Lakota), Goddess festivals: Isis (Egypt), Litha (N. Africa), Yellow Corn Mother (Taino), Ishtar (Babylonian).

Aug. 2: Lammas/Mid-Summer: first harvest, breaking bread, goddesses of abundance: Green Corn Ceremony (Creek), Corn Mother (Hopi), Amaterasu (Japan), Hatshepsut's Day (Egypt).

Sept. 22: Equinox/Fall: gather and store, ripeness, goddesses: Tari Pennu (Bengal), Old Woman Who Never Dies (Mandan), Chicomecoatl (Aztec), Black Bean Mother (Taino).

Oct. 31: Samhain/Mid-Fall: underworld journey, ancestor spirits, Hallowmas/Halloween/Festivals of the Dead around the world, Sukkoth (Jewish harvest/wine festival).

¤ *musawa and Nell Stone 2000*

Sources: *The Grandmother of Time* by Zsuzsanna E. Budapest, 1989; *Celestially Auspicious Occasions* by Donna Henes, 1996; and *Songs of Bleeding* by Spider, 1992

A Southern Hemisphere Look at the Seasons

As you turn the calendar pages through the wheel of this year, **We'Moon** seasonal Holydays are interpreted from a Northern Hemisphere perspective. Summer and Winter, Spring and Fall are at opposite times of the year than in the Southern Hemisphere. If you live in the Southern Hemisphere, you might want to transpose descriptions of the Holydays to match the seasons in your area. To give a whole earth perspective, we are including the seasons (*Killa*) in Quechua, the most common Amerindian language spoken by millions of people in the Andes. 75% of the people of Bolivia today identify as indigenous and 12 million people speak Quechua. We are also including Quechua as one of the four languages rotating through the calendar pages.

Summer

end December–January: *Qhapaquintiraymi killa*—festival of the hummingbird (time of many flowers) month—starts the first new moon after the December Solstice and lasts the whole period of the moon.

end January–February: *Qhapmiy killa*—season of the rain month

end February—March: *Jatunpuquy killa*—large production month

Fall

end April–May: *Pachapuquy killa*—harvest of the earth month

end May–mid June: *Ariwaki Killa*—festival of the moon month

Winter

mid June–mid July: *Aymuray killa*—festival of the sun month

mid July–early August: *Chakraqunakuy killa*—obtaining Earth month

early August–early September: *Chakrayapuy killa*—preparing the Earth month

Spring

early September–early October: *Tarpuy killa*—planting month

early October–November 1: *Pawqarwara killa*—season of green month

November 2–December 2: *Ayamarqay killa*—festival of the souls month

The Quechuan's Incan roots promote the worship of the Pachamama, the Earth Mother. Their lives are governed by her cycles. This is seen even in the Quechua names of the month. Killa means both month and moon . . . In the Southern Hemisphere, not only the seasons are opposite; the moon is inverted too! Just as the Quechua language and its spelling changes in different regions, so may the interpretation and significance.

© Katrina Klemens 2001

INTRODUCTION TO THE THEME: GREAT MOTHER

*INVOCATION: Great Mother, Divine Aspect of all Being, accept our offering: all the thoughts, feelings, stories, poems, and images in this **We'Moon**, all our reflections of you. Thank you for inspiring and empowering the creativity that flows through these pages. Thank you for being the ground and spirit of our experience and for allowing us to participate in your blessed creation here and now. Be with us as we move through the 13 Moons of this year! May we'moon open to the treasures, the lessons, the gift of your presence in everything that happens through the cycles to come. Bless those who touch and are touched by this **We'Moon**. Together, we cast a circle around the sacred space of this world. We open our hearts to receive your love and guidance. We raise our power, individually and collectively, to mater-realize your Spirit, our true Selves, in all we are and do. Help us to find the source of oneness greater than all that appears to oppose You in our lives. May your harmony and balance be restored to Earth-life. Blessed Be. Amamma*

"God was female for at least the first
200,000 years of human life on earth."

© *Monica Sjöö and Barbara Mor 1987,*
from The Great Cosmic Mother (see p. 43)

Whatever does it mean to speak of "God," in the first place? To imagine Divine Spirit is to reach beyond all form. She is ineffable—who can name Her? We can only *point* toward Source with all our God/Goddess language, our metaphors and symbols for that Power which creates, sustains, ends life. We know from archeological discoveries and feminist scholarship that the earliest peoples honored the image of God-the-Mother. No wonder: they were paying attention to observable experience. What a holy, astonishing power belongs to woman; that she can birth, and feed, another person from her body! The wonder is that patriarchal religions conceived the absurd, exclusive notion of male deity as Creator. **We'Moon** challenges the stranglehold of patriarchal symbology and brings forward spiritual expression infused with

Divine Female imagery. **We'Moon '03** is devoted to The Great Mother in Her myriad aspects, not as a female version of some remote God-Up-There, but as immanent in all existence, in the wholeness of life, death and rebirth.

While ancient peoples revered the Earth as the Great Mother Goddess, most of us have not grown up with this understanding. We have had to find our way back to Her. For us (Bethroot and musawa), politics and spirituality braided together in our individual paths to the Goddess. Bethroot had preacher-ancestors and was steeped in liberal theology through college and graduate school; musawa grew up in a non-religious family with humanitarian values, schooled in Spirit by Mother Nature. We both had our political coming out, and spiritual deepening, in the Civil Rights Movement of the sixties; our work continued in the Peace Movement, Women's Liberation, in lesbian community and eventually on women's lands. For over 30 years, we, and women all over the world, have been creating a new, living tradition of earth-based, Goddess-centered spiritual practice. We have dug into history, mythology, imagination, soul-depths, soil-depths—and have remembered/invented/celebrated reverential connection to Spirit whom we dare image as Female. We redress the balance of centuries in which spiritual language and practices, especially in Western cultures, have been His. Our very prayers to Her make revolution!

The same strands running through our personal herstories thread into the re-emergence of the Goddess in collective consciousness over the past fifty years. The spiritual is political, is personal . . . in the interweave of Great Mother's web. Earth scientists now call our planet Gaia (an ancient Greek goddess), recognizing what indigenous peoples have always known: She is a living, self-healing being who holds all life in Her balance. Archeological evidence dating back to the Neolithic period (circa 10,000 BCE) suggests that ancient societies were cooperative, egalitarian, non-violent, earth-centered. These survival values are as urgently relevant now, when Man's exploits endanger the natural balance, as they were in tribal times when Nature's harmony was intact. As we reconnect with the primordial reality of the most ancient Goddess whose body is the Earth, the pendulum swings back toward a world view that affirms the interdependent web of life. The Great Mother is at work in this monumental shift enacted by worldwide movements challenging the globalization of violence, dominance and greed. Holding all beings in Her embrace, She cycles and recycles even patriarchy; its universal antagonisms are the death throes of an unsustainable world order.

Pervasive as air, resourceful as earth, life-sustaining as water, transformative as fire, Great Mother is as subtle as a paradigm shift, and as earth-shaking. In the patriarchal equation, Woman and Nature, once held sacred, became the negative "other," the wild and instinctive shadow side of existence, to be controlled and exploited. She does get wild! Her stormy elemental extremes (hurricanes, earthquakes, floods, volcanoes) command occasional attention in a world transfixed by violence and bad news. Her devastation—the destruction of whole peoples, cultures, species, habitats—is the worst news of all. Her sacred power is not to be denied, however. The extent of Her dominion is obvious when attempts are made to replicate what Mother Nature did perfectly before human intervention. It takes enormous effort to restore ecological balance, to support the self-healing human body under siege, to eliminate artificially induced toxins. For Her, and for our survival, we must commit to fundamental recreation of planetary health. As cells of Her body, we mobilize in Her healing response. Great Mother's resilience is greater than the death-culture's violations. She is larger than life, larger than death.

We'Moon '03 is a prayer to The Great Mother: a book of praise and thanksgiving, filled with art and writing by we'moon sharing their devotions to Her through the 13 Moons. Take refuge in these pages; be inspired and comforted by the depth and joy of these offerings. The Great Mother is celebrated here as the Earth, Source of all life. She is the ancient rock of being, blessing Her creation through the ages, through the cycles of seasons and generations. We'moon encounter Her in Nature, loving Her with naked feet, immersing themselves in Her forests, meeting up with Her wild animal Self. They tell stories of Her healing powers and worship Her as Goddess-in-Body through sexuality, pregnancy, childbirth, creativity of all kinds. The Moon pages resonate with Love as the heartbeat of Great Mother. Sometimes Her gift is elusive, and we'moon struggle to feel connected to Goddess-presence. To embrace Her is to embrace contradictions and mysteries. She gives death as well as life. Gaia is invincible; She is also wounded. **We'Moon '03** cries out on behalf of this precious Earth, invoking the Great Mother's power to liberate the planet and all Her creatures from devastation.

By whatever name we call upon—*Goddess, Great Spirit, Higher Power*—let us be inspired to live our love and direct it toward the healing of Earth and all beings. Chant with us the names of the 13 Moons, with honor to Her vast expanse and, coming full circle, to Her depth in each of us:

© *musawa and Bethroot Gywnn 2002*

Gaia
© *Rosa Davis 2001*

SHE CREATES ALL
SHE IS AGELESS
SHE CHANGES
SHE HEALS
SHE LIBERATES
SHE EMBODIES
SHE CONNECTS
SHE GIVES BIRTH
SHE ABOUNDS
SHE NURTURES
SHE INSPIRES
SHE GIVES DEATH
SHE IS ALL LOVE
SHE IS YOU!!!

The Woman Whose Body Became the Earth: Mythology for Re-Creation

Once there was a woman whose body became the Earth.
Her cells changed, turning from human form
     to animal, vegetable, mineral.
A cool stream pebbled down her throat and her center
became a pool with floating water lilies.
Her spine became an old Cedar, her breasts grew into hillsides.
She took a breath and her lungs made grasses and grains.
The sun rose over the cave of her ribs and all the colors
of the desert mesa were etched along the horizon.
The woman squatted down and her womb poured forth a fertility
that swam and crawled and galloped and flew;
that chirped and squeaked, grunted and meowed and hissed.
And all this life made its way through the terrain of her flesh
until she was very full.

Once there was a woman whose body became the Earth—
and became it, and became it and became it—
until the woman was no longer Woman.
All thought stopped.
The trees breathed. The mountains trembled.
The tides rose and fell under the eye of the Moon.
And the Earth rolled round and round in the satin black sky.
No time passed. What was, Was.
The striving, dreaming, scheming, willful, wonderful, conflicted,
clear consciousness of human mind slept deep *within her*
(within her) and the Earth rested.
Breathing. The Earth rested.
Stretching. The Earth rested.
And more no time passed.
And the Woman whose body had become the Earth,
who held all creatures inside herself, and all the wild places
from pole to pole, rested, too.

excerpt © Christina Baldwin 2001

0. SHE CREATES ALL

Moon 0: December 19–January 2
Full Moon in ♊ Gemini: Dec. 19; Sun in ♑ Capricorn: Dec. 21

Creation
© *Jennifer Lynn Shifflet 1991*

December '02

diciembre ──── ⅅⅅⅅ lunes ────

♉ ## Monday
16

☽□♃	5:40 am	
♄△♅	1:36 pm	
☽□♅	9:11 pm	v/c

Mother and
Spirit Children
¤ *Cathryn Tinker 2001*

──── ♂♂♂ martes ────

♉
♊ ## Tuesday
17

☽→♊	5:43 am
♄PrG	5:46 am
☉♂♄	9:28 am
☉⚹♅	11:50 am
☽△♆	11:34 pm

──── ☿☿☿ miércoles ────

♊ ## Wednesday
18

♃△♀	5:40 am
☽⚹♃	4:14 pm
☽☍♀	4:18 pm

──── ♃♃♃ jueves ────

♊
♋ ## Thursday
19

☽♂♄	6:53 am	
☽△♅	7:30 am	
☉☍☽	11:10 am	v/c
☽→♋	3:30 pm	

──── ♀♀♀ viernes ────   Full Moon in ♊ Gemini 11:10 am PST

♋ ## Friday
20

☿⚺♃	1:58 pm
☽△♂	2:43 pm
☽△♀	5:46 pm

ALL ASPECTS IN PACIFIC STANDARD TIME; ADD 3 HOURS FOR EST; ADD 8 HOURS FOR GMT

Prayer Of Thanksgiving

Oh, Great Goddess, Creatress of all things,
     hear your children's prayer of thanks
     for this our Mother Earth,
Who with seed of star power
     has given us volcano, wind and cloud,
     spider, tiger, human child,
     golden grasses—grain to feed our bodies.
Oh, Great and Loving Earth-Mother,
     your gifts nourish us
     and give us strength.
We find you more beautiful in
     every sunrise.
You, whose rich, dark soil
     has given us birth,
Whose ample arms hold us in warm embrace
     wide as the summer sky,
     deep as thunder's song.
May we be worthy. May all your children, in
     all forms and in all places be richly
     blessed and may
We know our place in the Great Harmony.

excerpt © Saya Wolf 1995

♋
♌
     ♄♄♄   sábado

Saturday
21

☽☌♅   1:31 am   v/c
☉→♑   5:14 pm
☽→♌   10:48 pm

Solstice

Sun in Capricorn 5:14 pm PST

○○○   domingo

♌

Sunday
22

☽☌♆   3:27 pm
☽□♂   11:51 pm

December

december

♌

))) maandag

Monday
23

☽□♀	3:34 am	
☽☌♃	6:07 am	
☽△♀	6:56 am	
☽✶♄	7:27 pm	
☽☍♅	8:58 pm	v/c

♂♂♂ dinsdag

Tuesday
24

♌
♍

☽→♍	4:05 am	
☉△☽	8:48 am	
♀□♃	5:26 pm	

☿☿☿ woensdag

Wednesday
25

♍

☽✶♂	6:56 am	
☽□♀	11:24 am	
☽✶♀	11:25 am	
☽△♅	9:45 pm	
☽□♄	11:09 pm	v/c

♃♃♃ donderdag

Thursday
26

♍
♎

☽→♎	7:53 am	
☿⚹♄	4:07 pm	
☉□☽	4:31 pm	
☽△♆	11:54 pm	

Waning Half Moon in ♎ Libra 4:31 pm PST

♀♀♀ vrijdag

Friday
27

♎

☽✶♃	1:08 pm	
☽✶♀	2:41 pm	
♂□♃	11:22 pm	

webs are built
from the most
basic female instinct.
are what hold
the world together.
are at once
nests and traps

i am the spider.
i am the fly.
excerpt © Donna Henes 1977

ALL ASPECTS IN PACIFIC STANDARD TIME; ADD 3 HOURS FOR EST; ADD 8 HOURS FOR GMT

Creating the Cosmos

© *Jan Wright 1998*

♎︎
♏︎

Saturday
28

☽△ħ	1:49 am	
☽△♅	4:09 am	
☽□♅	4:15 am	v/c
☽→♏︎	10:41 am	
☉⚹☽	11:05 pm	

♏︎

Sunday
29

☽□♆	2:36 am
☽□♃	3:19 pm
☽PrG	4:58 pm
☽♂♂	5:26 pm
☽♂♀	11:48 pm

MOON 0

December/January

diciembre/enero ──── ☽☽☽ lunes ─────────────

♏︎ ☾ **Monday**
♐︎   **30**

☽□♅ 6:39 am
☽⚹♂ 9:04 am v/c
☽→♐︎ 1:01 pm

© *Deborah Koff-Chapin 1989*

Gaia

──────────── ♂♂♂ martes ─────────────

♐︎ ☾ **Tuesday**
         31

☽⚹♆ 5:04 am
☽△♃ 5:26 pm
☽☌♀ 7:48 pm

──────────── ☿☿☿ miércoles ─────────────

♐︎ ☾ **Wednesday**
♑︎   **1**

☽☍♄ 6:10 am
☉☌♆ 8:10 am
☽⚹♅ 9:23 am v/c
♀⊼♄ 10:14 am
☽→♑︎ 3:42 pm

January 2003

──────────── ♃♃♃ jueves ─────────────

♑︎ ☾ **Thursday**
         2

☿R 10:19 am
☉☌☽ 12:23 pm

New Moon in ♑︎ Capricorn 12:23 pm PST

──────────── ♀♀♀ viernes ─────────────

♑︎ ☾ **Friday**
♒︎   **3**

☽⚹♂ 4:22 am
♀□♅ 12:38 pm
☽⚹♀ 1:36 pm
☽☌♅ 4:56 pm v/c
☽→♒︎ 7:56 pm

─────────────────────────────────────

ALL ASPECTS IN PACIFIC STANDARD TIME; ADD 3 HOURS FOR EST; ADD 8 HOURS FOR GMT

Woman as Potter

From the very first time she threw that hunk of clay on the wheel, she said, I'm going to throw a hell of a world. And from the rich recesses of the cool, dark earth, she hollowed out a bowl, a hand-held crater, into which she collected the rain. And as the rain shimmered down outside, she held the image of her world, and the redwoods and cedars drank deep from their roots, silhouetted against the silvery cusp of the moon. And as the arc of the moon tipped up on her pointed toes, the woman as potter settled her weight down on her hips, and gravity danced between them like lightning in the hills and rocked them in the deep rhythmic pull of the tides.

And as the carpet of leaves below hugged tightly around the chest of earth mother, the stars whirled around the elliptic on the potter's wheel, and as autumn spun through winter to spring, the little bulbs pushed their prayered hands up through the carpet of leaves, and the vision of woman as life-giver grew strong. No torn and tattered maiden, no servant, no rib; this woman was warrior, minstrel of fire, storm lover and mother of birth. You could see her splinter flint from her anvil, fire stones into stars in her kiln, wrack forth life like thunder, while her prayers ushered forth oracular and her children claimed life with both hands.

© *Julie Weber 2000*

---------------- ላላላ sábado ----------------

≈ **Saturday**

4

☽♂♆ 1:22 pm

---------------- ☉☉☉ domingo ----------------

≈ **Sunday**

5

☿✶♀	12:00 am	☽□♂	1:18 pm
☽♂♃	1:46 am	☽△♄	3:48 pm
☽✶♀	5:22 am	☽♂♅	8:21 pm

Through Her Cracks

We hike the corridor of the Andes and are changed.

We climb a narrow path, each groove cut deep, a prayer.

Holy ground as long as any story knows.

Cascades on every side are at the level of our eye.

How faithfully the path stitches us to earth.

We rise to meet the Andean sky—

Clouds sail the blue of each horizon.

We make our pilgrimage to where earth's joy erupts.

Unseen guardians draw a curtain all around the springs.

Their ancient presence sets this site like a ring sets a jewel.

Through Her cracks, hot juice bursts!

Pours out to heal Her children.

Her ecstasy has been boiling over as long as the Andes have been.

The mind cannot grasp how slowly She changes.

She sends Her essence out to meet us.

Her love runs and pools. Runs!

Her gift of healing springs without cease, teaching

hundreds of generations   what giving   can be.

¤ *Sue Silvermarie 2001*

I. SHE IS AGELESS

Moon I: January 2–February 1

New Moon in ♑ Capricorn: Jan. 2; Full Moon in ♋ Cancer: Jan. 18; Sun in ♒ Aquarius: Jan. 20

Pachamama
© *Hrana Janto 1991*

January
Januar

———— ☽☽☽ Montag ————

♒
♓
Monday
6

☽☐♀   12:44 am v/c
☽→♓   2:57 am
☉⚼♃   5:34 pm

———— ♂♂♂ Dienstag ————

♓
Tuesday
7

♀→♐   5:07 am
♂⚼♄   10:36 am
☉⚹☽   11:47 am
☽☐♀   2:35 pm

———— ☿☿☿ Mittwoch ————

♓
♈
Wednesday
8

☽☐♄   1:08 am
☽△♂   2:02 am
☽⚹♅   3:55 am v/c
⚸ApG 11:12 am
☽→♈   1:15 pm
☽△♀   4:09 pm
☿⚹♂   4:18 pm

———— ♃♃♃ Donnerstag ————

♈
Thursday
9

☽⚹♆   9:01 am
☿⚼♄   11:30 am
☽△♃   9:23 pm

———— ♀♀♀ Freitag ————

♈
Friday
10

☽△♀   2:41 am
☉☐☽   5:15 am
☽☐♅   10:43 am
☽⚹♄   1:02 pm
☽ApG 4:34 pm
☽⚹♅   7:10 pm v/c

Waxing Half Moon in ♈ Aries 5:15 am PST

ALL ASPECTS IN PACIFIC STANDARD TIME; ADD 3 HOURS FOR EST; ADD 8 HOURS FOR GMT

Goddess 101

The mysteries of female biology dominated human religious and artistic thought, as well as social organization, for at least the first 200,000 years of human life on earth. The first human images known to us are the so-called Venuses found in Upper Paleolithic remains (35,000–10,000 B.C.). From the way these statues are positioned and located in cave hearths, niches, and graves, they are interpreted as cult images—the Mother Guardians of the daily life, death and rebirth of the people. These Venuses, carved from stone, bone, and ivory, and shaped from clay, are magic images of the mysterious power of the female to create life out of herself, and to sustain it.

In the world's oldest creation myths, the female god creates the world out of her own body. The Great Mother everywhere was the active and autonomous creatrix of the world . . . and unlike the aloof and self-righteous patriarchal gods who only recently usurped her mountain-throne, the ancient Goddess was always there—alive, immanent—within her creation; no ontological scapegoater, she was wholly responsible for both the pain and the good of life. This concept of a female earth as the source of cyclic birth, life, death, and rebirth underlies all mythological and religious symbology; it is the source of all religious belief. It is important to grasp the time dimension involved: God was female for at least the first 200,000 years of human life on earth.

© *Barbara Mor and Monica Sjöö 1987; reprinted from* The Great Cosmic Mother
with permission of HarperCollins Publishers Inc.

———————————— ♄♄♄ Samstag ————————————

♈ ◗ Saturday
♉   ‖

☽→♉	1:48 am
☉☌☿	12:02 pm
♂□♅	8:47 pm
☽□♆	9:59 pm

———————————— ☉☉☉ Sonntag ————————————

♉ ◗ Sunday
            12

☽□♃	9:36 am
☿PrG	11:25 am
☽△♉	5:20 pm
☉△☽	11:36 pm

January
enero

☽☽☽ lunes

♉ ♊

Monday
13

☽□♅ 7:54 am
☽☍♂ 9:44 am v/c
☽→♊ 2:08 pm
☉⊼♄ 6:39 pm

Who can imagine You,
Queen of Humanity
unfolding over
millions of years.
Loveradiant Beauty,
You are Ourselves
as we shall one day be.

¤ *Janine Canan 2001*

♂♂♂ martes

♊

Tuesday
14

☽☍♀ 4:02 am
☽△♆ 9:51 am
☽⚹♃ 8:16 pm

☿☿☿ miércoles

♊ ♋

Wednesday
15

☽☍♇ 2:41 am
☽☌♄ 11:29 am
☽△♅ 6:16 pm v/c
☽→♋ 11:56 pm

♃♃♃ jueves

♋

Thursday
16

☿⊼♃ 10:21 am
♂→♐ 8:22 pm

♀♀♀ viernes

♋

Friday
17

♀⚹♆ 2:35 am
☽☍☿ 2:54 am

Tarxien Goddess
© *Monica Sjöö 1994*

♋
♌

Saturday

18

☉☍☽	2:48 am	v/c
☽→♌	6:29 am	
☽△♂	8:11 am	

Full Moon in ♋ Cancer 2:48 am PST

♌

Sunday

19

☽☍♆	12:26 am
☽△♀	4:08 am
☽♂♃	8:33 am
☽△♀	3:31 pm
☽⚹♄	10:45 pm

MOON I

January
januari

♌
♍

Monday
20

☉→♒	3:53 am	
☽⚼♅	5:46 am	v/c
☿☌♄	7:11 am	
☽→♍	10:32 am	
☽□♂	2:40 pm	

Sun in Aquarius 3:53 am PST

♍

Tuesday
21

♀△♃	7:35 am
☽△♅	7:40 am
☽□♀	11:44 am
☽□♇	6:46 pm

♍
♎

Wednesday
22

☽□♄	1:34 am	v/c
☽→♎	1:23 pm	
☿D	5:08 pm	
☉△☽	5:49 pm	
☽⚹♂	7:53 pm	

♎

Thursday
23

☽△♆	6:55 am
☽□♅	10:12 am
☽⚹♃	1:38 pm
☽PrG	2:27 pm
☽⚹♀	6:37 pm
☽⚹♇	9:34 pm

♎
♏

Friday
24

☽△♄	4:05 am	
☽△♅	11:48 am	v/c
☽→♏	4:09 pm	

ALL ASPECTS IN PACIFIC STANDARD TIME; ADD 3 HOURS FOR EST; ADD 8 HOURS FOR GMT

Year at a Glance for ♒ AQUARIUS (Jan. 20–Feb. 18)

The last seven years have been full of unpredictable havoc while Uranus—agent of change—was transiting your sign. From the necessary breakdown of a stagnant, stuck personality, through some wild experimentation and a desperate need for space and independence—as Uranus begins its shifts out of Aquarius into Pisces—you begin the work of steadying this new self. Uranus does return to your sign of Aquarius for one last burst between March and September 2003. Some unexplored facet of your nature may burst out, surprising everyone this year, especially if you have anything you've been hiding. It's a last opportunity to shapeshift into a more authentic way of presenting yourself to the world.

Unexpected changes in economics nudge you to innovate. Windfalls appear through unexpected sources as your economic base and values begin to change rapidly. Crises encourage the development of skills you otherwise would not have considered. Experiment with sensible risks. Don't leave a job until you have thoroughly explored ways to make it more exciting and interesting.

What will help you? Partners are supportive, a professional alliance is likely to be profitable. The assistance of a professional whether it be a lawyer, healer or counselor will be particularly helpful in expanding your perspective and your options. A change made in August or September releases you from some limiting circumstance and is ultimately for the best.

June onwards is a good time to acquire more efficient methods or skills, especially those that will improve health or work. Diminish waste or scattering of your energy. Your nerves are extremely sensitive and benefit from a spiritually based workout, such as yoga or sacred dance.

© *Gretchen Lawlor 2002*

The Star
© *Lynn Dewart 1998*

———————————— ♄♄♄   zaterdag ————————————

♏ ☽ **Saturday**
25

⊙□☽ 12:33 am	☽⚹♀ 1:58 pm
☽□♅ 9:57 am	☽□♃ 4:08 pm
♀☌♀ 9:59 am	⊙⚹♂ 9:26 pm

Waning Half Moon in ♏ Scorpio 12:33 am PST

———————————— ⊙⊙⊙   zondag ————————————

♏ ☽ **Sunday**
26

☽□♅ 3:14 pm v/c	
☽→♐ 7:26 pm	
♀☌♇ 8:16 pm	

January
Qhapaqintiraymi killa

))) Killachaw

♐

Monday

27

☽♂♂	7:02 am
☉⚹☽	8:00 am
☽⚹♆	1:38 pm
☿⊼♃	5:51 pm
☽△♃	7:16 pm

♂♂♂ Atichaw

♐
♑

Tuesday

28

☽♂♀	4:36 am	
☽♂♀	10:13 am	
☽☍♄	10:43 am	
♀☍♄	4:13 pm	
☽⚹♅	7:26 pm	v/c
☽→♑	11:30 pm	

☿☿☿ Quyllurchaw

♑

Wednesday

29

♃⊼♇	10:26 am

♃♃♃ Illapachaw

♑

Thursday

30

☽♂♉	2:34 am	v/c
☉♂♆	3:32 pm	

♀♀♀ Ch'askachaw

♑
♒

Friday

31

♆ApG	12:18 am
☽→♒	4:44 am
☽⚹♂	10:21 pm

All over the lands of earth
I see the labyrinth's way
returning and you my daughters
following silver threads.
Praise be.

excerpt ¤ Cora Greenhill 2001

ALL ASPECTS IN PACIFIC STANDARD TIME; ADD 3 HOURS FOR EST; ADD 8 HOURS FOR GMT

Labyrinth
□ *Witchhazel Wildwood 2001*

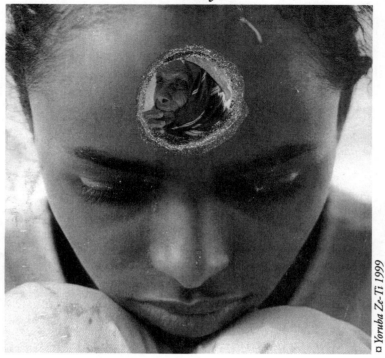

□ *Yoruba Ze-Ti 1999*

Imbolc

Imbolc marks the midpoint between Winter Solstice and Spring Equinox. Sap begins to run in the trees and green shoots emerge from the quiet earth. In the Celtic lands, great Imbolc fire festivals were held honoring the Goddess Brigit. Brigit is the bringer of knowledge to humanity. She is the keeper of the wells of inspiration. Her fire is the flame of creative invention.

In today's world, greed and the lust for power have turned humankind's capacity for creation into self-destruction. We strip-mine our Earth's precious minerals, log her oxygen-producing forests and dam her life waters. We have invented toxins, pesticides and radioactive poisons. Weapons of mass destruction capable of ending all life on earth in an instant lie waiting to be used.

Brigit's true creative gifts are forged with compassion and are for the good of all. Light a beeswax candle on an altar of green cloth or earth. Ask Brigit for inspiration on how your creative tools can be used as instruments of healing for the earth. Know that as you manifest your creativity you are changing the world.

© *Ginny Salkowski 2002*

Communication

I can feel the mental tendril of

a mind close to mine,

and suddenly distances are spanned

and I am surrounded by beloved spectres,

their ghostly lips brimming with womynly wisdom,

kind thoughts and expanding visions

that fill me with hope, courage, and the

knowledge of a million earthbound years.

◻ *Trisia Eddy 2001*

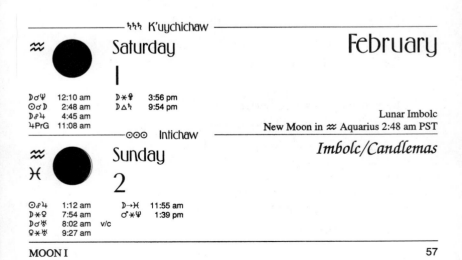

──────── ♄♄♄ K'uychichaw ────────

≈ **Saturday**

1

February

☽☌♆	12:10 am	☽⚹♀	3:56 pm
☉☌☽	2:48 am	☽△♄	9:54 pm
☽☍♃	4:45 am		
♃PrG	11:08 am		

──────── ☉☉☉ Intichaw ────────

Lunar Imbolc
New Moon in ≈ Aquarius 2:48 am PST

Imbolc/Candlemas

≈
♓ **Sunday**

2

☉☍♃	1:12 am	☽→♓	11:55 am
☽⚹♀	7:54 am	♂⚹♆	1:39 pm
☽☌♅	8:02 am	v/c	
♀⚹♅	9:27 am		

Changing Woman

I am the tender bud waiting hidden
     in the branch;
I burst forth in spring
     at the first sign of warmth.
I am young and succulent, burgeoning
     with promise, tart
And sweet and juicy.

Opening, growing, taking shape—a full-bodied leaf,
     noble and prime,
I breathe with a million million of my sisters,
     doing the green work of Creation.
Every summer morning I rise and open to the hot,
     luscious light,
I pull the sun into my cells and give birth
     to life everlasting.

I am the flaming orange banner, the brilliant
     gold and brown, crackling in autumn winds,
Falling, whirling, dancing in the cold,
     crystalline air, dropping, floating
Resting, nourishing the seed.

I am the open space between the branches
     where the new moon rests with stars
On a winter's eve, the tree slumbers,
     my tender buds wait.
The night is long and I am content
     for I feel the great earth turning
     in the dark.

II. SHE CHANGES

Moon II: February 1–March 2

New Moon in ♒ Aquarius: Feb. 1; Full Moon in ♌ Leo: Feb. 16; Sun in ♓ Pisces: Feb. 18

Abundance: Tree of Life
© *Marie LoParco 2000*

February
Februar

 ♓   ## Monday
3

☽□♂   9:22 am

♓
♈   ## Tuesday
4

☽□♀   12:53 am
☽⚹♅   1:48 am
♀→♑   5:27 am
☽□♄   6:53 am   v/c
☽→♈   9:44 am
☽□♀   11:24 pm

♈   ## Wednesday
5

♂△♃   11:25 am
☽⚹♆   7:24 pm
☽△♃   10:47 pm
☽△♂   11:34 pm

♈   ## Thursday
6

☉⚹☽   8:37 am
☿☍♄   10:31 am
☽△♀   12:32 pm
☽⚹♄   6:28 pm
☽□♅   7:20 pm

♈
♉ ## Friday
7

☽⚹♅   6:22 am   v/c
☽→♉   9:59 am
☽ApG   2:05 pm
☽△♀   6:06 pm

ALL ASPECTS IN PACIFIC STANDARD TIME; ADD 3 HOURS FOR EST; ADD 8 HOURS FOR GMT

Ix Chel

Mayan Moon Goddess, Mother, Grandmother of Change.
Serpent of the Heavens, endlessly recreating
Yourself. Old Woman Spider, center of the world's web,
eternally weaving and reweaving the fabric of life itself.

You sit at your loom, sing with your nesting weaver bird,
stroke each soul between your fingers,
weave us together in all our differences.

Healer and renewer, you send refreshing rain,
watch over women in childbirth
and with your sacred rabbit, scribe of lunar calendars,
compose herbs to ease and mend us,
welcome us to your sacred island, Isla Mujeres.

Oh, solitary and independent wanderer,
lover of nocturnal creatures
in your ever changing constancy
touch me with your light,
be my midwife for creation.

□ Antonia Matthew 2001
artwork: Spider Woman Series © Donna Henes 1987

ħħħ   Samstag

♉   **Saturday**

♉   8

☉✶♀	7:31 am
☽□Ψ	8:20 am
☽□♃	10:54 am

☉☉☉   Sonntag

♉   **Sunday**

♊   9

☉□☽	3:11 am	
☽△♅	2:55 pm	
☽□♅	7:28 pm	v/c
☽→♊	10:45 pm	

Waxing Half Moon in ♉ Taurus 3:11 am PST

February
febrero

⟩⟩⟩   lunes

♊   ## Monday
10

☽△♆   8:47 pm
☽⚹♃   10:26 pm

Dreaming the Divine
□ *Nadine Butterfield 2001*

♂♂♂   martes

♊   ## Tuesday
11

☉△♄   1:45 am
☽☍♂   7:10 am
☽☍♀   1:15 pm
☽♂♄   6:29 pm
☉△☽   8:00 pm

☿☿☿   miércoles

♊
♋   ## Wednesday
12

☽△♅   6:29 am   v/c
☽→♋   9:19 am
☿→♒   5:00 pm

♃♃♃   jueves

♋   ## Thursday
13

☽☍♀   4:22 am   v/c

♀♀♀   viernes

♋
♌   ## Friday
14

♀⚼♃   7:34 am
☽→♌   4:04 pm
☽☍♉   9:08 pm

ALL ASPECTS IN PACIFIC STANDARD TIME; ADD 3 HOURS FOR EST; ADD 8 HOURS FOR GMT

a romance

the sun drops down to another country,
and the sky opens to an ocean, darker and deeper than those
at the edge of our shores.
stars swoon and dip into the night like drops of paint left behind.
they shimmer and shriek, so sharp i'd surely prick my finger.
i wish for wings, for the tail of a mermaid. i must move.
i pull open the door to the backyard: here are fireflies spinning,
grass breathing, crickets chanting.
there she is, the moon, in her best dress, coming to court me.
she lifts her skirts like a can-can dancer, tempting me, and i nearly
faint with anticipation and relief. once, it's true, she was an orphan,
singing mournfully from her post in the charred night.
but since then i have learned the names of ancient women and
taken the ribbons from my hair.
i remember that i am also daughter and mother. like the stars,
i too have burned and screamed and died for things.
and now there is weaving and digging and dancing.
so she comes for me each month, as i shake myself out of
these chains and touch my bare feet to the skin of the earth,
the sweet shell of the sacred queen.
and we glide hand in hand like lovers.

© Sara Baker 2001

ኣኣኣ sábado

♌ ◐ **Saturday**
15

☽☍♆	11:40 am
☽☌♃	11:49 am

⊙⊙⊙ domingo

♌
♍ ○ **Sunday**
16

♃☍♆	1:12 am	♂☌♀	8:00 am	
☽△♂	1:38 am	⊙☍☽	3:51 pm	
☽△♀	1:55 am	☽☍♅	5:18 pm	v/c
☽✶♄	6:14 am	☽→♍	7:22 pm	

Full Moon in ♌ Leo 3:51 pm PST

February
februari

♍

Monday
17

☉☌♅ 1:38 pm
♀☌♌ 1:39 pm
☽△♀ 9:13 pm

Kundalini Rising
© *Michelle Waters 1998*

————♂♂♂ dinsdag ————

♍
♎

Tuesday
18

☽□♀ 3:51 am
☽□♂ 5:48 am
☽□♄ 7:56 am   v/c
♅ApG 1:07 pm
☉→♓ 6:00 pm
☽→♎ 8:48 pm

————☿☿☿ woensdag ————

Sun in Pisces 6:00 pm PST

♎

Wednesday
19

☽PrG 8:20 am
☽△♅ 12:07 pm
☽✶♃ 2:34 pm
☽△♆ 3:30 pm

————♃♃♃ donderdag ————

♎
♏

Thursday
20

☽□♀ 2:39 am   ☿☍♃ 11:12 am
☽✶♀ 5:06 am   ☽△♅ 8:29 am   v/c
♂☍♄ 6:14 am   ☽→♏ 10:09 pm
☽△♄ 9:08 am   ☿☌♆ 10:50 pm
☽✶♂ 9:16 am

————♀♀♀ vrijdag ————

♏

Friday
21

☉△☽ 2:04 am
☽□♃ 3:52 pm
☽□♆ 5:20 pm
☽□☿ 7:25 pm
♄D 11:41 pm

ALL ASPECTS IN PACIFIC STANDARD TIME; ADD 3 HOURS FOR EST; ADD 8 HOURS FOR GMT

Year at a Glance for ♓ PISCES (Feb. 18–March 20)

Uranus—lightning flash of inspiration and unexpected change—enters Pisces for the first time since the 1920's on March 3, 2003. You will be one of its major "spark carriers" during the next seven years. If you can be flexible, this can be an extraordinary and exhilarating time for you. A streak of genius and a gift for innovation helps as you instinctively channel something new welling up from the collective psyche.

In the last 2 1/2 years you were less visible, inwardly preoccupied with establishing a solid launching platform. The first half of 2003 offers opportunities for you to shift from no longer vital habits, locations or positions and set sturdier foundations in place. Fall 2002 through August 2003 is also an excellent period for health improvements; you experience greater physical strength and vitality. Pisceans have sensitive constitutions; if your body has to heal or recover, there will be assistance at this time.

People are particularly supportive of you, especially from August onwards. A patron, benefactor or collaborator opens doors. It's a good time to work with others. Do not rely solely upon promises; stretch yourself and experiment but do so with an eye for enduring growth. Personal setbacks come from excessive willfulness or lack of accountability. Strengthen your creative gifts with a steady commitment to crafting their emergence. Take yourself seriously as an artist, a lover or a parent. Something greater than yourself is desiring to come into form through you at this time and will require your devotion. © *Gretchen Lawlor 2002*

Blessed Be
◻ *Jules Bubacz 1998*

─── ᚺᚺᚺ zaterdag ───

♏

Saturday
22

☽⚹♀ 9:08 am
☽□♅ 11:15 pm v/c

─── ☉☉☉ zondag ───

♏
♐

Sunday
23

☽→♐ 12:46 am
☉□☽ 8:46 am
♀⚹♄ 11:45 am
☽△♃ 6:40 pm
☽⚹♆ 8:45 pm

Waning Half Moon in ♐ Sagittarius 8:46 am PST

February/March

Qhaqmiy killa/Jatuñpuquy killa

DDD Killachaw

Monday
24

D⚹♅ 5:05 am
D♂♀ 11:05 am
D☍♄ 3:16 pm
D♂♂ 8:28 pm

♂♂♂ Atichaw

Tuesday
25

D⚹♅ 3:50 am   v/c
D→♑ 5:11 am
☉⚹D 5:45 pm

☿☿☿ Quyllurchaw

Wednesday
26

☿⚹♀ 10:34 am

♃♃♃ Illapachaw

Thursday
27

D♂♀ 4:58 am   v/c
D→♒ 11:24 am
☿△♄ 10:51 pm

♀♀♀ Ch'askachaw

Friday
28

D☍♃ 5:41 am
D♂♆ 9:04 am
☉⚻♃ 1:16 pm

ALL ASPECTS IN PACIFIC STANDARD TIME; ADD 3 HOURS FOR EST; ADD 8 HOURS FOR GMT

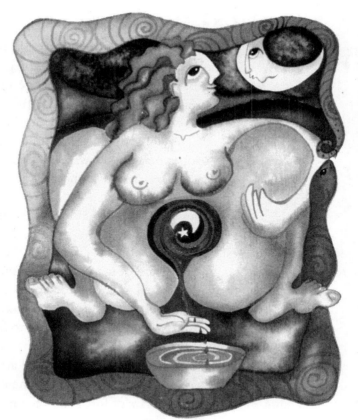

Resacralize the Feminine
© *Katheryn M. Trenshaw 1999*

ᛝᛝᛝ K'uychichaw

 ♒︎
♓︎

Saturday

1

☽∗♀	12:12 am	☽∗♂	3:56 pm	
☽△♄	4:39 am	☽♂♅	6:30 pm	v/c
☽♂♉	8:54 am	☽→♓	7:26 pm	

⊙⊙⊙ Intichaw

♓︎

Sunday

2

| ♀→♒︎ | 4:40 am |
| ⊙♂☽ | 6:35 pm |

New Moon in ♓ Pisces 6:35 pm PST

MOON II

My Great Mother Story

When I was a troubled child of 12 searching for love, I became pregnant. On April 20, 1961 at the age of 13, I gave birth to a beautiful baby girl who was whisked over my head in the delivery room to the arms of secret adoptive parents. I was left alone with sadness, sorrow and shame. It was not my choice nor was it the choice of many young girls then. Society was full of shame and blame that masked its real need for more babies for childless, affluent couples of the post war era. My family thought they were doing the right thing for the baby. I was not figured in, after all, I had made my bed . . . There was no counseling then, only silence and closed records. After being hidden away for months, I returned to school to finish the eighth grade just 2 weeks after the birth.

I couldn't speak about it for years. Luckily, I discovered art and love of nature, animals, beauty and many wonderful women who came into my life through the long years of loss. This to me is the Great Mother in my life! She has led me to greater love, peace and given me so many gifts. She has shown me that out of darkness can come light and out of pain comes joy.

In March 2001, I found my daughter! I traveled 3000 miles to celebrate her 40th birthday with her. We cried, held each other and told our stories. She is a beautiful woman with a heart full of love for people, animals, art and nature. I was told by the woman from the internet site, where we were matched, to give her something of me after our first meeting. It was easy to decide to give her this painting as I spent every day of my pregnancy painting it. My beloved grandmother framed it and I kept it with me for 40 years. Now it hangs in my daughter's bedroom and she and I are building our friendship. We are writing a book together. I am not searching anymore, I am full circle complete.

photo and writing © Amarah K. Gabriel 2001

III. SHE HEALS

Moon III: March 2–April 1

New Moon in ♓ Pisces: March 2; Full Moon in ♍ Virgo: March 18; Sun in ♈ Aries: March 20

She Finds Healing
© *Megaera 1998*

March

März

Mother Nature's the cure,
Take at least
Three times a day!

excerpt ◻ Lorye Keats Hopper 2001

──────── ☽☽☽ Montag ────────

♓

Monday

3

☽□♀	9:36 am
☽□♄	2:14 pm
♂⚹♅	11:30 pm

──────── ♂♂♂ Dienstag ────────

♓
♈

Tuesday

4

☽□♂	5:04 am	v/c
☽→♈	5:30 am	
☽⚹♀	10:44 am	
☿♂♅	1:16 pm	
♂→♑	1:17 pm	
☿→♓	6:04 pm	
☿⚹♂	9:01 pm	

──────── ☿☿☿ Mittwoch ────────

♈

Wednesday

5

☽△♃	12:13 am
☽⚹♆	5:06 am
☽△♀	9:07 am

──────── ♃♃♃ Donnerstag ────────

♈
♉

Thursday

6

☽⚹♄	1:58 am	
☽⚹♅	5:10 pm	v/c
☽→♉	5:36 pm	
☽△♂	8:35 pm	

──────── ♀♀♀ Freitag ────────

♉

Friday

7

☽⚹☿	1:34 am
☉⚹♆	4:38 am
☽□♀	5:42 am
☽ApG	8:35 am
☽□♃	12:22 pm
☽□♆	5:57 pm

───────────────────────────────

ALL ASPECTS IN PACIFIC STANDARD TIME; ADD 3 HOURS FOR EST; ADD 8 HOURS FOR GMT

Naked Foot

Take your shoes off and walk with me, in the soft grass,
On the smooth stone, on the warm sand, on the cool soil.
Your feet can be a simple prayer . . .
The naked Earth loves nothing more than the naked touch
Of your naked foot on her naked self.
She'll squish mud between your toes
And give you flowers which make the air
Smell beautiful when you dance on her without shoes or fences
Or boundaries or barriers between her body and yours.
Yes. You really can speak with your feet
It's an ancient sign-language
Between things which feel each other all over
The Earth, look, nothing else here in this forest is wearing shoes,
And she is strong enough to bear the weight of giant trees.
Which means your foot upon her flesh is light
As a kiss.

© *Felix 2001*

The writer of this poem suffers from severe rheumatoid arthritis in both feet . . . one of her favourite therapies is cool, cool mud which soothes the pain and reconnects her to the Earth. She has done a series of artworks exploring this relationship between feet and the Earth, and this poem is an attempt to explore the same theme in words.

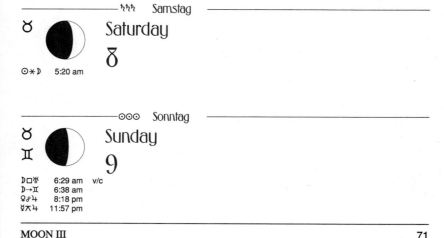

———————— ꕔꕔꕔ   Samstag ————————————
♉   Saturday
          ♉
☉⚹☽   5:20 am

———————— ⊙⊙⊙   Sonntag ————————————
♉   Sunday
♊   9
☽□♅   6:29 am   v/c
☽→♊   6:38 am
♀☍♃   8:18 pm
♉⊼♃   11:57 pm

March
marzo

♊ Monday

10

☽⚹♃	12:49 am	⛢→♓	12:53 pm
☽□♉	12:58 am	☉□♀	1:51 pm
☽△♀	1:21 am	☽☍♀	10:29 pm
☽△♆	6:53 am	☉□☽	11:15 pm

Waxing Half Moon in ♊ Gemini 11:15 pm PST

──────── ♂♂♂ martes

♊
♋ Tuesday

11

☽♂♄	3:24 am	v/c
☽→♋	6:12 pm	
☽△⛢	6:19 pm	

──────── ☿☿☿ miércoles ────────

♋ Wednesday

12

☽☍♂	3:28 am
♀♂♆	10:35 am
☽△♉	9:13 pm

──────── ♃♃♃ jueves ────────

♋ Thursday

13

☉□♄	3:38 am	
☉△☽	1:13 pm	v/c

──────── ♀♀♀ viernes ────────

♋
♌ Friday

14

☽→♌	2:06 am
☿⚹♇	8:58 am
☽♂♃	5:31 pm
☽☍♆	11:36 pm

ALL ASPECTS IN PACIFIC STANDARD TIME; ADD 3 HOURS FOR EST; ADD 8 HOURS FOR GMT

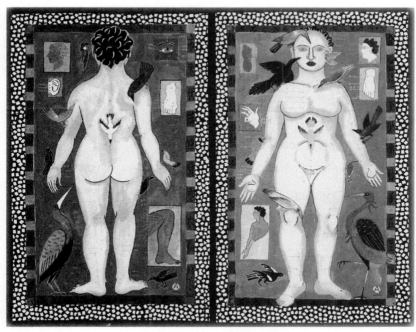

Acupuncture with Birds
© *Anna Oneglia 1998*

───────── ♄♄♄ sábado ─────────

♌ 🌙

Saturday

15

☽☍♀	5:10 am
☽△♃	12:55 pm
☿ApG	3:22 pm
☽⚹♄	5:24 pm v/c
♀□♀	11:19 pm

──── ☉☉☉ domingo ────

♌
♍ 🌙

Sunday

16

☽→♍	5:52 am
☽☍♅	6:23 am
☽△♂	6:43 pm

MOON III   73

Into the Woods

Once a year I go into the woods. Not *to* the woods, *into* the woods. I travel there, and then I drop myself in, I burrow myself in, I bury myself in the woods. Not under the dirt like a mouse or a snake or a gopher, not literally. I submerge myself in what it is to be a piece of nature.

Once a year I leave the concrete and the whooshing of cars and the jangle of the telephone, the intercom, the emergency broadcasting system. Once a year I leave the pantyhose and the push-up bra and the shoes that match the outfits that squish. Once a year I leave the men and the boys and the whistles and the questions and the requirements and the human resources department and the mall.

I sleep close to the ground so I can smell dirt, be cooled by soft breezes. I walk with no shoes so I can feel grass, sand, sticks and stones digging into my too-soft feet that have forgotten. I stand in the rain, which always comes, so I can taste the cleaning in the air. I eat food prepared by loving women hands. I watch them take food from root to pot to plate and it's clean and fresh. I take in what it is to be a piece of nature. I chew it up. I volley it around in my mouth, swish and roll. I swallow it. I take it into myself, like myself into the woods and I am renewed. I am empty and full and covered in rain and dirt and sweat and mud and I am clean.

Once a year I go into the woods and I incubate.

Once a year I go to the womb and I am whole.

© *Julianne Skai Arbor 2000*

Spring Equinox

The first day of spring has arrived. In Greek mythology, Persephone, the Goddess of Spring, returns from the underworld and is reunited with her mother Demeter, Goddess of the Earth. As Mother Earth rejoices in her daughter's embrace, life bursts forth from the soil. Plants send up new growth in response to the longer daylight hours. There is a swell of energy for everything fresh and new.

Healing our connection to our inner child is a powerful ritual of renewal for spring. Too many of us have received wounds in our childhoods which we keep hidden in the underworld of our souls. Many more of us see the wounds of the earth and feel pulled into sinking depressions. Like Persephone, we must remember to emerge from our dark places to reclaim our love, laughter and hope for life.

Build an altar in the earth with colored eggs, images of hope and your words of self-healing. Plant a circle of spring bulbs around it. Water your magic circle by dancing around it three times. Sprinkle glitter all around. Invite a child to help. © *Ginny Salkowski 2002*

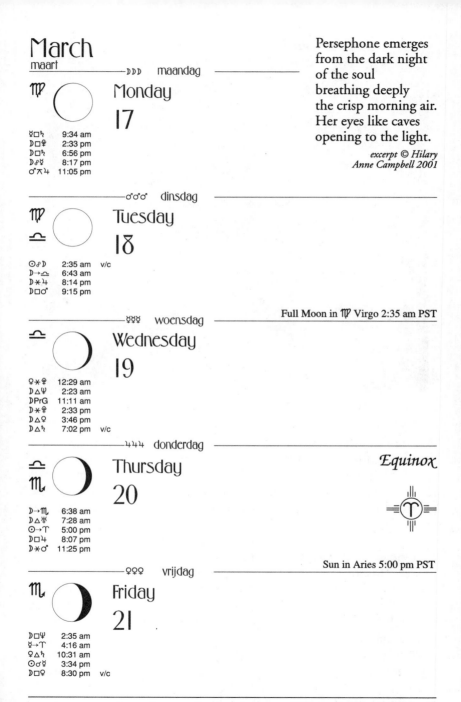

March
maart
───── ⊃⊃⊃ maandag ─────

♍

Monday
17

♉□♄	9:34 am	
☽□♀	2:33 pm	
☽□♄	6:56 pm	
☽☌♉	8:17 pm	
♂⚹♃	11:05 pm	

Persephone emerges
from the dark night
of the soul
breathing deeply
the crisp morning air.
Her eyes like caves
opening to the light.

excerpt © Hilary
Anne Campbell 2001

───── ♂♂♂ dinsdag ─────

♍
♎

Tuesday
18

☉☍☽	2:35 am	v/c
☽→♎	6:43 am	
☽⚹♃	8:14 pm	
☽□♂	9:15 pm	

Full Moon in ♍ Virgo 2:35 am PST

───── ☿☿☿ woensdag ─────

♎

Wednesday
19

♀⚹♀	12:29 am	
☽△♆	2:23 am	
☽PrG	11:11 am	
☽⚹♀	2:33 pm	
☽△♀	3:46 pm	
☽△♄	7:02 pm	v/c

───── ♃♃♃ donderdag ─────

♎
♏

Thursday
20

☽→♏	6:38 am	
☽△♅	7:28 am	
☉→♈	5:00 pm	
☽□♃	8:07 pm	
☽⚹♂	11:25 pm	

Equinox

♈

Sun in Aries 5:00 pm PST

───── ♀♀♀ vrijdag ─────

♏

Friday
21

☽□♆	2:35 am	
♉→♈	4:16 am	
♀△♄	10:31 am	
☉☌♉	3:34 pm	
☽□♀	8:30 pm	v/c

ALL ASPECTS IN PACIFIC STANDARD TIME; ADD 3 HOURS FOR EST; ADD 8 HOURS FOR GMT

Year at a Glance for ♈ ARIES (March 20–April 20)

In the last few years you've been trying on new roles as you reinvent yourself, catalyzed by your contacts with open minded, far-sighted people. You're thriving in this social matrix of forward thinking individuals. In 2003, you want to put your ideals into action, becoming a religious, spiritual or political activist. In 2003, be watchful for unrealistic yearnings or short lived rebellious escapism. There is a "divine discontent" in you, some dissatisfaction with what you have achieved so far. Do not obsess on past failures or the inadequacy of your successes. Surprising inspirations and glimpses of future developments will present themselves. Watch your dreams, they may be revealing the next chapter in your life.

Home and family will occupy a considerable amount of your time this year. You feel the constraints of an existing home or responsibilities towards family hemming you in. You may feel like the only one who isn't getting what you want. Things that you have been putting up with in your domestic life will have to be dealt with now. This is an excellent time to do emotional house cleaning, perhaps with the help of therapy. Buried memories can erupt explosively, ultimately for the better, though disturbing in the moment, tending to appear from nowhere to shock you and those close to you. They provide opportunity to expose the weak links or deeply entrenched complexes in your make-up and clear away old emotional debris.

In 2003, you tap into a well of creative and flamboyant self-expression. Your infectious enthusiasm arouses playmates, maybe lovers, especially pre-September. You get people onto your bandwagon by making whatever you do look like so much fun. © *Gretchen Lawlor 2002*

Mother Tree
© *Krista Lynn Brown 2000*

ℳ ♐   ♄♄♄   zaterdag

Saturday
22

☽→♐	7:33 am	☽△♉	11:55 am
☽□♅	8:36 am	♀R	9:13 pm
☉△☽	10:24 am	☽△♃	9:26 pm

♐   ☉☉☉   zondag

Sunday
23

☽⚹♆	4:27 am
☽☌♀	5:20 pm
☽☍♄	10:32 pm

March
Jatunpuquy killa

Planting Prayer
Leaves, roots,
flowers, fruits:
Be ye well
and by my toil,
grow ye strong
within this soil.

© *Anne Renarde 2001*

————》》》 Killachaw ————————

♐
♑

Monday
24

☽⚹♀ 3:58 am v/c
☽→♑ 10:48 am
☽⚹♅ 12:06 pm
☉□☽ 5:51 pm

————♂♂♂ Atichaw ———— Waning Half Moon in ♑ Capricorn 5:51 pm PST

♑

Tuesday
25

☽□♅ 12:24 am
☿△♃ 6:27 am
☽♂♂ 10:16 am v/c

————☿☿☿ Quyllurchaw ————————

♑
♒

Wednesday
26

☽→♒ 4:51 pm

————♃♃♃ Illapachaw ————————

♒

Thursday
27

☉⚹☽ 4:47 am
☽☍♃ 7:59 am
☿⚹♆ 9:36 am
♀→♓ 10:14 am
☽♂♆ 4:14 pm
☽⚹♅ 5:28 pm

————♀♀♀ Ch'askachaw ————————

♒

Friday
28

♀♂♅ 4:44 am
☽⚹♀ 6:12 am
☽△♄ 12:27 pm v/c
☿□♂ 6:12 pm
☉△♃ 9:31 pm

———————————————————————

ALL ASPECTS IN PACIFIC STANDARD TIME; ADD 3 HOURS FOR EST; ADD 8 HOURS FOR GMT

Scent of the Mother

Born from morning earth
pure lavender
yarrow sharp as warrior's pains
mountain joy of marjoram
bless our hands with memory

woven into ancient knowing
sage against the mind's betrayal
lemon balm of battered spirits
thyme all-healing
help & guide us

once forgotten sister wisdom
parsley in a sunless season
sweet verbena feverbane
dream-ease of valerian
scent the ageless winds that whisper

from the Mother
teach us home.

© Ann K. Schwader 2001
artwork: Medicine Woman © Janah Wickett Breidenbach 2001

───────────── ㅅㅅㅅ K'uychichaw ─────────────

≈
ℋ

Saturday
29

☽→ℋ   1:26 am
☽♂♅   3:18 am
☽♂♀   5:36 am
♅□♃   10:11 pm

───────────── ☉☉☉ Intichaw ─────────────

ℋ

Sunday
30

☽⚹♂   9:06 am
☽□♀   4:12 pm
☽□♄   10:59 pm v/c

I Am the Goddess

I am the Goddess
and I speak now from
the mouth of all women.

I am the Earth,
the cradle of creation.
In the creases of my
inner thighs lies your salvation.

Every particle of your being
has been brought forth
from the fiber of my body.

Your muscles are made of
proteins from the plants you
trample under foot
without a thought.

You have covered my naked
sacred body with a garment
of cement. I feel restricted;

I cannot dance and
undulate my rippling torso
where I have been paved over,
deforested, wrapped in plastic.

Uncover me. Peel back the layers
of what you call progress.
I am so much more
beautiful naked than clothed.

Stand before me,
feel your feet planted
in my moist soil.

Feel the roots shoot
from the bottom of
your feet to the mud
and the heat way
way down deep below.

See how the legs of any woman
are the pillars of a temple
growing up like redwoods
from their roots below
the ground.

Worship me in that temple
Worship me in that temple

Worship me now
Worship me now!

© *La Tigresa/Dona Nieto 2002*

La Tigresa reads this poem, bare-breasted and "vulnerable like Mother
Earth," as she confronts logging trucks to protest the destruction of
old growth redwood forests.

IV. SHE LIBERATES

Moon IV: April 1–May 1

New Moon in ♈ Aries: April 1; Full Moon in ♎ Libra: April 16; Sun in ♉ Taurus: April 20

Blue Raven Warrior
© *Lynda Healy 2000*

March/April
März/April

ⅮⅮⅮ　Montag

♓
♈

Monday
31

☿△♀　1:13 am
☽→♈　12:04 pm

April

♂♂♂　Dienstag

♈

Tuesday
1

☽△♃　4:09 am
☉☌☽　11:19 am
☽⚹♆　1:21 pm
♂☌♄　4:44 pm
☿⚹♄　8:29 pm
☽□♂　11:58 pm

New Moon in ♈ Aries 11:19 am PST

☿☿☿　Mittwoch

♈

Wednesday
2

☽△♀　3:57 am
☽⚹♄　11:16 am
☉⚹♆　12:32 pm
☽☌♉　2:05 pm　v/c

♃♃♃　Donnerstag

♈
♉

Thursday
3

☽→♉　12:20 am　　☽⚹♀　6:14 pm
☽⚹♅　2:47 am　　♃D　7:04 pm
♀⚻♃　3:24 am　　☽ApG　8:29 pm
☽□♃　4:43 pm

♀♀♀　Freitag

♉

Friday
4

☽□♆　2:12 am
☽△♂　4:15 pm　v/c

ALL ASPECTS IN PACIFIC STANDARD TIME; ADD 3 HOURS FOR EST; ADD 8 HOURS FOR GMT

The Source

We know she lives. She is the voice of the newborn
and the Ancestor, the gaze of the last white tiger
and the flower that breaks through the road.
She is the red thread of life in all of us;
she is tomorrow and we cry for her: *Mother, free us.*

excerpt © Rose Flint 2001   artwork: Gaia's Cry © Katherine E. Schoelkopf 2000

ħħħ Samstag

Saturday

5

♀→♉	6:37 am
☽→♊	1:24 pm
☽□♅	4:05 pm

☉☉☉ Sonntag

Sunday

6

♀✶♅	12:27 am
☽✶♃	6:46 am
☽□♀	3:07 pm
☽△♆	4:16 pm

Daylight Savings Time begins 2:00 am PST

April
abril

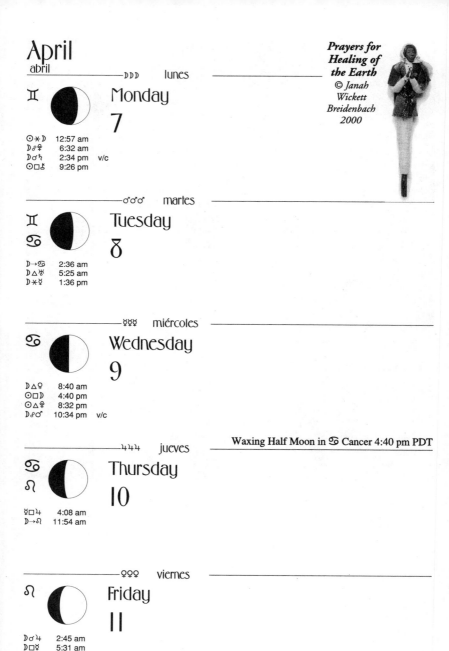

⟶ⅮⅮⅮ lunes

Monday
7

☉✶☽ 12:57 am
☽☍♀ 6:32 am
☽♂♄ 2:34 pm v/c
☉□♅ 9:26 pm

♊

—⟶♂♂♂ martes

Tuesday
8

♊
♋

☽→♋ 2:36 am
☽△♅ 5:25 am
☽✶♉ 1:36 pm

—⟶☿☿☿ miércoles

Wednesday
9

♋

☽△♀ 8:40 am
☉□☽ 4:40 pm
☉△♀ 8:32 pm
☽☍♂ 10:34 pm v/c

—⟶♃♃♃ jueves

Waxing Half Moon in ♋ Cancer 4:40 pm PDT

Thursday
10

♋
♌

♉□♃ 4:08 am
☽→♌ 11:54 am

—⟶♀♀♀ viernes

Friday
11

♌

☽♂♃ 2:45 am
☽□♉ 5:31 am
♀✶♄ 10:50 am
☽☍♆ 11:14 am
☽△♀ 11:33 pm

Prayer

Hail Nerthus! Anti-war Goddess of old. Where are You,
Nerthus? Come. Come now. Come running
 with your red wagon bumping over the battlefield.
The battlefields have become supermarkets, restaurants,
 bus stops, refugee camps, churches, temples, mosques.
Hurry! The soldiers have become children.
Just say the word, and guns will not fire. One glance
from You, grenades will not explode, bombs will fall flat.
Come, with Your holy force field,
turn landmines into fruits for starving peoples.
Lift one finger, mighty Nerthus, and trigger Peace.
Monkeywrench the machines of war with Your Love,
dull the blade, catch the missile, grab the detonator.
Pile Your wagon high with dead weapons,
cart them off the edge of earth.
Charm bullets into rain for thirsty ground.
Goddess! Send us Mercy, irresistible.
Flood the halls of power, the tents of the dispossessed
with Mercy.
Still with Mercy the command to shoot, bulldoze, launch.
Inspire with Mercy the passion to mend.
Pour out Mercy, O Nerthus, to the ends of the earth.
Hurry! Nerthus, Hurry!

excerpt © Bethroot Gwynn 2002

ᚻᚻᚻ sábado

♌ ☽ Saturday
♍   12

☉△☽	3:31 am		☽☍♅	7:53 pm
☽✶♄	7:18 am	v/c	♀□♇	11:03 pm
♂⚼♄	7:30 am			
☽→♍	5:07 pm			

☉☉☉ domingo

♍ ☽ Sunday
      13

| ☽△♉ | 2:40 pm |
| ♉□♆ | 4:27 pm |

April

———— ☽☽☽ maandag ————————————

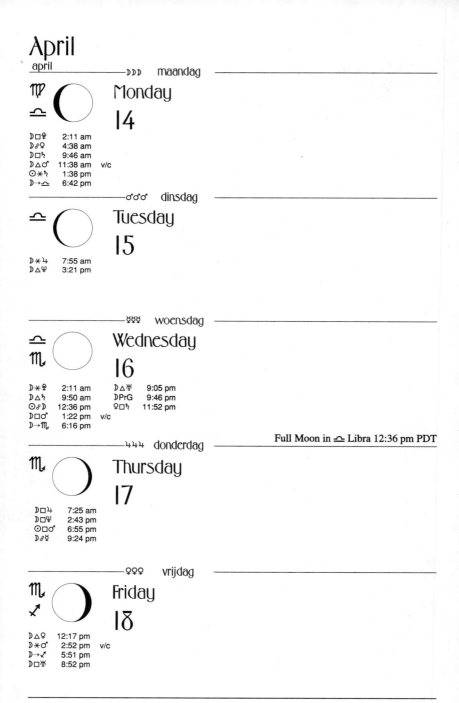

♍
☐   **Monday**
♎   **14**

☽□♀	2:11 am
☽☍♀	4:38 am
☽□♄	9:46 am
☽△♂	11:38 am v/c
☉⚹♄	1:38 pm
☽→♎	6:42 pm

———— ♂♂♂ dinsdag ————————————

♎   **Tuesday**
      15

☽⚹♃	7:55 am
☽△♆	3:21 pm

———— ☿☿☿ woensdag ————————————

♎   **Wednesday**
♏   **16**

☽⚹♀	2:11 am	☽△♅	9:05 pm
☽△♄	9:50 am	☽PrG	9:46 pm
☉☍☽	12:36 pm	♀□♄	11:52 pm
☽□♂	1:22 pm v/c		
☽→♏	6:16 pm		

———— ♃♃♃ donderdag ———————— **Full Moon in ♎ Libra 12:36 pm PDT**

♏   **Thursday**
      17

☽□♃	7:25 am
☽□♆	2:43 pm
☉□♂	6:55 pm
☽☍♅	9:24 pm

———— ♀♀♀ vrijdag ————————————

♏   **Friday**
♐   **18**

☽△♀	12:17 pm
☽⚹♂	2:52 pm v/c
☽→♐	5:51 pm
☽□♅	8:52 pm

———————————————————————————

ALL ASPECTS IN PACIFIC DAYLIGHT TIME; ADD 3 HOURS FOR EDT; ADD 8 HOURS FOR GMT

Year at a Glance for ♉ TAURUS (April 20–May 21)

Taurus has a gift for growing anything in poor soil, both literally and metaphorically. In the last few years, necessity has called up the best of your resourcefulness. Applaud yourself for the valuable emotional, mental and/or spiritual abundance that has emerged through your efforts.

In order for you to be successful at this time, your work must serve a larger good, whether social service, environmental concerns or even public art. Be wary of speculative or risky ventures, as your usually pragmatic eye is obsessed with seeing what it wants to see, not what is actually happening. Networking with strong willed, strong minded people exposes you to unexpected possibilities for your future you would never have dreamed up on your own. You need the encouragement of others and will work hard to strengthen your web of community. Training or schooling improves your communication skills, adds confidence and clarity of expression. Your mind is ready for the discipline.

The first half of 2003 is good for improving your home life, whether that be renovating, moving or just appreciating family and roots. The second half brings out more playfulness and heightened creativity. This is a good year to thrust yourself out into the world. People will be intrigued. If you have children, they will be going through a positive period, where their efforts to become more than they have been will be rewarded. If you are not already romantically involved, the chances of meeting someone are high, especially in the second half of the year. Existing loves blossom from holidays or playful activities. You are more able to be yourself, with a sunny ease and without apology.

© *Gretchen Lawlor 2002*

Salt Springs Wild Women
© *Amarah K. Gabriel 2000*

♐ ♄♄♄ zaterdag

Saturday
19

☿△♄	3:10 am
☽△♃	7:31 am
☽⚹♆	2:59 pm

☉☉☉ zondag

♐ ♑
Sunday
20

☽♂♀	2:06 am	☽→♑	7:20 pm
☉→♉	5:03 am	☉△☽	8:24 pm
☽♂♄	10:55 am	☽⚹♅	10:38 pm
☽□♀	6:02 pm v/c		

Sun in Taurus 5:03 am PDT

April
Pachapuquy killa

♑

Monday
21

♀✶♂	1:50 am
♀→♈	9:18 am
♂→♒	4:48 pm

♑
♒

Tuesday
22

☿⊼♀	12:27 am	
☽△☿	5:40 am	v/c
☉✶♅	5:57 am	
☽→♒	11:58 pm	

♒

Wednesday
23

☽♂♂	1:27 am
☽✶♀	3:52 am
☉□☽	5:18 am
☽☍♃	3:50 pm
☽♂♇	11:58 pm

Waning Half Moon in ♒ Aquarius 5:18 am PDT

♒

Thursday
24

☽✶♀	12:22 pm	
☽□☿	1:48 pm	
☽△♄	11:19 pm	v/c

♒
♓

Friday
25

☽→♓	8:02 am
☿R	8:59 am
☽♂♅	12:05 pm
☉✶☽	6:30 pm

ALL ASPECTS IN PACIFIC DAYLIGHT TIME; ADD 3 HOURS FOR EDT; ADD 8 HOURS FOR GMT

Great Mothers Birthing the Future
© *Selina di Girolamo 2001*

♓

Saturday
26

☿R   4:59 am
☽□♀   10:18 pm

⊙⊙⊙ Intichaw

♓
♈

Sunday
27

☽⚹♉   12:04 am
☽□♄   10:18 am   v/c
☽→♈   6:54 pm

Holy Yoni

About nine thousand years ago, the communities who lived around the Mediterranean Sea venerated a goddess supreme in Her creative powers of seduction and fruition. She was the generous Mother of Creation, Queen of Heaven and Earth. Her generative heat, lust and love were the forces which maintained all life. She guided all growth, and especially loved lovers and art, beauty and heart. She was later called Ishtar, Isis, Cybele, Inanna, Aphrodite, Yemaya. She was not shy.

The vulva, representing as it does the passageway through which we enter life, was probably the first religious symbol of humankind. The Sanskrit, *Jagad Yoni*, translates as *womb of the world*, its shape clearly characterizing woman's external genitalia. The yoni has survived as a central sacred image in several cultures and can be observed in Druid temples, domed synagogues and basilica and the soaring arches which grace Hindu and Arabic places of prayer. Even the familiar horseshoe, which is still hung as protection over the thresholds of houses and barns, owes its power to its shape—a stylized vulva.

Cowrie shells, perfect, miniature yonis have long been universally prized for use as ritual paraphernalia. Twenty-thousand-year-old skeletons have been discovered which were decked out in elaborate cowrie shell decorations. Their name comes from Kauri, another appellation of the goddess, Kali-Cunti. The Greek word for cowrie, *kteis,* also means *vulva.*

In these ancient sacred images we can recognize the holiness implicit in the female sexual experience. Freely exchanged, unabashed and bold, sex was seen as authentic religious expression. Although this erotic attitude toward worship was all but annihilated by the puritanical and judgmental Judeo-Christian-Islamic cultures, this primal, carnal knowledge of the universal order surfaces in our language today. Sex and prayer are inextricably linked etymologically. *Venerate* and *venereal* both stem from the same root—the Latin name of the licentious Roman Goddess of Love, Venus. And the word, *lust* in the old Germanic language meant, *religious joy.*

excerpt © Donna Henes 2001

V. SHE EMBODIES

Moon V: May 1–May 30

New Moon in ♉ Taurus: May 1; Full Moon in ♏ Scorpio: May 15; Sun in ♊ Gemini: May 21

Lotus
¤ Melissa VanTil 2000

April/May

April/Mai

April/Mai

I Only Have Thighs for You
◻ *Angela Hrabowiak 2000*

ⅮⅮⅮ Montag ———

♈

Monday
28

☽⚹♂	2:34 am
☽☌♀	12:09 pm
☽△♃	12:56 pm
♀△♃	8:19 pm
☽⚹♆	9:13 pm

♂♂♂ Dienstag ———

♈

Tuesday
29

☽△♀	10:19 am	
☉□♃	12:32 pm	
☽⚹♄	11:12 pm	v/c

☿☿☿ Mittwoch ———

♈
♉

Wednesday
30

☽→♉	7:26 am	
☽⚹♅	12:01 pm	
☽□♂	6:25 pm	
☿⚻♀	12:37 pm	
☽ApG	12:40 am	

♃♃♃ Donnerstag ———

♉

Thursday
1

☽□♃	2:09 am	
☉☌☽	5:15 am	
☽□♆	10:09 am	
☽☌♅	10:27 pm	v/c

May
Beltane

New Moon in ♉ Taurus 5:15 am PDT

♀♀♀ Freitag ———

♉
♊

Friday
2

♀⚹♆	5:57 am
☽→♊	8:27 pm

ALL ASPECTS IN PACIFIC DAYLIGHT TIME; ADD 3 HOURS FOR EDT; ADD 8 HOURS FOR GMT

© *Jennifer Beam 2001*

Beltane

This holy day on the cusp of summer is ablaze with passion. Maypoles are danced around, symbolically uniting the male and female energies within the Goddess' tree of life. Lovers jump the Beltane fire to release old grievances. Everywhere the abundance of nature is encouraged and appreciated.

On Beltane we revel in the sexual nature of our female bodies. We honor the sacred mysteries of bleeding, birthing and holding our wise blood within. With the population of the earth at six billion people, our Mother Earth is straining to feed and shelter us all. Our female creative powers are abundant, yet we must use them wisely to ensure that all life on earth is sustained.

This Mayday take time to honor your sexual powers. Find a place to build a fire and dress in green, the color of abundance. Dance or make love in the firelight. Focus on anything you want to increase in your life and toss handfuls of sweet herbs into the fire as offerings to the Goddess. Affirm that our bodies are sacred and perfect just the way they are. Know that we have control over our bodies: choices about sexuality and reproduction are ours to make. © *Ginny Salkowski 2002*

Open

Cosima Hewes 2000

Artichoke

She's feminine by nature
jewel of the earth
you might say she's guarded
I say she's complex;
with her layers of petals
standing erect
while soft under bellies
caress their living source.

You might say she's aloof
I say it's in your approach.
She thrives on airy fingertips
and gentle nibbles.

Read her like a book
tear off each page

and savor her slowly.
She gives you all you need to
know
without words
just the taste of her story
printed on your tongue
as her journey unfolds
and slides down your throat

she lies naked before you
with nothing to offer
but her heart
moist
and
delicious!

© Timothi Jane Graham 2001

Forepray: to the Great One
Invocation to Ignite Desire

Shakti! Your fiery yoni
rouses. Wake us!
Kameshvara! Mother of Desire
For the sacrament of the body,
claim and consecrate us now.
Kali and Pele! Prepare us
to erupt—to stream.

Artemis, Ishtar!
May we who would
penetrate your mysteries
dare dissolve in you.
Sex Goddesses you
dance and carouse
as One. Infuse us
with your fever heat.
With your revels, Great One,
charge the body of creation!

¤ *Sue Silvermarie 2001*

ħħħ　Samstag

♊ **Saturday**

3

☽□♅	1:11 am
☽△♂	10:34 am
☽⚹♃	3:30 pm
☉□♆	5:18 pm
☽△♆	11:02 pm

⊙⊙⊙　Sonntag

♊ **Sunday**

4

☿△♄	1:30 am
☽⚹♀	3:39 am
☽☍♀	11:46 am

May
mayo

Monday
5

☽♂♄ 1:43 am v/c
☽→♋ 8:42 am
☽△♅ 1:26 pm

Silbury Hill
© *Chesca Potter 1990*

Tuesday
6

♀□♅ 7:39 am
☉⚹☽ 4:02 pm
☽⚹♀ 5:03 pm
☽□♀ 9:21 pm v/c

Wednesday
7

☉♂♀ 12:21 am
♀△♇ 10:36 am
☽→♌ 6:46 pm

Thursday
8

♂☍♃ 10:36 am
☽♂♃ 1:11 pm
☽☍♂ 1:17 pm
☉△♅ 6:12 pm
☽☍♆ 7:16 pm
☽□♀ 10:51 pm

Friday
9

☉□☽ 4:53 am
☽△♇ 6:34 am
♀PrG 7:01 am
☽△♀ 11:03 am
☽⚹♄ 8:13 pm v/c

Waxing Half Moon in ♌ Leo 4:53 am PDT

ALL ASPECTS IN PACIFIC DAYLIGHT TIME; ADD 3 HOURS FOR EDT; ADD 8 HOURS FOR GMT

Newporter

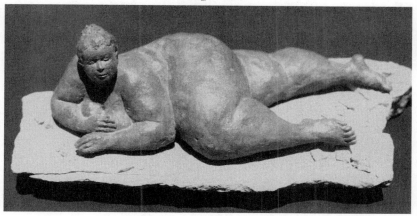

□ *Joyce Ann Mudd 2001*

And she saw that she looked like the Goddess Mothers she had just seen. The thousands of little fat gals unearthed were not meant as a singular idea of reproduction or menstruation, but they represented creativity, abundance, renewal, bounty of Earth and self. She left the museum juicy, full, and ripe with possibility.

excerpt □ *Deb-RA Sawers 2001*

———— ♄♄♄   sábado ————

♌
♍

Saturday
10

☽→♍   1:31 am
☉⅂♀   3:30 am
☽☍♅   5:55 am

———— ☉☉☉   domingo ————

♍

Sunday
11

☽△♅   1:38 am
☽□♀   10:53 am
☉△☽   1:14 pm

May
mei

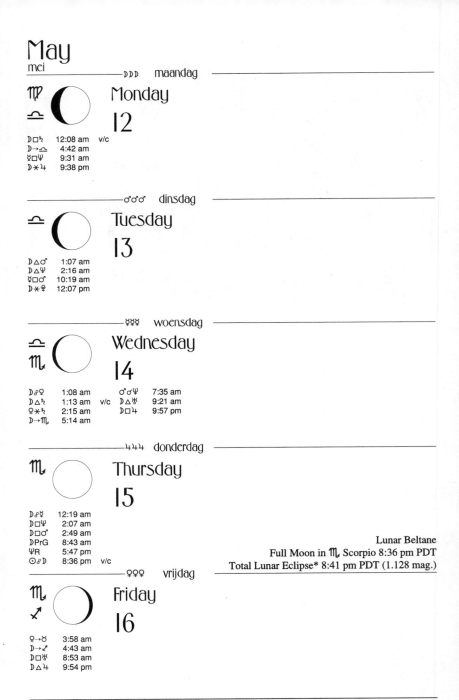

———⟫⟫⟫ maandag ———————————

Monday
12

☽□♄	12:08 am	v/c
☽→♎	4:42 am	
☿□♆	9:31 am	
☽✶♃	9:38 pm	

———♂♂♂ dinsdag ———————————

Tuesday
13

☽△♂	1:07 am
☽△♆	2:16 am
☿□♂	10:19 am
☽✶♀	12:07 pm

———☿☿☿ woensdag ———————————

Wednesday
14

☽☍♀	1:08 am		♂☌♆	7:35 am
☽△♄	1:13 am	v/c	☽△♅	9:21 am
♀✶♄	2:15 am		☽□♃	9:57 pm
☽→♏	5:14 am			

———♄♄♄ donderdag ———————————

Thursday
15

☽☍♅	12:19 am	
☽□♆	2:07 am	
☽□♂	2:49 am	
☽PrG	8:43 am	
♆R	5:47 pm	
☉☍☽	8:36 pm	v/c

Lunar Beltane
Full Moon in ♏ Scorpio 8:36 pm PDT
Total Lunar Eclipse* 8:41 pm PDT (1.128 mag.)

———♀♀♀ vrijdag ———————————

Friday
16

♀→♉	3:58 am
☽→♐	4:43 am
☽□♅	8:53 am
☽△♃	9:54 pm

* Eclipse visible from the Americas, Africa and Europe

The Goddess Tree

I lean my body
into the bark
of the Goddess Tree

until my voice
becomes one
with Hers
tumbling into roots
and sky.

excerpt © Pesha Joyce Gertler 2001
artwork: Girltree ¤ Melissa VanTil 2000

♄♄♄   zaterdag

   ♐

Saturday
17

☽⚹♆	1:45 am
☽⚹♂	4:18 am
☽☌♀	11:26 am

☉☉☉   zondag

   ♐
♑

Sunday
18

☽☍♄	1:41 am	☽⚹♅	9:27 am
☽→♑	5:03 am	☽△♀	9:32 am
♀⚹♅	8:39 am	☽△♅	11:38 pm

May

Ariwaki Killa

♑

Monday
19

☿□♃ 4:47 pm
☿D 12:33 am

♑
♒

Tuesday
20

☉△☽ 6:29 am v/c
☽→♒ 8:01 am
☽□♀ 5:50 pm

♒

Wednesday
21

☽□♅ 3:55 am
☽☍♃ 4:10 am
☉→♊ 4:12 am
☽♂♆ 7:33 am
☽♂♂ 2:53 pm
☽⚹♀ 6:21 pm

Sun in Gemini 4:12 am PDT

♒
♓

Thursday
22

☽△♄ 11:49 am v/c
☽→♓ 2:41 pm
☉□☽ 5:31 pm
☽♂♅ 7:51 pm

Waning Half Moon in ♓ Pisces 5:31 pm PDT

♓

Friday
23

☽⚹♀ 7:10 am
☽⚹♄ 12:50 pm
☿□♃ 6:22 pm

ALL ASPECTS IN PACIFIC DAYLIGHT TIME; ADD 3 HOURS FOR EDT; ADD 8 HOURS FOR GMT

Year at a Glance for ♊ GEMINI (May 21–June 21)

Gemini have a naturally restless, unconventional nature and are currently dealing with a ferocious itch to demonstrate to the world their originality and genius. In 2003 there are likely to be sudden moves, especially for financial or professional advantage. Take on some project and do so with economy and resourcefulness. If you focus upon acquisition of money or stuff as reward, you will be frustrated. Don't base decisions upon nervous financial appraisals; increased creativity and self-esteem are more available and valuable. Take note of repetitive impulses and themes as important keys to your life in the next 3–5 years.

In the past three years you have been finishing with an old project and realigning your self to something even closer to your essence. This shift has entailed some isolation, discipline and the acquisition of skills to help you communicate more effectively. Before you leap out of an existing job, consider other ways to express your original spark. Experiment with skills or talents that you have left dormant as hobbies or sidelines, they could turn lucrative in the next couple of years. Restlessness may make you irritable, belligerent and undependable; find a place to let it out, or you may be looking for a new job in spite of yourself.

2002 was a watershed year for you. A compelling encounter may still be having a transformative effect upon you. You need profound interactions at this time; they help you change and become more powerful. If you are already involved, you and your partner are less willing to skate around on the surface. You are generous and compassionate with yourself; family ties will be good support and comfort.

© *Gretchen Lawlor 2002*

Women of the Night
© *L.A. Hecht 1999*

----------------- ᚻᚻᚻ K'uychichaw -----------------

♓ **Saturday**

24

☉□♅ 12:37 am
☽□♀   3:19 am
☽□♄ 10:33 pm   v/c
♂⚹♀ 11:58 pm

-----◎◎◎ Intichaw -----

♓
♈ **Sunday**

25

☽→♈ 12:59 am
☉⚹☽   9:02 am

May/June

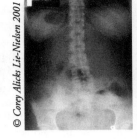

© Corey Alicks Lie-Nielsen 2001

—》》》 Montag —————

♈

Monday
26

♀□♃	12:29 am
☽△♃	12:58 am
☽✶♆	3:22 am
☽△♀	3:08 pm
☽✶♂	5:02 pm
♅♂♀	5:04 pm

————♂♂♂ Dienstag —————

♈
♉

Tuesday
27

♀□♆	12:01 am	
♅□♆	9:17 am	
☽✶♄	11:41 am	v/c
☽→♉	1:32 pm	
☽✶♅	7:12 pm	

————☿☿☿ Mittwoch —————

♉

Wednesday
28

☽ApG	6:05 am
☽□♃	2:39 pm
☽□♆	4:18 pm
☽♂♅	5:57 pm
☽♂♀	8:57 pm

————♃♃♃ Donnerstag —————

♉

Thursday
29

| ☽□♂ | 8:53 am | v/c |

————♀♀♀ Freitag —————

♉
♊

Friday
30

☽→♊	2:32 am
☽□♅	8:10 am
♀△♎	10:58 am
☉♂☽	9:20 pm

Annular Solar Eclipse* (3 min., 37 sec.) 9:09 pm PDT
New Moon in ♊ Gemini 9:20 pm PDT

* Eclipse visible from the Arctic Circle, Europe and parts of Asia and Africa

On Seeing My X-Ray

It was placed on the light box for viewing, peering:
a piece of film exposing my innermost secrets.
Irreverent hands pointing:
sacroiliac, pelvis, vertebrae,
even the flesh of my breasts.
I was not prepared for the eerie beauty of it;
my structure laid bare;
a luminous map of my very core.
Don't touch it, I wanted to say, *my pelvis is sacred;*
five babies have been cradled there
reading the messages left to each other
etched in my bones.
My power lies there—I am a Mother:
I have held all of creation in my mother-bones,
the entire universe at my sacrum.
Those bones have opened like the gates of Heaven,
moving with geological force,
pouring forth the sun, the moon, the oceans and skies—
All that exists is before us
as we gaze into the holy book of my bones.

© *Corey Alicks Lie-Nielsen 2001*

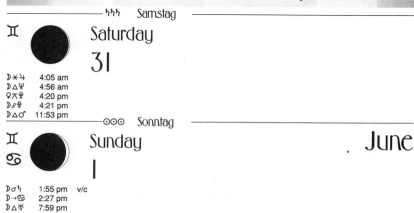

—————————— ♄♄♄ Samstag ——————————

♊

Saturday
31

☽⚹♃	4:05 am
☽△♆	4:56 am
♀⚺♀	4:20 pm
☽☍♀	4:21 pm
☽△♂	11:53 pm

——————— ☉☉☉ Sonntag ———————

♊
♋

Sunday
1

☽♂♄	1:55 pm	v/c
☽→♋	2:27 pm	
☽△♅	7:59 pm	

. June

Wild Things

The golden glow of sunset calls me out to walk in the mountains near my home. I am often rewarded on these walks with gifts from Gaia: antlers, feathers, rainbows, glorious sunsets and animal encounters. I have come face to face with some of the wild four legged creatures who live here: coyotes, javalina, deer, fox and mountain lion. There is a moment when we are frozen in time. Our eyes meet, we stare into each others' souls and their wildness ignites my wildness. Sometimes I bring my hands to my heart and bow to their sacredness. Then, they turn and disappear through the pine trees.

During these brief encounters, I am aware that I have come face to face with the Great Mother. These wild creatures are her emissaries and to look into their eyes is looking into the eyes of Gaia, Earth Goddess. I am grateful. Blessed Be!

VI. SHE CONNECTS
Moon VI : May 30–June 29
New Moon in ♊ Gemini: May 30; Full Moon in ♐ Sagittarius: June 14; Sun in ♋ Cancer: June 21

Freedom
© Marie LoParco 1998

June
junio

————— ☽☽☽ —— lunes —————

Monday
2

☿△♄ 12:54 am
♃☍♆ 7:55 pm

Summer's Reflection
© *Lynda Healy 2001*

————— ♂♂♂ —— martes —————

Tuesday
3

☽⚹♅ 1:54 am
☽⚹♀ 9:27 am v/c
♅⚻♀ 3:37 pm
♄→♋ 6:28 pm
☉△♆ 7:27 pm

————— ♀♀♀ —— miércoles —————

Wednesday
4

☉⚹♃ 12:14 am
☽→♌ 12:25 am

————— ♃♃♃ —— jueves —————

Thursday
5

☽☍♆ 12:55 am   ☽□♅   3:12 pm
☽☌♃ 1:36 am   ♀□♂   4:53 pm
☉⚹☽ 3:17 am   ☽☍♂ 10:55 pm
☽△♀ 11:19 am   ☽□♀ 11:18 pm v/c

————— ♀♀♀ —— viernes —————

Friday
6

☽→♍ 7:51 am
☽⚹♄ 8:26 am
☽☍♅ 12:55 pm
♅R 11:58 pm

Sister Maiden

i remember when
we laughed together so hard
it was impossible to remember we had
lived so many years without laughing
i felt you iron weighted
like a steamer train
in a pattern we wished to forget
and you told me of a song you used
to sing in fourth grade
when you still felt time
stretching before you
and you saw yourself free
of sunday dresses
and good manners

i remember when
we sat together under
the pruned hedges laughing
like we had no teachers
reveling in the freedom
you were teaching me
the light filtering through
painting the leafy print of branches
on your arms and face
halo of your long black hair
wavy and unmanageable
and i think of the first time
i saw the Goddess
and she was in you.

© *Nicolle Morris 2000*

ħħħ sábado

♍

Saturday
7

⊙□☽   1:28 pm
☽□♀   4:54 pm
⊙⊼♄   8:27 pm

⊙⊙⊙ domingo

Waxing Half Moon in ♍ Virgo 1:28 pm PDT

♍
♎

Sunday
8

☽△♅   1:36 am
☽△♀   9:27 am   v/c
☽→♎   12:30 pm
☽□♄   1:33 pm
♀PrG   2:22 pm

June
juni

——— ⅅⅅⅅ   maandag ———

♎ Monday
9

☽△♆ 10:32 am
☽✶♃ 12:26 pm
☉✶♀ 1:44 pm
☽✶♀ 7:50 pm
☉△☽ 8:17 pm
♀→♊ 8:32 pm

——— ♂♂♂   dinsdag ———

♎ ♏ Tuesday
10

☽△♂ 10:00 am v/c
☽→♏ 2:39 pm
☽△♄ 4:05 pm
☽△♅ 7:15 pm
☿□♂ 10:48 pm

——— ☿☿☿   woensdag ———

♏ Wednesday
11

☽□♆ 11:48 am
☽□♃ 2:14 pm

——— ♃♃♃   donderdag ———

♏ ♐ Thursday
12

♀□♅ 3:56 am
☽□♂ 12:11 pm
☽☍♅ 2:51 pm v/c
☽→♐ 3:12 pm
☽PrG 4:29 pm
☿→♊ 6:34 pm
☽□♅ 7:43 pm
☽☍♀ 9:07 pm

——— ♀♀♀   vrijdag ———

♐ Friday
13

☽✶♆ 12:04 pm
☽△♃ 3:05 pm
☽☌♀ 8:58 pm

The Source
Life is a question
of connection or separation.
What you truly desire
is already true,
for we are reflections
in the Mother's eyes.

excerpt © Myra Dutton 2001

ALL ASPECTS IN PACIFIC DAYLIGHT TIME; ADD 3 HOURS FOR EDT; ADD 8 HOURS FOR GMT

Goddess
¤ *Witchhazel Wildwood 2001*

───── ♄♄♄ zaterdag ─────

♐
♑

Saturday

14

☉☍☽	4:16 am		☽→♑	3:38 pm	
☽⚹♂	2:05 pm	v/c	☽☍♄	5:56 pm	
♀□♅	3:04 pm		☽⚹♅	8:12 pm	v/c

───── ☉⊙☉ zondag ─────

Full Moon in ♐ Sagittarius 4:16 am PDT

♑

Sunday

15

───────────────────────────

June
Aymuray killa

───── ☽☽☽ Killachaw ─────

♑
♒

Monday
16

☽→♒ 5:41 pm
♂→♓ 7:25 pm

Beginning Prayer
© Durga Bernhard 1999

───── ♂♂♂ Atichaw ─────

♒

Tuesday
17

☽△♉ 5:50 am
☽△♀ 9:36 am
☽☌♆ 4:08 pm
☽☍♃ 8:52 pm

───── ☿☿☿ Quyllurchaw ─────

♒
♓

Wednesday
18

☽✶♀ 1:52 am
☉△☽ 6:08 pm   v/c
☽→♓ 10:57 pm
☽☌♂ 12:39 am

───── ♃♃♃ Illapachaw ─────

♓

Thursday
19

☽△♄ 2:35 am
☽☌♅ 4:03 am
☽□♉ 8:32 am
☽□♀ 9:49 pm

───── ♀♀♀ Ch'askachaw ─────

♓

Friday
20

☽□♀ 9:24 am
♀△♆ 9:52 am
☿△♆ 1:32 pm
☿☌♀ 8:53 pm

ALL ASPECTS IN PACIFIC DAYLIGHT TIME; ADD 3 HOURS FOR EDT; ADD 8 HOURS FOR GMT

Year at a Glance for ⊙ CANCER (June 21–July 22)

You may still be sloughing off an old life-skin in the first months of 2003. A great lassitude in these early months responds to solitude and sleep, helping you shed, like a snake, this significant era. Health issues at this time will respond best to detoxifying programs and therapies that work with underlying emotional/psychological issues.

Be wary of potential liaisons offered prior to June, they may be associated with your past rather than your future and could end up holding you back. Some bold effort on your part late–2001 through mid–2002 gave you a chance to display yourself as an innovator and achiever and 2003 is not too late to follow up on contacts that presented themselves at that time. These connections will prove valuable in years ahead, don't let them slip away.

By June, you are ready to begin to mould a new sense of identity. It's time to prove you can work hard and take on responsibilities. You may find yourself in over your head in terms of skills, constantly struggling to live up to what is expected of you. Experience or "on the job training" are your very best teachers. Both successes and failures will be immensely useful, don't waste time criticizing yourself. You are laying material foundations for the next 12 years. You are being challenged to think in radical and innovative ways. Exposure to new ideas may come through travel, through unusual educational opportunities or even solely through a change in residence. Rapport with people while journeying will be instant and electrifying, introducing you to possibilities for your future that you would not have come to on your own.

© *Gretchen Lawlor 2002*

⊱⊱⊱ K'uychichaw

♓		**Saturday**			*Solstice*

21

⊙□☽	7:45 am	v/c
☽→♈	8:06 am	
♃⊼♇	10:02 am	
⊙→⊙	12:10 pm	
☽□♄	12:36 pm	

Waning Half Moon in ♓ Pisces 7:45 am PDT
Sun in ⊙ Cancer 12:10 pm PDT

⊙⊙⊙ Intichaw

♈ **Sunday**

22

♉⊼♇	7:53 am	☽△♃	4:49 pm	
☽⚹♆	9:33 am	☽⚹♉	5:51 pm	
♉⚹♃	10:55 am	☽△♀	8:28 pm	v/c
☽⚹♀	3:03 pm	♂△♄	9:21 pm	

Summer Solstice

The longest day of the year lights our ability to love and connect in community. Summer Solstice corresponds with the full moon and to the mother ocean. It is the time for hand fastings, wish making and dancing in fairy rings. Litha the Celtic Goddess of abundance and Yemaya the African orisha of the ocean are honored with offerings of honey and roses.

As summer flourishes around us we are reminded of the interconnectedness of all life. No being is alone on this planet, we exist in relationship to each other. The artificial barriers we impose to keep us from nature and our communities are a loss of our power. Racism, sexism and other social divisions within the human family can leave us weak and isolated. Modern inventions such as television, computers and automobiles box us away from the sun and fresh air we need for life.

As summer reaches her peak, let us reclaim the wisdom of the bee, the tree, the web and the spiral. Get outside and meet your neighbors. Have a community ritual or potluck. Source yourself in nature by walking in a forest or on the beach. Join hands with family and friends around a fire. Celebrate diversity. © *Ginny Salkowski 2002*

A Line Dance

Lady of the Beasts

remember: the continous flow of ecstatic connection

remember: the time of unified vision and creation

remember: the days are long and lovely

remember: you are cherished

excerpt ¤ Elizabeth Roberts 2001

June
Juni

eye-breasts
© *Lieve Snellings 2001*

ⅮⅮⅮ Montag

 ♈
♉

Monday
23

♀⚼♂	1:52 am
☿☍♀	9:46 am
♀✶♃	11:07 am
♂♂♅	1:02 pm
☽→♉	8:15 pm

♂♂♂ Dienstag

 ♉

Tuesday
24

☉✶☽	1:11 am	♄△♅	4:34 pm
☽✶♄	1:34 am	♀☍♀	7:00 pm
☽✶♅	1:45 am	☽ApG	7:19 pm
☽✶♂	2:11 am	☉△♂	8:54 pm
☉♂♄	6:39 am	☽□♆	10:15 pm
☉△♅	8:08 am		
♄ApG	11:43 am		

☿☿☿ Mittwoch

 ♉

Wednesday
25

☽□♃	6:41 am	v/c

♃♃♃ Donnerstag

 ♉
♊

Thursday
26

☽→♊	9:13 am
☽□♅	2:36 pm
☽□♂	5:02 pm

♀♀♀ Freitag

 ♊

Friday
27

☽△♆	10:46 am
☽✶♃	8:03 pm
☽☍♀	9:30 pm

Flotsam

I invite her to my home. She says to me *what's all this junk you have here?* She is pointing at a large oval copper-coloured plate that was my grandmother's favourite serving plate. On this plate there are two blackbird feathers that I came across while walking this morning, and a pine cone that my sister sent to me, and a string of amethyst beads that I sometimes wear, and a picture that I found last spring of a she-wolf with her cubs, and a windfall apple from my garden and a yellow scarf that was a gift from a friend.

I tell her *it is flotsam.*

She stares at me, confused. So I explain that this is my altar, that its contents change constantly according to what the universe floats my way. I explain to her that this altar is a reflection and an acknowledgement, a comfort and a challenge, a reminder of the past and the present and the future.

A week later she invites me to her home. In the middle of a shelf in a bookcase, there is a space between the books. And in the space there is a little wooden tray, carved into the shape of a ladybird. And on the tray there are five sea shells and a child's drawing of a butterfly.

Flotsam, she says.

¤ Fi Benson 2001

ħħħ Samstag

♊
♋

Saturday
28

☽☌♀	6:00 am	
☽☌♉	7:31 pm	v/c
☽→♋	8:52 pm	

☉☉☉ Sonntag

♋

Sunday
29

☽△♅	1:59 am	
☽☌♄	3:14 am	
♉→♋	3:17 am	
☽△♂	6:07 am	
☉☌☽	11:39 am	v/c

New Moon in ♋ Cancer 11:39 am PDT

Why Being Pregnant is Like Being an Apple

If you were to divide me in half, open me up across the middle with a line that starts where my hipbones end, I would look like an apple when you separate its top from its bottom. My insides would be a star-flower, filled with seeds as brown as the earth, packed with enough potential and magic to grow taller and stronger and more beautiful than I'll ever be.

My body has become a secret even from me, planning and changing and brewing with a knowledge that I'm not privy to. If you could find the right spot to listen, and press your ear against me like a seashell or a locked door, you could hear whispers of old wisdom and snake logic siphoning through me like static down a wire.

My breasts feel like ripe fruit, responding to a cultivation older than love. Their curves follow the roundness of green and red things, filling and colouring and growing heavy for plucking. As girls we used to pretend we had breasts by putting apples against our flat nipples and it was then we felt we knew what it meant to be womyn.

If you could taste me, or really study the colour of my flesh, it would have the pink tint and flavour of an apple whose brightness has soaked through its skin to permeate its whole being. My own mother told me that pink apples are lucky—there is no way of knowing if you have one until a part of it is in a part of you.

I feel like I want to gather and preserve and bake and taste things sweet and sticky and full of spices and sugars. I want my heat to soften and toast things until they smell better than heaven and home mixed together. I think all my cells have been filled with sweet-tart juice that would drip out at the lightest touch.

I remember being afraid of heights everywhere but in an apple tree that my mother taught me to climb, filling my shirt with apples to bring back down to earth, their smooth skins resting against my belly, thrilling it with their solidity and weight.

And so I sit in my kitchen, feeling circular and content, to wait until a harvest moon.

◻ *Alison D. Hauch 2000*

VII. SHE GIVES BIRTH

Moon VII: June 29–July 28

New Moon in ♋ Cancer: July 29; Full Moon in ♑ Capricorn: July 13; Sun in ♌ Leo: July 22

In Full Bloom
© *Jennifer Lynn Shifflet 1996*

June/July
junio/julio —————— ⊅⊅⊅ lunes —————

Monday
30

☿△♅   8:27 am
☿☌♄   6:14 pm
⚵PrG 10:18 pm

Mama
⌗ *Kit Skeoch 2001*

————— ♂♂♂ martes —————

Tuesday
1

♃△♀   5:47 am
☽→♌   6:13 am
☿△♂   5:06 pm

July

————— ☿☿☿ miércoles —————

Wednesday
2

☽☍♆   5:39 am
☽△♀   3:31 pm
☽☌♃   4:05 pm

————— ♃♃♃ jueves —————

Thursday
3

☽⚹♀   11:06 am v/c
☽→♍   1:16 pm
☽☍♅   5:50 pm
☽⚹♄   8:15 pm

————— ♀♀♀ viernes —————

Friday
4

☽☍♂   12:28 am   ☉⚻♆   4:28 pm
☽⚹♅   9:39 am   ☽□♀   9:15 pm v/c
♀→♋   10:39 am   ☿⚻♆   10:30 pm
☉⚹☽   11:22 am

—————————————————————————————————————

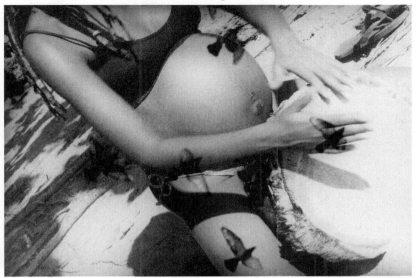

© *Lilian de Mello 1999*

Child, I awaken every night to the insistent beating of your heart.

You strike out and my vast belly rattles with staccato life.

It is a shaman's drum, the taut skin played from within.

excerpt © Clare McCall 1999

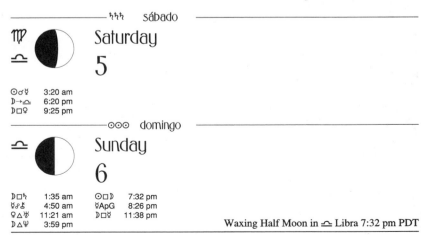

ħħħ   sábado

♍ Saturday
♎ 5

☉♂♉	3:20 am
☽→♎	6:20 pm
☽□♀	9:25 pm

⊙⊙⊙   domingo

♎ Sunday
6

☽□♄	1:35 am	☉□☽	7:32 pm
♉☌♃	4:50 am	☿ApG	8:26 pm
♀△♅	11:21 am	☽□♉	11:38 pm
☽△♆	3:59 pm		

Waxing Half Moon in ♎ Libra 7:32 pm PDT

July
juli

──────────))) maandag ──────────

Monday
7

D⚹♀   1:11 am
D⚹♃   3:23 am   v/c
☿⊼♃   9:44 am
☉☌♇   11:17 am
D→♏   9:43 pm

Great Mother Gives Birth
© *Dánahy Sharonrose 2001*

────────── ♂♂♂ dinsdag ──────────

Tuesday
8

♀☌♄   1:30 am
D△♅   1:51 am
D△♄   5:13 am
D△♀   5:32 am
D△♂   10:15 am
D□♇   6:41 pm

────────── ☿☿☿ woensdag ──────────

Wednesday
9

☉△D   1:49 am
D□♃   6:35 am
D△☿   10:58 am   v/c
D→♐   11:48 pm

────────── ♃♃♃ donderdag ──────────

Thursday
10

D□♅   3:46 am
☉⊼♀   4:57 am
D□♂   12:56 pm
DPrG   3:08 pm
D⚹♆   8:20 pm

────────── ♀♀♀ vrijdag ──────────

Friday
11

♀△♂   12:28 am
D☌♀   5:13 am
D△♃   8:53 am   v/c

───────────────────────────────────────

ALL ASPECTS IN PACIFIC DAYLIGHT TIME; ADD 3 HOURS FOR EDT; ADD 8 HOURS FOR GMT

For a moment, labor carries me beyond myself.

The night hangs heavy with remnants of the day's heat.

Crickets chirp. The lake lingers in the breeze,

wafting through the room like a subtle perfume.

The earth calls, and I start to fly.

The topography looks suspiciously like a woman.

Breasts here. Bellies there. Forests of invitations.

Then an earthquake hits. The ground rumbles, and I fall.

My breasts. My belly. My rolling hills.

Forest fires and churning rivers.

Clear mountain lakes and audacious volcanoes.

I race into a cave.

Deep within the darkness a light penetrates from the other side.

I run toward it, suddenly afraid I might die, because the vision looks suspiciously like the near death experience I've heard about.

Then I realize the cave is a tunnel.

The earth is a tunnel.

I am a tunnel.

¤ *Connee L. Pike 2001*

ℏℏℏ zaterdag

♐
♑ ◯ Saturday

12

☽→♑   1:21 am
☽⚹♅   5:14 am
☽☍♄   9:37 am
☽⚹♂   3:17 pm
☽☍♀   6:15 pm

⊙⊙⊙ zondag

♑ ◯ Sunday

13

♉→♌   5:10 am
⊙☍☽ 12:21 pm   v/c

Full Moon in ♑ Capricorn 12:21 pm PDT

July

Jawqaykuski killa

☽☽☽ Killachaw

♑ ♒

Monday

14

☽→♒ 3:38 am
☽☍☿ 7:21 am
☿⚻♅ 8:42 am
♀⚻♆ 12:25 pm

Who is
coming?
sky baby
moon child

excerpt ¤ Heidi Marion 2001

♂♂♂ Atichaw

♒

Tuesday

15

☽☌♆ 12:52 am
☽✶♇ 10:20 am
☽☍♃ 3:57 pm v/c

☿☿☿ Quyllurchaw

♒ ♓

Wednesday

16

☽→♓ 8:14 am
♀☍⚷ 10:05 am
☽☌♅ 12:16 pm
☽△♄ 6:18 pm

♃♃♃ Illapachaw

♓

Thursday

17

☽☌♂ 1:01 am
☽△♀ 1:51 pm
☽□♇ 4:50 pm

♀♀♀ Ch'askachaw

♓ ♈

Friday

18

☿⚻♂ 12:36 am
☉△☽ 7:49 am v/c
☽→♈ 4:20 pm
♀⚻♇ 8:26 pm

All aspects in Pacific Daylight Time; add 3 hours for EDT; add 8 hours for GMT

Birthing a Dragon

She walks

> with the moon
> in her belly

Along the

> river's edge
> before dawn

Lifting a

> dragon from
> folds of skin

She moves

> low and sweet
> her tail on the wind.

¤ *Tami Kent 2001*

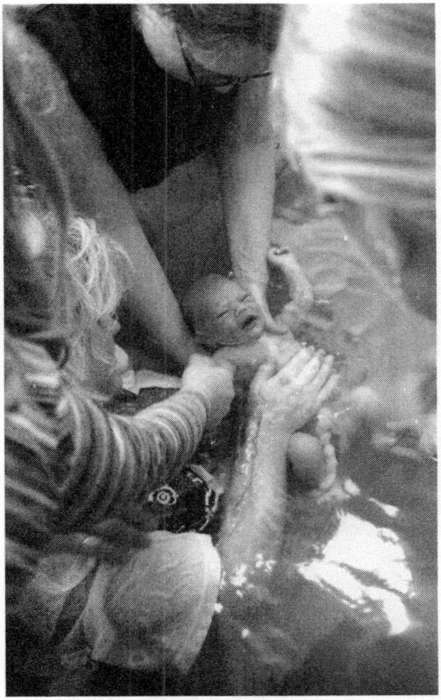

Waterbirth
© *Annie Ocean 1999*

ꜣꜣꜣ K'uychichaw

♈ Saturday
19

☽□♄	3:40 am
♉☌♆	1:58 pm
☽⚹♆	4:11 pm
☽△♅	4:35 pm

⊙⊙⊙ Intichaw

♈ Sunday
20

☽△♀	2:58 am
☽□♀	6:29 am
☽△♃	11:30 am
♉⚻♇	7:14 pm

July
Juli

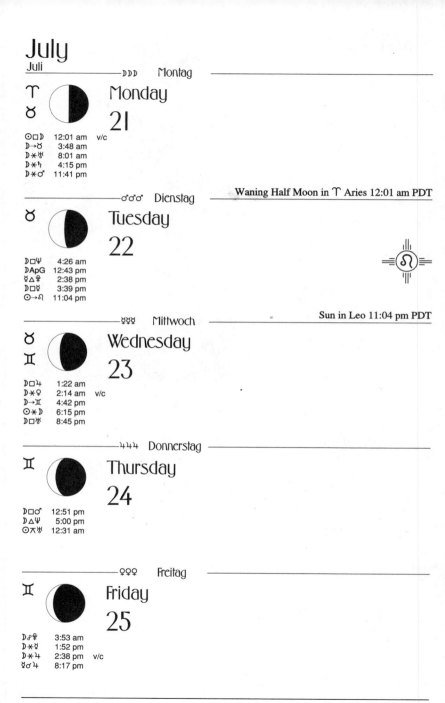

—DDD— Montag

♈
♉

Monday
21

⊙□D 12:01 am v/c
D→♉ 3:48 am
D✳♅ 8:01 am
D✳♄ 4:15 pm
D✳♂ 11:41 pm

—♂♂♂— Dienstag

Waning Half Moon in ♈ Aries 12:01 am PDT

♉

Tuesday
22

D□♆ 4:26 am
DApG 12:43 pm
☿△♀ 2:38 pm
D□☿ 3:39 pm
⊙→♌ 11:04 pm

—☿☿☿— Mittwoch

Sun in Leo 11:04 pm PDT

♉
♊

Wednesday
23

D□♃ 1:22 am
D✳♀ 2:14 am v/c
D→♊ 4:42 pm
⊙✳D 6:15 pm
D□♅ 8:45 pm

—♃♃♃— Donnerstag

♊

Thursday
24

D□♂ 12:51 pm
D△♆ 5:00 pm
⊙⊼♅ 12:31 am

—♀♀♀— Freitag

♊

Friday
25

D☍♀ 3:53 am
D✳♉ 1:52 pm
D✳♃ 2:38 pm v/c
☿♂♃ 8:17 pm

ALL ASPECTS IN PACIFIC DAYLIGHT TIME; ADD 3 HOURS FOR EDT; ADD 8 HOURS FOR GMT

Year at a Glance for ♌ LEO (July 22–Aug. 23)

Jupiter, planet of opportunity and expansiveness, entered Leo in August 2002 and will be there until September 2003. Launch yourself into some new project, study or sphere of influence. People will respond well to your confidence and style. This occurs only every 12 years, so use it! (What did you launch 12 years ago or regret not doing?) Walk your talk rather than keeping things at the idea or intention stage.

To act in an inspiring way and be respected and recognized by others is truly Leo's path. Success depends on sincerity of heart, as Leo can slip from generosity and courage to extravagance and self-aggrandizement. Soaring idealism and an amplified imagination in the early months are best used in artistic expression.

Cautions in this essentially positive time—watch over-extension or pompousness. This is not a time to cast off all pre-existing projects and responsibilities. It is rather a time to breathe fresh life into the ones that have an enduring value and slowly withdraw energy from the ones that have reached their peak. Associations will be formed for the sake of new and unusual purposes, where you experiment with collaborative efforts in less self-serving or traditional ways.

A chapter in your life suddenly ends and another begins, associated with the circumstances of someone close to you (especially July born Leos). Although the overall flavor of the year financially is quite positive, some caution is suggested in the choice of professional partnerships (especially for Leos born early August). Intimately and sexually you feel curious and ready. This could invigorate an existing relationship or you could meet someone who really sets your socks on fire.

© *Gretchen Lawlor 2002*

She Is Welcomed
© *Megaera 1998*

ħħħ   Samstag

♊
♋   Saturday
    26

☽→♋   4:23 am
☽△♅   8:07 am
☽♂ħ   5:29 pm
☽△♂   11:53 pm

⊙⊙⊙   Sonntag

♋   Sunday
    27

Gift Giving and the Goddess

Women's labour is gift labour and it is the basis of co-muni-cation (muni means gifts in Latin), the giving of free gifts together, which forms the co-muni-ty. In fact by nurturing our children we form both the bodies and the minds of the people who make up the community. This material non-sign communication involving giving and receiving without a pay back, is what makes us human generation after generation.

By taking off the eyeglasses of exchange we can see Mother Earth not as the adversary or as raw material for our profit- making activities but as the great gift giver. Each of the four elements has a different gift quality. Fire can be given to others without losing it, water nurtures life freely making up most of our body mass, earth gives us ground, space and innumerable gifts of plant and animals, while air flows from a high pressure to a low pressure area, from where there is more to where there is less.

When we create a society in which gift giving has become the human norm, our spirituality will be liberated and we will recognize the goddess in each other and the earth. Though some of us may feel that we are already experiencing this phenomenon, we have to remember the dire situation society is in and try to turn our gift giving towards the big picture. Protesting against patriarchy is a spiritual necessity. We must mother society, mother the future, mother our Mother the Earth and our human mothers as well as our children. As we call upon the ancient goddesses of our own and other cultures we empower ourselves with their gifts and we are also respecting the need of the people of the past not to have lived in vain. When we look at our planet from space we see that here we are living in comparative eden. Using the energy of the sun, the earth has created all this abundance of life. She is the creative receiver-and-giver. We must honour her processes. When we have restored the gift giving way we will all be able co muni cate with the spirits of nature who have no gender script. Our psychic abilities cannot develop because the contents of our minds have been made manipulative by our economics. Perhaps if we create a gift based society we will be able to form a community with the spirits of the dead as well, a practical heaven on earth.

excerpt ¤ Genevieve Vaughan 1999

III. SHE ABOUNDS

Moon VIII: July 28–August 27
New Moon in ♌ Leo: July 28;
Full Moon in ♒ Aquarius: Aug. 11;
Sun in ♍ Virgo: Aug. 23

Awaiting the Harvest
© *Karen Russo 2000*

July/August
julio/agosto

♋
♌

Monday
28

☽☌♀	12:25 pm	v/c
☽→♌	1:17 pm	
♀→♌	9:25 pm	
☉☌☽	11:53 pm	

♂♂♂ martes

New Moon in ♌ Leo 1:17 pm PST

♌

Tuesday
29

♂R	12:36 am
☽☍♆	11:08 am
☽△♀	9:06 pm

☿☿☿ miércoles

♌
♍

Wednesday
30

☿→♍	7:05 am	
♀⊼♅	8:16 am	
☽☌♃	8:46 am	v/c
☽→♍	7:27 pm	
☽☌☿	8:58 pm	
☽☍♅	10:34 pm	

♃♃♃ jueves

♍

Thursday
31

☽⚹♄	8:21 am
☿☍♅	11:24 am
☽☍♂	1:13 pm

♀♀♀ viernes

♍
♎

Friday
1

August

| ☽□♀ | 2:02 am | v/c |
| ☽→♎ | 11:48 pm | |

ALL ASPECTS IN PACIFIC DAYLIGHT TIME; ADD 3 HOURS FOR EDT; ADD 8 HOURS FOR GMT

Nurture the Seed
© *Joyce Radtke 1993*

Lammas

At Lammas we have reached the midpoint between Summer Solstice and Fall Equinox. It is the feast of first fruits and a celebration of the bountiful earth. Traditionally, breads were baked with the first grains and were offered to the Mother Goddess asking for protection on the harvest to come. Bonfires were built on the hilltops to ward off bad spirits and the ground was blessed with beer and moon blood.

The harvests of today differ from any the world has ever known. Huge "agribusinesses" produce tons of a single crop with the use of chemical fertilizers, pesticides and genetic engineering. This intensive food production is a major source of pollution. In spite of this mass production however, for most people in the world, food is still a scarce resource. 35,000 children die of starvation every day.

For Lammas this year take some action on the issue of food. If you planted a garden, offer some of your first bounty to a needy person in the name of the Goddess. Buy your food as organic and local as possible to support sustainable agriculture. Call your congress person and ask for labeling of genetically engineered foods. Go vegetarian.

© *Ginny Salkowski 2002*

artwork: The Sower © Agnes Nyanhongo 2001   photo: © Cora Greenhill 2001

Wheat

She is the bread I break upon my table now. Long before the churches took HER body and made it HIS, she was eaten on tables and Thanked for her bounty. Long before crucifixes there were corn dollies. Long before, and long after, there will be fields full of ripe, yellow, waving stems of wheat, rounding in the sun and offering the life of soil, wind, water and miracle to us, to eat, today. Food connects us all to each other, all over the world . . . Give us now this daily bread . . . Everyday I bless my food and this what I say:

Bless the Earth and the Sun, and the marriage between the two
which brings forth all life
Bless the hands through which this food has passed
along its journey.
Bless those who reap, those who sow, those who till,
those who buy and those who sell.
May all be touched by the abundance with which I
now find myself.
And a blessing to this table, that when we eat this food,
we will take its energy on into
The world, to do good things with.

© Felix 2001

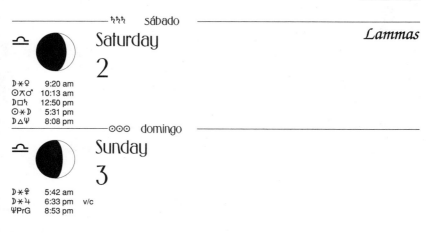

ᚻᚻᚻ sábado

Saturday
2

Lammas

♎

☽⚹♀ 9:20 am
☉⚻♂ 10:13 am
☽□♄ 12:50 pm
☉⚹☽ 5:31 pm
☽△♆ 8:08 pm

☉☉☉ domingo

Sunday
3

♎

☽⚹♀ 5:42 am
☽⚹♃ 6:33 pm v/c
♆PrG 8:53 pm

August

augustus ――――――― ☽☽☽　maandag ―――――――

♎︎
♏︎

Monday

4

☽→♏︎	3:12 am	☽□♀	5:33 pm
☽△♅	5:57 am	☽△♂	7:56 pm
☉☌♆	6:54 am	☿⚹♄	8:12 pm
☽⚹♅	4:11 pm	☽□♀	11:14 pm
☽△♄	4:32 pm		

――――――――――――― ♂♂♂　dinsdag ―――――――

♏︎

Tuesday

5

☉□☽	12:28 am	
♀⚻♂	7:02 pm	
☽□♃	10:22 pm	v/c

Las Papayas
□ *Jules Bubacz 1998*

―――――――――――― ☿☿☿　woensdag ――――――― **Waxing Half Moon in ♏︎ Scorpio 12:28 am PDT**

♏︎
♐︎

Wednesday

6

☉⚻♆	2:03 am
☽→♐︎	6:11 am
☿☍♂	6:12 am
☽PrG	7:02 am
☽□♅	8:47 am
☽□♂	10:28 pm

――――――――――――― ♃♃♃　donderdag ―――――――

♐︎

Thursday

7

☽□☿	12:12 am	♀☍♆	9:18 am
☽△♀	1:19 am	☽☌♀	11:35 am
☽⚹♆	2:01 am	☿⚻♆	8:37 pm
☉△☽	7:02 am		

――――――――――――― ♀♀♀　vrijdag ―――――――

♐︎
♑︎

Friday

8

☽△♃	2:01 am	v/c
☽→♑︎	9:02 am	
☽⚹♅	11:31 am	
♀⚻♆	5:55 pm	
☽☍♄	11:11 pm	

―――――――――――――――――――――――――――――――――

ALL ASPECTS IN PACIFIC DAYLIGHT TIME; ADD 3 HOURS FOR EDT; ADD 8 HOURS FOR GMT

Garden Sabbats

Garden is peace
black dirt caked under my nails
buckets of manure and compost
hauled from the pile
waiting to be spread
damp black earth turned
scenting the breezes.
This is ever evolving; never finished
i envision what it will look like and feel like
when the spring broccoli is ready to eat
when the corn is tall,
when the tomatoes are red ripe
when the fall cabbage is heading
when the mulch is spread and cold frames are up
when . . .
what is happening in my garden is what is happening in my life.
My rituals and sabbats are celebrated here
With the seasons of tilling, planting,
and bedding down for the winter,
i am tilling, planting, and bedding down myself
Garden is my soul worked in a physical way.

Brussel Sprouts
□ *Janice Iliffe-Lewis 1990*

© Nicolle Morris 2001

ħħħ zaterdag

♑ **Saturday**
9

☽⚹♂ 12:56 am
☿△♃ 6:01 am
☽△♅ 7:57 am   v/c

☉☉☉ zondag

♑
≈ **Sunday**
10

☉△♀ 1:42 am
☽→≈ 12:23 pm

August

Chakraqunakuy Killa))) Killachaw

excerpt ¤ Tatiana Bourdillon
de Blanco 2000

♒

Monday

11

☽☌♆	8:35 am
☽☍♀	6:17 pm
☽✶♀	6:39 pm
☉☍☽	9:48 pm
♀△♀	10:19 pm

Lunar Lammas
Full Moon in ♒ Aquarius 9:48 pm PDT

───── ♂♂♂ Atichaw ─────

♒
♓

Tuesday

12

☽☍♃	11:35 am	v/c
☽→♓	5:19 pm	
☽☌♅	7:38 pm	
♂△♄	7:55 pm	
♅□♀	8:01 pm	

───── ☿☿☿ Quyllurchaw ─────

♓

Wednesday

13

| ☽☌♂ | 9:01 am |
| ☽△♄ | 9:19 am |

───── ♃♃♃ Illapachaw ─────

♓

Thursday

14

| ☽□♀ | 1:01 am | |
| ☽☍♅ | 3:29 am | v/c |

───── ♀♀♀ Ch'askachaw ─────

♊
♈

Friday

15

☽→♈	1:00 am
♀ApG	8:38 am
☽□♄	6:27 pm
☽✶♆	11:10 pm

───────────────────────────

ALL ASPECTS IN PACIFIC DAYLIGHT TIME; ADD 3 HOURS FOR EDT; ADD 8 HOURS FOR GMT

Harvest
© *Durga Bernhard 1987*

────── ᚼᚼᚼ K'uychichaw ──────

♈ ☽(moon)

Saturday
16

☽△⚷ 10:33 am
☽△♀ 10:55 pm
☉△☽ 11:49 pm

────── ⊙⊙⊙ Intichaw ──────

♈
♉

Sunday
17

☽△♃ 7:36 am   v/c
☽→♉ 11:52 am
☽⚹♅ 2:05 pm

August

August

☽☽☽ Montag

The Provider: Peru
© Elizabeth Staber 2001

♉

Monday 18

☽✶♂ 3:17 am
☽✶♄ 6:40 am
☽□♆ 10:54 am
☉☌♀ 11:05 am

♂♂♂ Dienstag

♉

Tuesday 19

☽ApG 7:24 am
☽△☿ 10:32 am
☉□☽ 5:48 pm
☽□♀ 6:36 pm
☽□♃ 9:29 pm v/c

Waning Half Moon in ♉ Taurus 5:48 pm PDT

☿☿☿ Mittwoch

♉
♊

Wednesday 20

☽→♊ 12:41 am
☽□♅ 2:43 am
☽□♂ 2:59 pm
☽△♆ 11:37 pm

♃♃♃ Donnerstag

♊

Thursday 21

♀☌♃ 3:23 am
☽☍♇ 11:29 am

♀♀♀ Freitag

♊
♋

Friday 22

☽□☿ 2:11 am
☉☌♃ 3:08 am
♀→♍ 4:35 am
♃ApG 10:34 am
☽✶♃ 10:45 am
☉✶☽ 11:15 am v/c
☽→♋ 12:44 pm
☽✶♀ 1:39 pm
☽△♅ 2:30 pm
♀☍♅ 9:49 pm

Year at a Glance for ♍ VIRGO (Aug. 23–Sept. 23)

By August 2003, you will be truly ripe to step into an exciting opportunity looming on your horizon. Some family history or old project is impeding your progress. Before August, finish it up, or have a ritual closure on the issue so it no longer pulls at your time and binds your soul (Virgo has a talent for ceremonial magic—use it).

Jupiter, planet of opportunities and new horizons enters Virgo on August 27, sending luck your way until September 25, 2004. Revel in the adventurousness, vitality and optimism it brings to you. At the same time Uranus, the electrifying lightning bolt of change and individuation, is also becoming more prominent in your life. Growth in influence is pretty well guaranteed for you with these two planets so prominent though it could be in a surprising new field of endeavor. Professional liaisons encourage you to step out of your tracks, just don't overshoot, stay self-reliant.

Virgo hungers to be the perfect healer or to develop the ultimate tool, technique or system. The determination and dedication you have poured into your work in the last few years should bear fruit and bring recognition, standing and opportunities for worthwhile collaborations. Your search for success is not merely outward directed effort, it is also a means of gaining inner validation—which is yours this year. An extreme urge for freedom may compel you to step away from the confines of existing partnerships or away from an established public/clientele. Or, it could be a partner who suddenly demands greater freedom and less leaning on. If not involved, romance is more than a possibility this year or the next, with someone unlikely or highly original.

© *Gretchen Lawlor 2002*

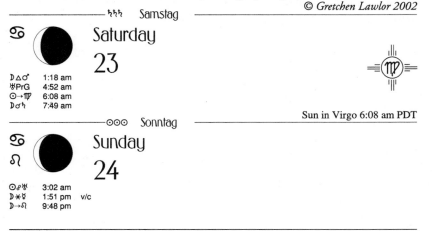

ħħħ Samstag

♋

Saturday
23

☽△♂   1:18 am
♅PrG   4:52 am
☉→♍   6:08 am
☽♂♄   7:49 am

Sun in Virgo 6:08 am PDT

⊙⊙⊙ Sonntag

♋
♌

Sunday
24

☉☍♅   3:02 am
☽⚹♉   1:51 pm   v/c
☽→♌   9:48 pm

Ma

The word for mother, world wide, is based on *ma*. *Ma* is the earliest form of the Indo-European root-word for mother, *mâter*, which is reflected in the Latin, *mäter;* the Greek, *métèr;* and the prehistoric Germanic, *möthar.* These, in turn, have become *madre* in Spanish and Italian, *mére* in French, *mae* in Portuguese; *mite'ra* in modern Greek; *mutter* in modern German, *moeder* in Dutch, *moder* in Swedish, *mör* in Danish, *mör* in Norwegian, and *mother* in English. Mother is *mat'* in Russian, *matka* in Polish and Czech, *majka* in Serbo-Croatian, *mayka* in Bulgarian, *anya* in Hungarian, *ema* in Estonian, *mate* in Latvian, *nana* in Albanian, *ima* in Hebrew, *anne* in Turkish and *omi* in classic Arabic. In the many languages of Sub-Saharan Africa, too, *ma* is prevalent; *mama* in Ibo and Hausa, *mma* in South African Sotho, *mbuta* in the Congo and *inate* in Ethiopian Amharic.

The similarity holds in Asia as well: *aamaa* in Nepali, *mae* in Thai, *nanay* in Philippino, *omoni* in Korean, *chomo* in Tibetan, *moqing* in Mandarin and *mama* in Cantonese. In the Telgu and Tamil languages of India, mother is *amma*, and she is *mata* in Hindi. In Pakistani, mother is *man*, which means "moon" and "wisdom."

The great primal Mother Goddesses, the creatrixes of nearly every culture, were invariably called Ma. The universal inspiration for the maternal appellation, *ma*, must then come from some inherent quality unique in the relationship with the mother. It is not difficult to imagine how this etymological concurrence might come to pass: A baby, cradled close, is nursing, along with the rich nourishment of her mother's bountiful body, she blissfully imbibes warmth, security, contentment, love. Mmmm, Mmma, mmmaa, mmaaaaaa. *Ma! Ma*, as in "maternal." *Ma*, as in "mammary." *Ma*, as in "mammal." *Mama* means "mother's breasts" in many places, and *ma* refers to "milk" as well as "mother." Certainly from the point of view of a dependent child, mother *is* milk.

The Great Goddess, divine maternal model, source and sustainer of all life, prototype single parent, was widely represented as a lactating mother. Abundant, ample-breasted, serene. Protective and nurturing. Full with the wherewithal to provide perfectly for the children whom She has created.

It is interesting to note that our galaxy is not only named for milk, it actually *means* milk. Galaxy is from the Greek, *gala*, "mother's milk," referring to Gala-Tea, the Milk Goddess, the galactic mother in classical Greek mythology.

excerpt © Donna Henes 1992

IX. SHE NURTURES

Moon IX: August 27–September 25

New Moon in ♍ Virgo: Aug. 27; Full Moon in ♓ Pisces: Sep. 10; Sun in ♎ Libra: Sep. 23

Mother and Child
© *Mara Friedman 1997*

August
agosto

Surcease
© S.L. Wilde 2001

---⟩⟩⟩ lunes---

♌

Monday
25

☽☍♆   6:14 pm

---♂♂♂ martes---

♌

Tuesday
26

☽△♀   5:00 am   v/c
♀☍♂   3:17 pm

---☿☿☿ miércoles---

♌
♍

Wednesday
27

♃→♍   2:26 am   ☉♂☽ 10:26 am
♂PrG 2:38 am   ☽☍♂ 12:35 pm
☽→♍   3:27 am   ☽♂♀   3:06 pm
☽♂♃   3:28 am   ☽✶♄   9:10 pm
☽☍♅   4:41 am

New Moon in ♍ Virgo 10:26 am PDT

---♃♃♃ jueves---

♍

Thursday
28

☿R   6:41 am
☽□♀   9:05 am
☉☍♂ 10:59 am
♀D   8:34 pm

---♀♀♀ viernes---

♍
♎

Friday
29

☽♂☿ 12:26 am   v/c
☽→♎   6:41 am
♃☍♅   9:37 pm

A Sleep

I love the time of day when
we lay together,
and the heavy mantle of Sleep
comes to cover us, and shepherds you into her domain.
The damp sweat of your brow
moistens the curve of my arm
as you are rhythmically lulled
into Sleep.
A rosebud mouth pulls at my breast,
and then, ever so slowly,
the nipple pink falls from your mouth to rest,
glistening against
the petal soft cheek.
The gentle arc of your brow softens.
The fairy-like wing of your lash quivers.
The grasp of your hand relaxes.
Your feet barely twitch as you cross the gate
into dreamland,
held as you are,
by the ancient arms of Sleep.

¤ Trisia Eddy 2001

ħħħ   sábado

Saturday
30

☽□ħ	12:16 am	
☽△Ψ	1:22 am	
☽✶♀	11:37 am	v/c
♀✶ħ	4:23 pm	

☉☉☉   domingo

Sunday
31

♀⊼Ψ	3:21 am		☽PrG	11:52 am
☽→♏	9:00 am		☽△♂	3:59 pm
☽△⛢	9:55 am		☉✶☽	11:06 pm
☽✶♃	10:35 am			

September
september

DDD maandag

♏

Monday
1

☽△♄	2:52 am
☽□♆	3:34 am
☽⚹♀	5:55 am
♀△⚷	7:37 am

Is This Heaven?

Is this heaven,
where God
greets everyone
with a big Motherly hug
and a romping laugh of joy?

¤ *Janine Canan 2001*

♂♂♂ dinsdag

♏ ♐

Tuesday
2

☽⚹☿	3:18 am	v/c
☽→♐	11:32 am	
☽□♅	12:19 pm	
☽□♃	1:55 pm	
☽□♂	5:42 pm	

☿☿☿ woensdag

♐

Wednesday
3

☉□☽	5:34 am
☽⚹♆	6:16 am
☉⚹♄	11:48 am
☽□♀	1:40 pm
☉⊼♆	3:31 pm
☽☌♇	4:55 pm

Waxing Half Moon in ♐ Sagittarius 5:34 am PDT

♃♃♃ donderdag

♐ ♑

Thursday
4

☽□☿	4:23 am	v/c
☽→♑	2:51 pm	
☽⚹♅	3:31 pm	
☽△♃	6:06 pm	
☽⚹♂	8:14 pm	
♄⊼♆	10:09 pm	

♀♀♀ vrijdag

♑

Friday
5

♀□♇	2:31 am
☉△⚷	3:53 am
☽☍♄	9:58 am
☉△☽	1:09 pm
☽△♀	10:39 pm

Kaite
© *Megaera 1995*

♑
≈

Saturday
6

☽△☿ 5:43 am v/c
☽→≈ 7:15 pm

≈

Sunday
7

♂☍♃ 1:00 pm
☽☌♆ 2:39 pm
☿☌♀ 10:35 pm

September

Chakrayapuy killa

☽☽☽ Killachaw

♒

Monday 8

☽✶♇ 2:01 am v/c
☿PrG 2:16 am

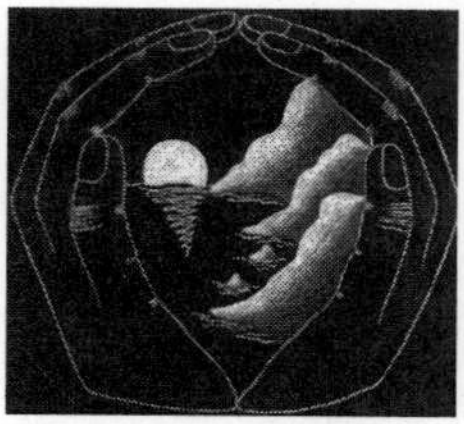

Nurtured by the Coast
© Zana 1998

♂♂♂ Atichaw

♒ ♓

Tuesday 9

☽→♓ 1:07 am
☽☌♅ 1:30 am
☽☌♂ 5:00 am
☽☍♃ 6:20 am
☽△♄ 10:05 pm

☿☿☿ Quyllurchaw

♓

Wednesday 10

☉□♇ 2:37 am
☽□♇ 9:05 am
☉☍☽ 9:36 am
☽☍☿ 10:56 am
☉☌☿ 6:57 pm
☽☍♀ 10:41 pm v/c

Full Moon in ♓ Pisces 9:36 am PDT

♃♃♃ Illapachaw

♓ ♈

Thursday 11

☽→♈ 9:09 am
☿□♇ 10:42 am

♀♀♀ Ch'askachaw

♈

Friday 12

☽✶♆ 6:01 am
☽□♄ 7:27 am
☽△♇ 6:40 pm v/c

Mothering Self

Folding my arms around my knees,
I am my own Mother.
I blow warm air down
on my body, smell gardenias,
lavender, blood and water.
My hair drapes around me,
and I grow within its shell.
Kali! Kali! Strengthen me!
Teach me to love her, this,
my Self as child. Teach me to love
Earth's children, their faces a garden
and their laughter
rain on the dry planet.

© *Susan H. Methvin 2001*

Home
© *Beth Budesheim 2001*

——————— ꙠꙠꙠ K'uychichaw ———————

♈
☽
♉

☽→♉   7:50 pm
☽✶♅   7:54 pm
☽✶♂   10:18 pm

Saturday
13

——————— ☉☉☉ Intichaw ———————

♉

☽△♃   3:38 am
☽□♆   5:29 pm
☽✶♄   7:26 pm
♅→♒   8:47 pm

Sunday
14

September

September

——————)))   Montag ——————

♉   **Monday**
15

☽△☿ 12:19 am
♀⊼♅ 8:37 am
♀→♎ 8:58 am
☉△☽ 5:47 pm

Young Edith
© *S.L. Wilde 1998*

—————— ♂♂♂ Dienstag ——————

♉
♊   **Tuesday**
16

☽ApG 2:20 am
♀⊼♂ 2:25 am
☽□♅ 8:25 am   v/c
☽→♊ 8:32 am
☽□♂ 10:17 am
☽△♀ 11:19 am
☽□♃ 5:35 pm

—————— ☿☿☿ Mittwoch ——————

♊   **Wednesday**
17

☽△♆ 6:22 am
☽□♉ 10:28 am
☽☍♀ 7:45 pm
♄D 9:09 pm

—————— ♃♃♃ Donnerstag ——————

♊
♋ **Thursday**
18

☉□☽ 12:03 pm
☿△♄ 3:36 pm
☽△♅ 8:50 pm   v/c
☽→♋ 9:07 pm
☽△♂ 10:14 pm

—————— ♀♀♀ Freitag ——————

Waning Half Moon in ♊ Gemini 12:03 pm PDT

♋   **Friday**
19

☽□♀ 6:44 am
☽✳♃ 6:59 am
☽♂♄ 8:53 pm
☽✳♅ 9:08 pm

ALL ASPECTS IN PACIFIC DAYLIGHT TIME; ADD 3 HOURS FOR EDT; ADD 8 HOURS FOR GMT

The Year My Mom Turned 50

The year my mom turned 50 we threw her a birthday party. It was probably the first birthday party my mom had had since before any of us were born. Imagine. Mom was good at going without. She just gave and gave and gave. It was easy to take advantage of her, easy to abuse the forever font of unconditional love and support, easy to forget to give it back.

That's why the party was such a big deal. It was our first adult recognition of all the time, energy and love she'd invested in us. As a gift, we documented that investment, with a photo collage. We cannibalized our photo albums: me and Mom in front of the Mother's Day cake I made her when I was five; all of us on a camping trip; New Year's eve in 1976; Mom and Dad in their Sheena and Tarzan outfits the year they met; Mom as a little girl. The centerpiece was her high school graduation photo, probably the last by herself, just for her, photo ever taken.

That collage is the one thing that's been on the wall in every home she's lived in since. It will always represent the only real bit of proof that we love her, that she knows it. With that party, represented by that collage still hanging on the wall, we told our mother that her life has made a difference. We told her, and she heard.

© Rebecca Rajswasser 2001

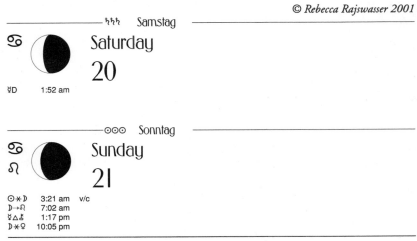

ħħħ Samstag

♋

Saturday
20

♉D   1:52 am

⊙⊙⊙ Sonntag

♋
♌

Sunday
21

⊙⚹☽   3:21 am   v/c
☽→♌   7:02 am
☿△♄   1:17 pm
☽⚹♀   10:05 pm

No I Can't Go Back Yet

I need to lie here.
I need to immerse myself.
I need to see nothing but green
for a little while.

I need to nourish my soul
to stroke it gently to life.
I need to lie on this ancient log
to soak up sky latticed leaves.
I need to wander my eye up
up up a trunk till I can't see.

I need to be here by the creek
to give my body to the ferns.
I need to breathe rich air
to receive my taste of soil.

Wilderness is no longer a luxury:
Just as my child needs milk from my breast,
this I need from my mother.

□ *Nirav Sumati 2001*

© Durga Bernhard 2001

Fall Equinox

At Fall Equinox we gather together to celebrate the harvest. Persephone now begins her journey below to the land of her grandmother, the crone of Samhain. From now on the nights will be longer, the air cooler and the energy will be moving downward into the roots.

The Equinox allows us a moment of balance to contemplate our accomplishments of the year, good or bad. Thanksgivings are made for abundance, regrets are expressed for losses. In times of hardship or illness in a community, the Equinox is a good time to offer healings and support to each other. Similarly, nurture the earth with healings of prayer and protest for any abuses done to her this year. Deepen your commitment to your activist path by finding what will nourish your spirit in times of darkness and trial.

Build an altar with harvest grains and apples. Light candles and bring out your drums. Sit in a circle with friends and take turns feeding and listening to each other. After your feast use your drum to aid in shamanic journeys where you follow Persephone into the underworld to gain wisdom. © *Ginny Salkowski 2002*

September
septiembre

☽☽☽ lunes

Monday 22

♌

☽☍♆ 2:40 am
☽△♇ 2:51 pm
☉⚻♅ 9:00 pm

♂♂♂ martes

Tuesday 23

♌
♍

☉→♎ 3:47 am
☉⚻♂ 8:54 am
☽☍♅ 12:33 pm v/c
☽→♍ 1:04 pm
☽☍♂ 1:25 pm
♀△♆ 10:03 pm
☽☌♃ 11:23 pm

Equinox

Sun in Libra 3:47 am PDT

☿☿☿ miércoles

Wednesday 24

♍

☽✶♄ 10:17 am
☽☌☿ 12:44 pm
☽□♇ 6:52 pm v/c

♃♃♃ jueves

Thursday 25

♍
♎

♀□♄ 8:21 am
♀□⚷ 8:27 am
♄☍⚷ 11:29 am
☽→♎ 3:49 pm
☉☌☽ 8:09 pm

New Moon in ♎ Libra 8:09 pm PDT

♀♀♀ viernes

Friday 26

♎

☽△♆ 9:13 am
☽□♄ 12:17 pm
☽☌♀ 2:46 pm
☽✶♇ 8:28 pm

Year at a Glance for ♎ LIBRA (Sept. 23–Oct. 23)

By mid–2003, you achieve a crowning moment as an authority in your field. In prestige, authority and position you will experience your greatest triumphs in the next couple of years, collecting the harvest of your past 7 years labors. If you don't feel ready, fake it. If you have worked hard and are willing to take on responsibilities, you'll soon grow into your own act.

In the last few years you've stretched your creative, pleasure-loving wings. Loosening up brought more childlike joy into your life, added flair and triggered undeveloped talents. This playfulness becomes a signature of your work and a beacon of attraction. Co-create with friends to move forward in ambitions or visions of the future, especially before September. September onwards you will be less inclined to push yourself. Some element of your life loses relevance and begins to fade. Let it go—within a year there will be something fresh and vital in its place.

Health issues arise from stepped up electricity and accelerated firing of synapses in your body. Stretching, dancing, progressive healing modalities and acupuncture will help channel excess energy through your system and decrease chances for accidents or burn out.

With the shift of Uranus into Pisces, take your creative style to work. Innovate, revolutionize. Flashes of insight provide fresh perspective on your gifts and assets. This may not be the year to throw in the towel at an old job, though plans that presently seem too radical or impractical may swiftly fall into place in your near future. Dare to dream. Experiment with short cuts and innovative teamwork to improve your reputation and enliven daily routines.

© *Gretchen Lawlor 2002*

Holding the World
© *Corey Alicks Lie-Nielsen 2000*

———— ♄♄♄   sábado ————

♎
♏

Saturday
27

♂D	12:52 am	
☽△♅	4:10 pm	v/c
☽→♏	4:52 pm	
☽△♂	5:04 pm	
☽PrG	10:53 pm	

———— ☉☉☉   domingo ————

♏

Sunday
28

☽✶♃	3:59 am
☿□♀	9:31 am
☽□♆	10:04 am
☽△♄	1:20 pm
☽✶♅	10:27 pm

Women Artists Gather

In the beginning, Grandmother Spider
brought light to the world and
empowered woman with the gift of creative thought.
We became potters and basket weavers so we could store
corn for the fallow times.
We became healers, using medicine given
by our Mother the Earth to cure the sick.
These things we did so life could go on.
With naked abandon, we danced a prayer of gratitude
beneath the harvest moon
as the Muse Polyhymnia played her sacred song.
For this, we burned as witches, yet still we danced,
and still we carried on.
Our great-grandmothers gathered to quilt,
spending hours stitching memories for warmth.
"I wore this dress to Seneca Falls," says one, holding a faded tatter
of sunflower calico.
"The harvest will soon be upon us and the fallow times here,"
says another.
They turn back to their work.
Life goes on.
Michelangelo, Matisse, Picasso are called
Great Masters of the Art World.
Where are you, Frida Kahlo, Camille Claudel?
Eleven books by women make the Modern Library List of the
One Hundred Best Novels.
Harper Lee's *To Kill a Mockingbird* didn't make the list at all.
We shake our heads, puzzled.
We paint; we write on.
Grandmother Spider is long forgotten, yet still she favors us,
weaving her web and binding us together
in sacred creative circle.
Women artists gather, and
together we live on.

© *Susan Trudeau 2001*

X. SHE INSPIRES

Moon X: September 25–October 25

New Moon in ♎ Libra: Sep. 25; Full Moon in ♈ Aries: Oct. 10; Sun in ♏ Scorpio: Oct. 23

Sacred Writing

© *Toni Truesdale 1997*

Thought Woman

Thought Woman is one of many names pervasive in tribal origin stories from all over the world for the essence of powerful feminine creative intelligence.

My intelligence is complete and unique. I am a wise descendant of Thought Woman, brilliant in my own creative ways, valuable to the Whole.

excerpt © Saya Wolf 1999

September/October

september/oktober

Monday
29

♏︎
♐︎

♀⚹♀ 10:53 am
☽□♅ 5:09 pm v/c
☽→♐ 5:57 pm
☽□♂ 6:14 pm

♂♂♂ dinsdag

Tuesday
30

♐︎

☉⚹☽ 5:27 am
☽□♃ 5:58 am
☽⚹♆ 11:27 am
☽♂♀ 11:11 pm

☿☿☿ woensdag

Wednesday
1

October

♐︎
♑︎

☽⚹♀ 2:37 am
☽□☿ 5:24 am
☽⚹♅ 7:25 pm v/c
☽→♑ 8:21 pm
☽⚹♂ 8:50 pm

♃♃♃ donderdag

Thursday
2

♑︎

☽△♃ 9:34 am
☉□☽ 12:09 pm
☽☍♄ 6:22 pm

♀♀♀ vrijdag

Waxing Half Moon in ♑ Capricorn 12:09 pm PDT

Friday
3

♑︎

☽□♀ 11:28 am
☽△☿ 3:40 pm v/c
☉△♆ 8:22 pm

ALL ASPECTS IN PACIFIC DAYLIGHT TIME; ADD 3 HOURS FOR EDT; ADD 8 HOURS FOR GMT

Earth-Art

I got an idea from an artist: that I could make an image or a sculpture from things I found in nature, photograph it and then leave it to die back into the earth. In this way, my art would not have to be separate from the Great mother. I have had many days of fun making a picture from leaves or berries on a rock or feathers, bird eggs, nests. I am struck by the intense creativity of the Earth, holding stones and feathers and berries and roots in my hands. These will be my brushes and these will be my colours. It is a new feeling, to make art that does not belong to me, and to work outdoors. It is a new form of Earth-worship, and play. The possibility of making art which exists as part of a forest, making me part of that forest, and its processes. Sitting on a red rock, in the middle of a river, I press flowers into a crack between stones and make a yellow moon. I arrange round stones in a pattern from big to small, like the moon emerging and disappearing in the sky. I leave these things then, for the birds, for the river, for the sky. And I feel like I understand a little, of how so many brilliant colours and animals and leaf-shapes exist; because the same creativity which makes me play by the river making pictures, is the same force which has lent beauty and variation to all life on this Earth. Life is born through play, and all life is her art.

© *Felix 2001*

ħħħ   zaterdag

Saturday
4

☽→♒   12:45 am
☽☌♇   7:35 pm
☉△☽   9:28 pm

☉☉☉   zondag

Sunday
5

☽⚹♀   8:32 am
☽△♀   11:12 pm
☉□☊   11:17 pm

October
Tarpuy Killa

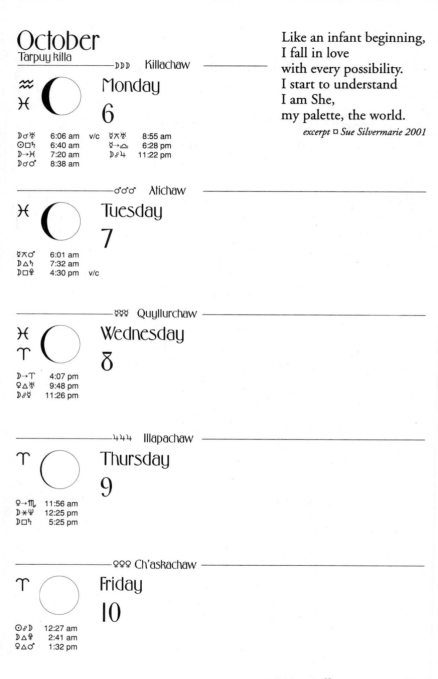

☽☽☽ Killachaw

♒ ♓

Monday
6

☽☌♅ 6:06 am v/c
☉□♄ 6:40 am
☽→♓ 7:20 am
☽☌♂ 8:38 am
☿⚻♅ 8:55 am
☿→♎ 6:28 pm
☽☍♃ 11:22 pm

Like an infant beginning,
I fall in love
with every possibility.
I start to understand
I am She,
my palette, the world.

excerpt ¤ Sue Silvermarie 2001

♂♂♂ Atichaw

♓

Tuesday
7

☿⚻♂ 6:01 am
☽△♄ 7:32 am
☽□♀ 4:30 pm v/c

☿☿☿ Quyllurchaw

♓ ♈

Wednesday
8

☽→♈ 4:07 pm
♀△♅ 9:48 pm
☽☍☿ 11:26 pm

♃♃♃ Illapachaw

♈

Thursday
9

♀→♏ 11:56 am
☽✶♆ 12:25 pm
☽□♄ 5:25 pm

♀♀♀ Ch'askachaw

♈

Friday
10

☉☍☽ 12:27 am
☽△♀ 2:41 am
♀△♂ 1:32 pm

Full Moon in ♈ Aries 12:27 am PDT

All aspects in Pacific Daylight Time; add 3 hours for EDT; add 8 hours for GMT

Offering to Mother Ocean
□ *Jules Bubacz 1996*

♈
♉

Saturday
11

11	☽✶♅	1:31 am v/c	☽✶♂	5:59 am
11	☽→♉	3:05 am	☽☌♀	7:37 am
11	☉✶♀	4:33 am	☽△♃	10:15 pm

⊙⊙⊙ Intichaw

♉

Sunday
12

11	☽□♆	12:02 am
12	☽✶♄	5:22 am
12	♉△♆	6:53 pm

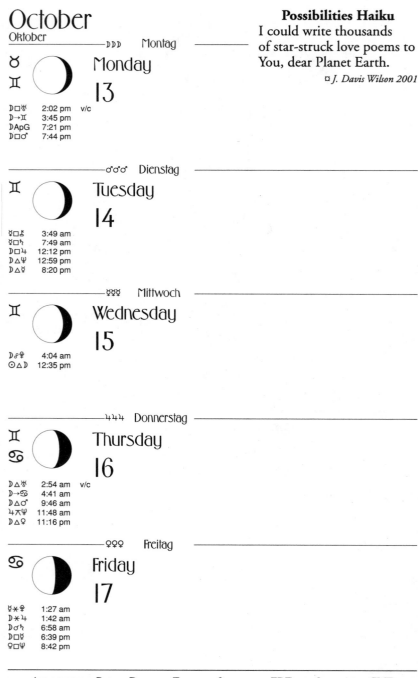

October
Oktober

————))) Montag ————

♉
♊

Monday
13

☽□♅	2:02 pm	v/c
☽→♊	3:45 pm	
☽ApG	7:21 pm	
☽□♂	7:44 pm	

———— ♂♂♂ Dienstag ————

♊

Tuesday
14

♉□♃	3:49 am
♉□♄	7:49 am
☽□♃	12:12 pm
☽△♆	12:59 pm
☽△♉	8:20 pm

———— ☿☿☿ Mittwoch ————

♊

Wednesday
15

☽☌♀	4:04 am
☉△☽	12:35 pm

———— ♃♃♃ Donnerstag ————

♊
♋

Thursday
16

☽△♅	2:54 am	v/c
☽→♋	4:41 am	
☽△♂	9:46 am	
♃⊼♆	11:48 am	
☽△♀	11:16 pm	

———— ♀♀♀ Freitag ————

♋

Friday
17

☿⚹♀	1:27 am
☽⚹♃	1:42 am
☽☌♄	6:58 am
☽□♉	6:39 pm
♀□♆	8:42 pm

ALL ASPECTS IN PACIFIC DAYLIGHT TIME; ADD 3 HOURS FOR EDT; ADD 8 HOURS FOR GMT

Playing for my Beloved Gaia

◻ *Zariah 2000*

Goddessong

Music
is the laughter
of the Goddess

And laughter
is her favorite
Music

◻ *Jessica North-O'Connell 1986*

♋︎
♌︎

Saturday

18

♀✶♃   2:33 am
☉□☽   5:31 am   v/c
☽→♌︎   3:41 pm

Waning Half Moon in ♋︎ Cancer 5:31 am PDT

♌︎

Sunday

19

☽☌♆   11:20 am
☽□♀   3:28 pm
♀✶⚷   11:43 pm

October
octubre

▷▷▷ lunes

♌
♍

Monday
20

20	☽△♀	1:18 am	
20	♀△♄	2:48 am	
20	☽⚹♅	11:54 am	
20	☉⚹☽	6:04 pm	
20	☽☍♅	9:18 pm	v/c
20	☽→♍	11:01 pm	

Muse
© Karen Bell 1999

♂♂♂ martes

♍

Tuesday
21

21	☽☍♂	5:45 am
21	☽♂♃	6:57 pm
21	☽⚹♄	10:08 pm

☿☿☿ miércoles

♍

Wednesday
22

22	☽⚹♀	2:20 am	
22	☽□♀	6:19 am	v/c
22	☉△♅	1:18 pm	
22	♆D	6:54 pm	

♃♃♃ jueves

♍
♎

Thursday
23

23	☽→♎	2:27 am
23	☉→♏	1:08 pm
23	☿△♅	1:57 pm
23	☽△♆	7:33 pm

Sun in Scorpio 1:08 pm PDT

♀♀♀ viernes

♎

Friday
24

23	☽□♄	12:10 am
24	☿→♏	4:20 am
24	♄☍♇	5:02 am
24	☽⚹♀	8:00 am

ALL ASPECTS IN PACIFIC DAYLIGHT TIME; ADD 3 HOURS FOR EDT; ADD 8 HOURS FOR GMT

Year at a Glance for ♏ SCORPIO (Oct. 23–Nov. 22)

2003 is a year for professional opportunities for Scorpio. Luck and good connections support your advancement. A position of leadership is likely to be offered you, especially September onwards, in recognition for your upbeat ability to motivate others. What may have felt like over-extension last year begins to feel more comfortable. If there is a particular lesson now, it is how to craft a good public image and then live up to it. Be cautious about borrowing money or getting involved in relationships—personal or professional—until you have made sure your own goals are well-defined and you understand others' unstated motivations. When you set your sights high and go for the best in projects and associates, you benefit from uniting your efforts.

You are completing several years of intense re-evaluation of life priorities, perhaps through conflict with another's differing values. A major source of security—a home, a relationship or family member—is less available for you. This is unsettling, though it has a hidden gift that is not yet apparent. Enduring comfort may be found in commitment to a spiritual journey, where you transfer your attachment to an old source of security into a journey towards greater inner stability. This break with the past releases a creative force in you, which will become more pronounced in the next few years. New experiences expand your consciousness, the artist in you is vital, inventive and innovative. The lover in you is attracted to highly creative liaisons. You are hungry to relate to others in a more authentic way, and old rigid patterns of relating break down. Experiment, play, there is good healing in it for you.

© Gretchen Lawlor 2002

--- ♄♄♄ sábado ---

♎
♏

Saturday
25

25	☽△♅	1:31 am	v/c
25	☉♂♉	2:58 am	
25	☽→♏	3:08 am	
25	☉♂☽	5:50 am	
25	☽♂♉	5:59 am	

☽△♂	11:17 am
♄R	4:42 pm
☽□♇	7:43 pm
☽✶♃	10:25 pm

Lunar Samhain
New Moon in ♏ Scorpio 5:50 am PDT

--- ☉☉☉ domingo ---

♏

Sunday
26

25	☽△♄	12:13 am
26	☽PrG	3:30 am
26	☽♂♀	11:53 am

Daylight Savings Time ends 2:00 am PDT

She Took Chris, Then Julie

Kali is on the prowl.
Watch out!—She springs without warning.
She has tasted fresh, young blood twice now among us.
Appetite whetted, She was not content with one ambush
not sated with one feast on healthy, vibrant woman flesh.
She struck again, aimed again deep into community heart
"Let me see," did She mutter through bloody fangs,
"where is the next, most robust morsel?"
Drunk, and hungry to eat promise again,
She sniffed the scent of joy
spit out the bitter suicide dregs of Her first kill
and, stealthy, crept among us—silent—
skilled in the art of surprise, drawn to pulsing happy vigor.

Not this one, we begged.
But Kali had made Her choice.
She let us touch and carry the body of our cherished friend,
watch irrevocable stillness,
the evolving purple, yellow, mottled bloom of cellular finish.
Then She insisted that we feed Her fiery maw
with this precious woman
who blazed into glory before our eyes.

Kali has only begun.
The two skulls around Her neck are a starter set.
She will be adding to Her necklace for years to come.
Old bones, wrinkled skin satisfy Her well enough,
they are Her staple fare.
But She went out of order,
broke into this clan and took our heirs.
This snatching of bright youth
Is aberration/Is outrage/Is Her prerogative
And we are stunned by her raw power, Her Absolute Mystery.
Shall we say Holy Mother? Can we say Blessed Be?

XI. SHE GIVES DEATH

Love is the Funeral Pyre
© Durga Bernhard 1999

Ah, She is impeccable—this teacher of fierce lessons.
Now we know, are reminded.
No holds are barred. No one is safe.
The only promise is that we will, each one,
look into Her grinning face
whenever She says, and be taken into Her Joy.
Her Mystery. Her Holiness.
Her Strange Mothering.
Shall we say Mercy? Shall we say Love?

Blessed Be.   *excerpt © Bethroot Gwynn 1998*

October
oktober

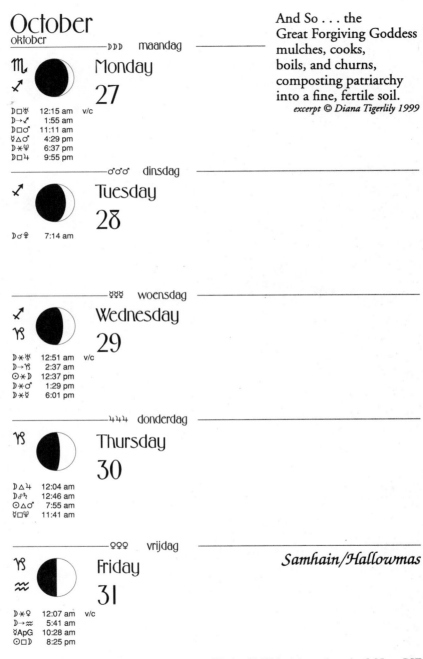

———— ☽☽☽ maandag ————

Monday

27

♏︎
♐︎

☽□♅   12:15 am   v/c
☽→♐   1:55 am
☽□♂   11:11 am
☿△♂   4:29 pm
☽⚹♆   6:37 pm
☽□♃   9:55 pm

And So . . . the
Great Forgiving Goddess
mulches, cooks,
boils, and churns,
composting patriarchy
into a fine, fertile soil.
excerpt © Diana Tigerlily 1999

———— ♂♂♂ dinsdag ————

Tuesday

28

♐︎

☽☌♀   7:14 am

———— ☿☿☿ woensdag ————

Wednesday

29

♐︎
♑︎

☽⚹♅   12:51 am   v/c
☽→♑   2:37 am
☉⚹☽   12:37 pm
☽⚹♂   1:29 pm
☽⚹♅   6:01 pm

———— ♃♃♃ donderdag ————

Thursday

30

♑︎

☽△♃   12:04 am
☽☍♄   12:46 am
☉△♂   7:55 am
☿□♆   11:41 am

———— ♀♀♀ vrijdag ————

Friday

31

♑︎
♒︎

☽⚹♀   12:07 am   v/c
☽→♒   5:41 am
☿ApG   10:28 am
☉□☽   8:25 pm

Samhain/Hallowmas

Waxing Half Moon in ♒ Aquarius 8:25 pm PST

ALL ASPECTS IN PACIFIC STANDARD TIME; ADD 3 HOURS FOR EST; ADD 8 HOURS FOR GMT

Samhain

© Fiona Murry McAuliffe 1997

Samhain marks the ending of a journey, the death before the rebirth. The nights are long and winter winds whip the fall leaves from their branches. The power of the spirit realm can be felt pressing in around us. This is the time of the Crone. She is honored by many names such as: Hecate, Cerridwen, Oya, grandmother, weaver and witch.

The Crone of death is ever present in our lives. Cancer, violence and species extinctions are on the rise. Activists struggling to win the "right to die" by choice are being met with fierce opposition from religious and medical institutions who seek to control our lives to the very end. Many fear death, yet support economic policies that destroy our quality of life.

Samhain is the time to connect with our ancestors for guidance on the year to come. Place pictures of the dead on an altar draped in black. Spend time in memories. Allow old griefs to surface and tears to flow. Using a dark mirror or bowl of water, gaze into the blackness of the future and ask any questions you need answered. As an ancestor of the next generation, ask yourself what history will you leave behind? *© Ginny Salkowski 2002*

Samhain: A Poetic Ritual at My Mother's Graveside

At this moment of gathering death's blessings
into the breast that succored me;
As your eyes stare in the Mother's Mystery
where I cannot follow;
Remember how my solid hands caressed your face
Though the Mother of All in her tenderness
smoothed the wrinkles.

I shovel the skin of our Mother onto your box
embracing you with Her
I alone among the mourners rejoice
knowing that my salt water tears will
gestate the sacred space of rebirth.
Just as you carried me into my holy body
I rise up chanting, circling
conjuring one moment of Mother communion
to last my lifetime.

The Mystery of two Mothers become One.
Come forth from the stone.
Let me hear your wisdom each morning in the wind tonings
of the oak outside my bedroom window.
Let me honor you each evening as the sky bleeds then deepens to
the unknowable well of endings and beginnings.
I rise up chanting, circling
conjuring a lifetime of Mother communion
to last a moment.

¤ Carolyn Lee Boyd 2000

Ritual Photo at my Mother's Grave
© Eileen Bellot 1999

Earth Angel
¤ *Joyce Ann Mudd 2001*

— ♄♄♄ zaterdag —

≈ **Saturday**

1

☽☌♆	12:09 am	♃⚹♄	9:13 am
☿⚹♃	4:48 am	☿⚹♇	12:19 pm
☽□♉	5:07 am	☽⚹♀	2:24 pm
☿△♄	5:17 am	♀□♅	4:43 pm

—☉☉☉ zondag —

≈
♓ **Sunday**

2

☽☌♅	9:51 am	
☽□♀	11:40 am	v/c
☽→♓	11:52 am	
♀→♐	1:42 pm	
☉□♆	10:54 pm	

MOON XI

November

Pawqarwara killa

☽☽☽ Killachaw

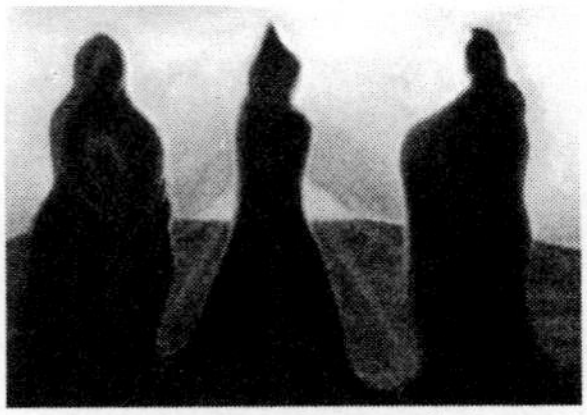

Mother, Maiden and Crone
© Jill Smith 1997

♓

Monday 3

☽☌♂ 3:21 am
☉△☽ 8:11 am
☽△♄ 12:37 pm
☽☍♃ 1:21 pm
☽△☿ 8:42 pm
☽□♇ 10:36 pm v/c

♂♂♂ Atichaw

♓ ♈

Tuesday 4

☽→♈ 9:02 pm

☿☿☿ Quyllurchaw

♈

Wednesday 5

☽△♀ 3:16 am
☉△♄ 3:24 pm
☽⚹♆ 5:33 pm
☽□♄ 10:49 pm

♃♃♃ Illapachaw

♈

Thursday 6

♃△⚷ 12:19 am
☽△♇ 9:26 am
☉⚹⚷ 11:21 am
☉⚹♃ 12:33 pm

♀♀♀ Ch'askachaw

♈ ♉

Friday 7

☽⚹♅ 6:16 am v/c
☽→♉ 8:29 am

All aspects in Pacific Standard Time; add 3 hours for EST; add 8 hours for GMT

Handiwork

A chanting pot of coffee.
My fingers flute the edge
of an apple pie.

Potatoes fall
like carved ivory
from my hand.

Drawn to ceremony
ghosts of my clan
gather in afternoon sunlight

dusted with flour. I smile
sharing a thousand years of ritual
with my ancestors.

And sigh knowing this
is the closest I can come
to holding my mother's hand.

□ Anne Bridgit Foye 2001

————————— ♌♌♌ K'uychichaw —————————

♉ ( ) Saturday

ठ

♅D	4:44 am	☽⚹♄	10:50 am
☽⚹♂	5:23 am	☽△♃	1:23 pm
☽☐♆	5:36 am	☉☍☽	5:13 pm

Full Moon in ♉ Taurus 5:13 pm PST
Total Lunar Eclipse* 5:20 pm PST (1.018 mag.)

————————— ☉☉☉ Intichaw —————————

♉ ( ) Sunday
♊

9

☽☍♉	1:44 pm	
☽☐♅	7:00 pm	v/c
☽→♊	9:14 pm	

———————————————————————————————

* Eclipse visible from the Americas, Africa, Europe and Asia

November

November ───────))) Montag ───────

♊ [moon image] ## Monday

10

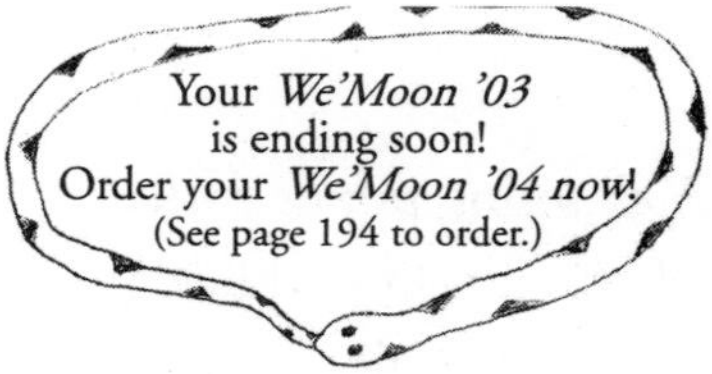

)ApG 4:04 am
)☍♀ 5:56 pm
)△Ψ 6:37 pm
)□♂ 8:42 pm

Your *We'Moon '03*
is ending soon!
Order your *We'Moon '04 now!*
(See page 194 to order.)

───── ♂♂♂ Dienstag ─────

♊ [moon image] ## Tuesday

11

♀✶Ψ 12:30 am
)□♃ 3:09 am
☿□♅ 6:05 am
)☍♀ 11:10 am
♃→♐ 11:19 pm

───── ☿☿☿ Mittwoch ─────

♊
♋ [moon image] ## Wednesday

12

)△♅ 7:57 am v/c
♀□♂ 9:27 am
)→♋ 10:10 am
♀⊼♄ 11:20 pm

───── ♃♃♃ Donnerstag ─────

♋ [moon image] ## Thursday

13

)△♂ 11:41 am
)♂♄ 12:05 pm
)✶♃ 4:22 pm
♂△♄ 9:27 pm

───── ♀♀♀ Freitag ─────

♋
♌ [moon image] ## Friday

14

☉△) 5:39 am v/c
♀□♃ 7:34 pm
)→♌ 9:48 pm

ALL ASPECTS IN PACIFIC STANDARD TIME; ADD 3 HOURS FOR EST; ADD 8 HOURS FOR GMT

Sacrifice

i'm dying dying shedding my skin
asking Ereshkigal to let me in
and the world falls apart around me—
my soul fractures and pieces of me
slough off like glaciers into the sea

soon the only thing left will be
that bright blue flame hidden deep within me—
my dragons have flown
my jewels turned to dust, my body to bone—
all i have left is my firefly heart twinkling
like sunlight on dew

dripping into you, goddess,
i'm dripping into you
                    descending

© *Kara Hunter Moon 2000*

Artwork: Mother of All the Living © *Kirsten D'Andrea Hollander 2000*

ካካካ   Samstag

♌   **Saturday**
     15

☽△☿   7:41 am
☽♂Ψ   6:12 pm

⊙⊙⊙   Sonntag

♌   **Sunday**
     16

☽△♀   6:28 am
☽△♃   9:50 am
⊙□☽   8:15 pm

Waning Half Moon in ♌ Leo 9:48 pm PST

November
noviembre

Feronia
© *Lynn Dewart 2001*

―――― ꙮꙮꙮ lunes ――――

♌
♍

Monday
17

☽☌♅	4:38 am	v/c
☽→♍	6:36 am	
♂✶♄	5:42 pm	
♀☌♅	5:51 pm	
☽□♅	11:04 pm	

―――― ♂♂♂ martes ――――

♍

Tuesday
18

☽✶♄	5:36 am
☽☍♂	9:41 am
☽☌♃	10:52 am
☽□♀	4:29 pm
☽□♀	6:40 pm
♅✶♆	11:43 pm

―――― ☿☿☿ miércoles ――――

♍
♎

Wednesday
19

☉✶☽	6:15 am	v/c
☽→♎	11:42 am	

―――― ♃♃♃ jueves ――――

♎

Thursday
20

☽△♆	5:38 am
♂☍♃	5:59 am
☽⚹♄	8:24 am
☽□♄	8:59 am
☽✶♅	9:03 am
☽✶♀	7:27 pm

―――― ♀♀♀ viernes ――――

♎
♏

Friday
21

☽✶♀	2:03 am	
☉□♅	9:14 am	
☽△♅	11:44 am	v/c
☽→♏	1:24 pm	

Year at a Glance for ♐ Sagittarius (Nov. 22–Dec. 21)

Sagittarius is always seeking something greater than herself. Mid–2002 through mid–2003 accentuates this upbeat reaching out for fresh goals. You have reached a significant point in your life and are eager to pursue something bigger. Travel is not only particularly enjoyable right now but broadens your mind and provides inspiration. If not physical travel, the pursuit of limitless subjects, such as law, religion, philosophy or astrology increase your ability to see the overall picture of life, as well as offering new directions for personal or professional advancement.

By the middle of 2003, you should have a good concept of the direction you would like your life to head. Now the shift is towards implementing the concept—which may take a few years to manifest fully. Through modeling your principles, with a basic belief in your direction and enthusiasm for your work, your reputation and sphere of influence will increase this year. Challenges? Of course. Relationships (personal and professional) continue to be the place to learn deep truths about yourself. Partners may feel restrictive; it is time for a re-negotiation of the contract between you. This will lead either to a deeper sense of yourself and a healthier capacity to meet others on equal ground or to the breakup of a relationship that you have outgrown.

An urge to relocate inflames many Sagittarians. Old security patterns are no longer working for you, be alert for a hastiness late summer through early fall. First try rearranging the furniture or remodeling the house. Metaphorically, you are doing what needs to occur on an inner level, changing old attitudes and security blankets. Look for new forms of stability that give you more emotional freedom.

© *Gretchen Lawlor 2002*

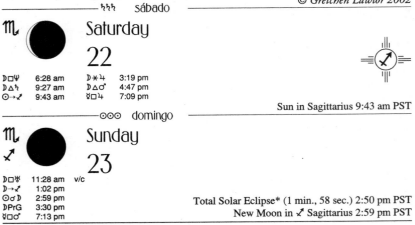

♄♄♄ sábado

♏

Saturday

22

☽□♆ 6:28 am
☽△♄ 9:27 am
☉→♐ 9:43 am
☽✶♃ 3:19 pm
☽△♂ 4:47 pm
☿□♃ 7:09 pm

Sun in Sagittarius 9:43 am PST

☉☉☉ domingo

♏
♐

Sunday

23

☽□♅ 11:28 am v/c
☽→♐ 1:02 pm
☉☌☽ 2:59 pm
☽PrG 3:30 pm
☿□♂ 7:13 pm

Total Solar Eclipse* (1 min., 58 sec.) 2:50 pm PST
New Moon in ♐ Sagittarius 2:59 pm PST

* Eclipse visible from Antarctica, Australia and southern Argentina

Surrender

This is a relationship of collaboration.

She provides the deep calling and a mother's true heart

And we provide the surrender

And the willingness.

She provides the direction and the momentum

And we provide the surrender

And the willingness.

She provides the steady encouragement and unwavering grace

And we provide the surrender

And the willingness.

She provides the rapture and the unyielding compassion

And we provide the surrender

And the willingness.

She is the call,

We are the yes.

She is the force,

We are the spinning.

She is the compass,

We are the footsteps.

A dance of collaboration, this one.

With my living, I dissolve into it.

¤ *Chandra Passero 1995*

XII. SHE IS ALL LOVE

Moon XII: November 23–December 23

New Moon in ♐ Sagittarius: Nov. 23; Full Moon in ♊ Gemini: Dec. 8; Sun in ♑ Capricorn: Dec. 21

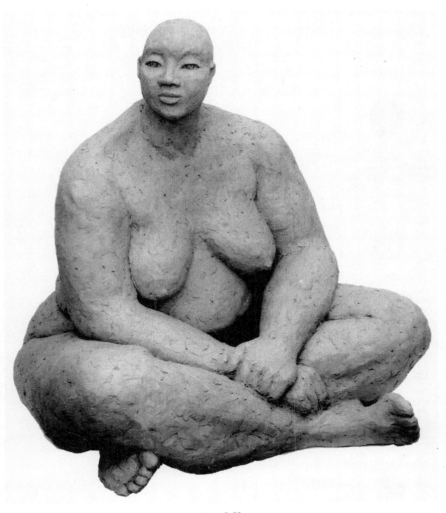

Buddha
¤ *Kit Skeoch 2001*

November
november

november

————))) maandag ————

♐

Monday
24

☽✶♆	5:53 am
☽□♃	3:00 pm
☽□♂	5:44 pm
☿☌♀	6:13 pm
☽☌♅	7:11 pm
☽☌♅	7:17 pm

———— ♂♂♂ dinsdag ————

♐
♑

Tuesday
25

☽☌♀	9:57 am	
☽✶♅	10:58 am	v/c
☽→♑	12:31 pm	
♀✶♅	10:22 pm	

———— ☿☿☿ woensdag ————

♑

Wednesday
26

☽☍♄	8:28 am	
♂□♀	3:24 pm	
☽△♃	3:37 pm	
♀→♑	5:07 pm	
☽✶♂	7:52 pm	v/c

———— ♃♃♃ donderdag ————

♑
♒

Thursday
27

☽→♒	1:48 pm
☉✶☽	11:24 pm

———— ♀♀♀ vrijdag ————

♒

Friday
28

☽☌♆	8:16 am
☽✶♀	11:09 pm

ALL ASPECTS IN PACIFIC STANDARD TIME; ADD 3 HOURS FOR EST; ADD 8 HOURS FOR GMT

Held In Grace
© Jennifer Lynn Shifflet 2000

ካካካ   zaterdag

≋
ℋ

Saturday
29

☽✶♉   10:47 am
☽♂♅   4:46 pm   v/c
☽→ℋ   6:25 pm

⊙⊙⊙   zondag

ℋ

Sunday
30

☽✶♀   2:05 am
⊙□☽   9:16 am
☽△♄   4:44 pm

Waxing Half Moon in ℋ Pisces 9:16 am PST

December
Ayamarq'ay killa

Prayers for Earth
□ *Nancy Blair 2000*

–––– ⊃⊃⊃ Killachaw ––––

♓   Monday

1

☽☍♃	2:18 am
☽□♀	6:28 am
☽♂♂	11:00 am
☿⚹♅	9:53 pm

–––– ♂♂♂ Atichaw ––––

♓
♈   Tuesday

2

☽□♅	1:39 am	v/c
☽→♈	2:56 am	
☿→♑	1:34 pm	
☽□♀	5:32 pm	
☉△☽	11:57 pm	

–––– ☿☿☿ Quyllurchaw ––––

♈   Wednesday

3

☽⚹♆	12:15 am
☽□♄	2:20 am
☉⚹♆	3:34 am
☽△♀	5:18 pm

–––– ♃♃♃ Illapachaw ––––

♈
♉   Thursday

4

☉□♄	2:56 am	
☽⚹♅	12:52 pm	v/c
☽→♉	2:30 pm	
☽△♅	8:25 pm	

–––– ♀♀♀ Ch'askachaw ––––

♉   Friday

5

☽□♆	12:38 pm
☽△♀	12:38 pm
☽⚹♄	2:20 pm

ALL ASPECTS IN PACIFIC STANDARD TIME; ADD 3 HOURS FOR EST; ADD 8 HOURS FOR GMT

Great Mother with Me

Great Mother, I am preparing myself to be fit for you to enter. I am trying so hard to get it right, setting the altar correctly, not fumbling my invocation.

But it is hard to open my heart so you may enter me; the hinge of my heart is fear-frozen—*but you have sent the Sun's new rising to warm me and that helps.* The handle of my heart refuses to turn through Time—*but you have sent the soft wind to unwind it and that helps.* The frame has clenched round the door to keep it shut and familiar, I push and push but cannot shift it *until you send a lioness to stand at my shoulder and help.* But I have no key. *No key!* I wail, and cry inconsolably *until you send the magical herb that opens all locks and place it on my lips. That green kiss helps.*

My heart swings open easily, like a lotus and I find space, stars in darkness, infinity.

Then I see how the flowers on the altar are your smile and that my cat has your eyes, your presence is in every candleflame, your grace in crystal and stone. I know now, that you are under and over and in, you are with me always; even in times when my heart closes and I have no memory, no words, no rituals—your love surrounds me, I hear your heartbeat inside my own.

© *Rose Flint 2001*

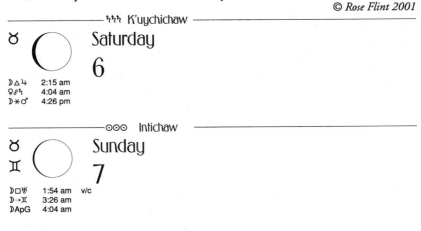

ᒡᒡᒡ K'uychichaw

ᚮ Saturday

6

☽△♃ 2:15 am
♀☍♄ 4:04 am
☽⚹♂ 4:26 pm

ⵔⵔⵔ Intichaw

ᚮ
♊ Sunday

7

☽□♅ 1:54 am v/c
☽→♊ 3:26 am
☽ApG 4:04 am

December

Dezember ──────── ⟩⟩⟩   Montag ──────

In this season of the white witch
remember the light
growing
like roses in the arctic

excerpt © Ellen Jaffe 1997

♊

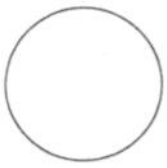

Monday

8

☽△♆	1:47 am
☉☍☽	12:37 pm
☽□♃	3:40 pm
☽☍♀	7:18 pm

──────── ♂♂♂   Dienstag ──────

Full Moon in ♊ Gemini 12:37 pm PST

♊
♋

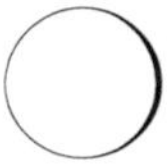

Tuesday

9

☽□♂	8:17 am	
☽△♅	2:48 pm	v/c
☽→♋	4:11 pm	

──────── ☿☿☿   Mittwoch ──────

♋

Wednesday

10

♀♂⚷	12:28 am
☉□♃	2:58 am
☽☍♅	10:17 am
☽♂♄	3:01 pm

──────── ♃♃♃   Donnerstag ──────

♋

Thursday

11

☽☍♀	3:55 am	
☽✶♃	4:09 am	
♀△♃	6:22 am	
☉♂♀	9:28 pm	
☽△♂	10:53 pm	v/c

──────── ♀♀♀   Freitag ──────

♋
♌

Friday

12

☽→♌	3:40 am
♀ApG	10:33 pm

Birth of the Moon
© *Mara Friedman 1996*

♌

Saturday

13

☽☍♆   1:15 am
♉☍♄   6:14 am
☽△♀   5:55 pm
☉△☽   9:39 pm

♌
♍

Sunday

14

♄⚹♆   4:48 am
☽☍♅   12:05 pm   v/c
☽→♍   1:07 pm

December

diciembre ———————))) lunes ———————————————

♍

Monday

15

☽✶♄ 9:37 am
☽△♅ 11:50 am
☽♂♃ 10:55 pm

——————— ♂♂♂ martes ———————————————

♍
♎

Tuesday

16

☽□♀ 1:45 am
♂→♈ 5:24 am
☉□☽ 9:42 am
☽△♀ 9:49 am v/c
☽→♎ 7:46 pm
☽☍♂ 8:25 pm

——————— ☿☿☿ miércoles ——————— **Waning Half Moon in ♍ Virgo 9:42 am PST**

♎

Wednesday

17

☿R 8:01 am
☽□♄ 2:51 pm
☽△♆ 3:28 pm
☽□♅ 5:42 pm

——————— ♃♃♃ jueves ———————————————

♎
♏

Thursday

18

☽✶♀ 6:28 am
☉✶☽ 5:50 pm
☽□♀ 6:53 pm
☽△♅ 10:39 pm v/c
☽→♏ 11:20 pm

——————— ♀♀♀ viernes ———————————————

♏

Friday

19

☽△♄ 5:04 pm
☽□♆ 6:02 pm
☽✶♅ 7:09 pm

Year at a Glance for ♑ CAPRICORN (Dec. 21–Jan. 20)

Capricorn hungers for an intellectual boost in 2003 to lift out of a mental rut. Recent or recurring crankiness and irritability, nervous problems and sleep disturbances are telling you your brain is restless with the fodder you've been giving it. Go for the sudden opportunity to undertake studies or to connect with a new crowd. This will feed your brain and blast away many former assumptions about life. Following upon some meaningful encounter in 2002, you begin the process of firming up a developing personal or professional relationship by mid–2003. You have a tremendous chance to learn a lot through one-on-one encounters right now, and you are ready for the experience.

Existing long-standing relationships may feel weighty and restrictive. Use the wisdom available at this time to clarify just what you are doing together, i.e., what has the arrangement been and what needs to be changed to make it more workable all around. Rewrite the contract. Some Capricorns will decide in 2003 that a significant relationship has served its purpose. A good closure can be effected well at this time with healing coming swiftly on the tail of recent stresses.

You are ready to step out into the light and share what you've discovered about life. After a few years of honing your skills behind the scenes, you are on your way to increasing worldly influence. You will do better with a new community who are more encouraging of your newly-found wacky and irreverent thinking than the old neighbors and friends who liked you as you were. In many ways the speed of change accelerates in 2003 for Capricorn; be encouraged—changes made this year will turn out well in the long run.

© *Gretchen Lawlor*

Goddess of Compassion
◻ *Susy Cremers Dolloff 1996*

ħħħ sábado

♏ Saturday
♐ 20

☽✶♃	5:52 am
♀→♒	10:32 pm
☽□♅	11:43 pm v/c

☉☉☉ domingo

♏ Sunday
♐ 21

Solstice

☽→♐	12:16 am	☽✶♆	6:23 pm
☽✶♀	12:25 am	♅♂♄	10:34 pm
☽△♂	4:54 am	☉→♑	11:04 pm
☉✶♅	3:34 pm		

Sun in Capricorn 11:04 pm PST

© *Jennifer Stratton 1996*

Winter Solstice

Winter Solstice is the longest night of the year. We are in the womb of the Goddess, the place of dreams and infinite possibilities. From this night on the sun returns longer each day, nurturing the child of spring who sleeps deep in the earth. Across the Northern Hemisphere celebrations are held focused on peace, giving and rebirth.

Winter Solstice corresponds to the dark moon. Although the frantic pace of modern culture presses on around us, the earth is calling us to look within. Deep in the still places of our minds lie visions for the future. What do you think the future will be like? Will it be the bleak, technology filled world ruled by violence, global corporations and warfare projected by the dominant culture? Or will we be able to draw on the Great Mother's power that is greater than all of that?

We can only create the future of love and sustainability we seek by having a clear vision of where we are going. Hold a community visioning circle on Solstice. Have friends and family bring gifts for the next seven generations. Draw pictures together of what your future will hold. Dream big and free. As the year progresses, manifest the future you want with your present actions. © *Ginny Salkowski 2002*

Winter Solstice
© Holli Zollinger 1999

Chrysalis Queen

The Mother of Darkness
Cailleach of old
powerful predator divine
beckons me into Her
labyrinthine lair when
deadness sucks
at my soul
coaxes me into
Her chrysalis cave
into Her black maw
of mystery where
She scrapes and scours me
grinds and binds me
boils me down to the bone
picked clean of all
that was wizened and worn
picked clean of all
that was suffering
I return to above
I give thanks for Her love
feel a seed in my womb
sleeping

as Her icy breath blows
as the solstice sun dawns
my seed of new life opens

¤ *Jane Redhawk 2000*

December
december

———— ☽☽☽ maandag ————

♐
♑

Monday
22

☽PrG 3:50 am
☽□♄ 5:56 am
☽☌♀ 8:18 am
☽⚹♅ 11:29 pm v/c
☽→♑ 11:55 pm

Virgin Mary
© Megaera 1997

———— ♂♂♂ dinsdag ————

♑

Tuesday
23

☉☌☽ 1:43 am
☽□♂ 6:29 am
☽☌☿ 2:04 pm
☽☍♄ 4:30 pm

———— ☿☿☿ woensdag ————

New Moon in ♑ Capricorn 1:43 am PST

♑

Wednesday
24

☽△♄ 5:52 am v/c

———— ♃♃♃ donderdag ————

♑
♒

Thursday
25

☽→♒ 12:13 am
♀⚹♂ 5:29 am
☽⚹♂ 9:07 am
☽☌♀ 9:17 am
☽☌♆ 7:20 pm

———— ♀♀♀ vrijdag ————

♒

Friday
26

☿□♂ 12:53 am
☽⚹♀ 10:18 am
☉☌☿ 5:11 pm

ALL ASPECTS IN PACIFIC STANDARD TIME; ADD 3 HOURS FOR EST; ADD 8 HOURS FOR GMT

Gaia Carols

I love the melodies of the old christmas carols, which conjure up for me childhood memories of long nights, warm fires, the scent of evergreen, and the laughter of friends gathering together to feast and exchange the gifts of the season. These melodies kindle deep pagan longings in me, and I have written new Wiccan verses to celebrate the Great Mother and her Daughters. This one is sung to the tune of "O Holy Night."

O blessed be!
The Goddess, she is smiling—
It is the smile of a Mother who loves.

Often confused
By worldly dreams beguiling,
We were afraid, and we knew not what of . . .

But now we see the truth about creation!
Now we see the lie behind the fear—
Throw back you head, and laugh with jubilation!
Laugh! Laugh! O laugh! The Goddess, She is here—

O laugh! O laugh! O laugh . . . For She is here!

◻ Carolyn Gage 2001

ℏℏℏ   zaterdag

≈
ℋ   Saturday

27

D♂♅	2:57 am	v/c	D⚹♅	10:02 am
D→ℋ	3:10 am		☉⚹D	1:16 pm
♅PrG	3:55 am		D△♄	9:07 pm

☉☉☉   zondag

ℋ   Sunday

28

| D☍♃ | 1:11 pm | |
| D□♀ | 4:03 pm | v/c |

Searching for the Divine

She was searching searching for the Divine, not Buddha
with that fig tree up his back or Christ with his bleeding hand
or Mohammed on the mountaintop;
something honest, whole as an apple.
Not distant wind in white pine nor sparkling boundary water,
not spire of Notre Dame piercing cloud nor frozen glacial peak;
something close necessary as breath.
Not April trillium or hovering angel-winged bird,
not beaded, bearded guru or stone goddess with swollen breast;
something sweet tender as newborn.
She was searching searching for the Divine.

Not goat-footed Pan or dizzy Sufi dancer
Not a medicine man with a sacred pipe
Not a saffron-robed Tibetan monk
Not a t.v. preacher with a big mouth
Not a banker with a closed book.

She was searching searching for the Divine.
She burned Pakistani incense, peered into crystals,
lit white candles, but god could not be kept on her little altar,
could not be kept in a good book, in a Holy City,
in a cave on a cross in Sunday School; god could not be kept
in a museum wrapped in a mummy skin; god could not be kept
silent in a little three letter word.
She grew wild as lightning in a snow storm.
Thus, the Divine found her,
exhausted as a Bear hibernating in sleep
Dreaming by a Yellow Spring listening to her heartbeat
a steady source of heat—
and when she awoke alone in her bed,
she found the Divine inside herself by Rising and Shining
like a Sun.

XIII. SHE IS YOU

Moon XIII: December 23–January 9

New Moon in ♑ Capricorn: Dec. 23; Full Moon in ♋ Cancer: Jan. 7

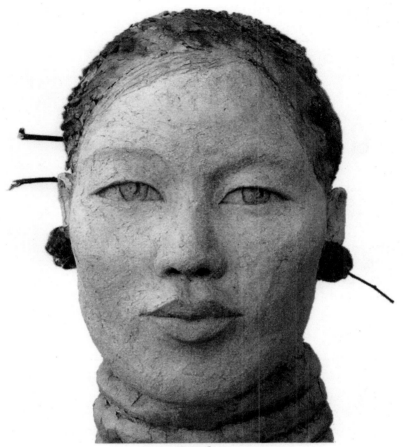

Mother
◻ *Kit Skeoch 2001*

Wear Your Dragon

Wear your dragon like you wear your clothes.
Don't convince yourself you are the clothes—
Just be seated in them.
The great mother dragon is already inside you,
Already clothed—
Just be seated in her.

◻ *Tatiana Bourdillon de Blanco 2001*

December/January
Dezember/Januar

Monday
29

♀⊼♄   12:38 am
☽→♈   10:08 am
☽□♅   12:19 pm
☉□♂   9:55 pm

♂♂♂   Dienstag

Tuesday
30

♅→♓   1:14 am   ☽⚹♆   8:36 am
☽♂♂   1:55 am   ♀♂♆   9:19 am
☉□☽   2:03 am   ☿⚹♅   11:30 am
☽□♄   5:09 am   ☿→♐   11:53 am
☽⚹♀   8:31 am

Waxing Half Moon in ♈ Aries 2:03 am PST

♀♀♀   Mittwoch

Wednesday
31

☽△♀   2:00 am
♄PrG   8:37 am
☉☌♄   12:57 pm
☽△♅   6:27 pm   v/c
☽→♉   9:02 pm
☽⚹♅   9:11 pm

♃♃♃   Donnerstag

Thursday
1

♂□♄   12:22 pm
☽⚹♄   4:34 pm
☉△☽   7:22 pm
☽□♆   8:44 pm

January 2004

♀♀♀   Freitag

Friday
2

☽□♀   3:28 am
☽△♃   11:21 am   v/c

Gifted Dancer

Mother, you gave me breath
and give it still
fire breath
dragon flame:
let me not waste this strength.

Yearn
© *Kimberly Beyer-Nelson 2001*

Mother, you gave me rhythm
beat of my heart
drum roll
thunder clap:
let me not waste this love.

Mother, you gave me joy
made me Joy God
lightning clouds
mountain peaks:
let me not waste this sight.

Mother, you gave me blood
coursing flow
storm flood
river riot:
let me not waste this freedom.

Mother, you gave me peace
made me Peace Queen
silence of starry night
satin sea:
let me not waste my wings.

¤ *Cora Greenhill 1999*

ℏℏℏ   Samstag

♉
♊   **Saturday**
3

☽→♊   9:58 am
☽□♅   10:21 am
☽ApG   12:21 pm
♃R   3:57 pm

⊙⊙⊙   Sonntag

♊   **Sunday**
4

☽✶♂   9:14 am
☽△♆   10:00 am
☽△♀   11:33 pm

January '04

Qhapaqintiraymi killa ⟩⟩⟩ Killachaw

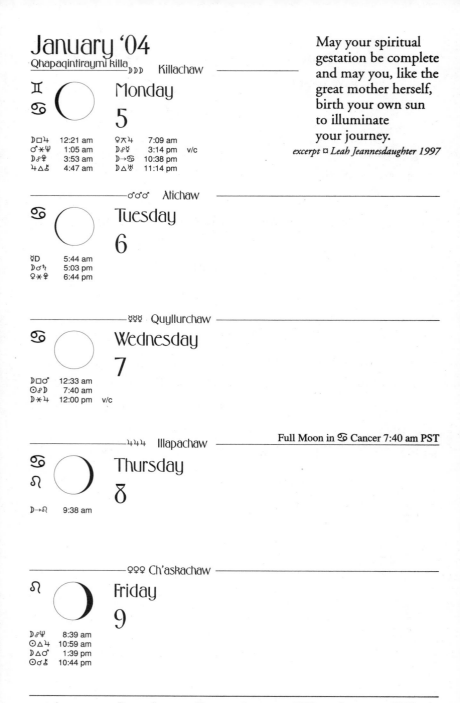

♊
♋
Monday
5

☽□♃	12:21 am		♀⚼♃	7:09 am	
♂✶♆	1:05 am		☽⚼♀	3:14 pm	v/c
☽⚼♀	3:53 am		☽→♋	10:38 pm	
♃△♄	4:47 am		☽△♅	11:14 pm	

*May your spiritual
gestation be complete
and may you, like the
great mother herself,
birth your own sun
to illuminate
your journey.*
excerpt ⌑ Leah Jeannesdaughter 1997

♂♂♂ Atichaw

♋
Tuesday
6

♅D	5:44 am
☽♂♄	5:03 pm
♀✶♀	6:44 pm

☿☿☿ Quyllurchaw

♋
Wednesday
7

☽□♂	12:33 am	
☉⚼☽	7:40 am	
☽✶♃	12:00 pm	v/c

♃♃♃ Illapachaw

Full Moon in ♋ Cancer 7:40 am PST

♋
♌
Thursday
8

| ☽→♌ | 9:38 am |

♀♀♀ Ch'askachaw

♌
Friday
9

☽⚼♆	8:39 am
☉△♃	10:59 am
☽△♂	1:39 pm
☉♂♄	10:44 pm

Eve
© *Sandra Stanton 1996*

HOW TO ORDER *WE'MOON* PRODUCTS

• **We'Moon '03:** datebook ($15.95 for lay-flat or spiral binding, or the Unbound edition)

• **We'Moon on the Wall 2003:** wall calendar ($12.95, full color, big 12" x 12" size)

• **Lunar Power Packet (LPP) '03:** notecards ($13 for a packet of 13 full color cards with envelopes + Lunar Power bumper sticker)

• **We'Moon '04 Products:** Contact Mother Tongue Ink for more information.

To place an order, request a catalogue of *We'Moon* products,
and/or get on our mailing list, contact MOTHER TONGUE INK
Call our toll free number: 877-693-6666 (877-0 WE-MOON)
write: P.O. Box 1395-A Estacada, OR 97023
email: matrix@wemoon.ws (subject "order")
Order online: www.wemoon.ws

HOW TO BECOME A *WE'MOON* CONTRIBUTOR

We'Moon is an exploration of a world created in Her image. We welcome artwork by, for and about womyn. Our focus on womyn is an affirmation of the range and richness of a world where womyn are whole unto themselves. Many earth-based cultures traditionally have womyn-only spaces and times, which, through deepening the female experience, are seen to enhance womyn's contributions to the whole of society. **We'Moon** invites all womyn who love and honor womyn to join us in this spirit, and we offer what we create from such a space for the benefit of all beings.

YOU, too, can become a **We'Moon** contributor! Here's how:

Step 1: Send us your request for a Call for Contributions, along with a self-addressed business size envelope (#10 USA) and adequate postage (US stamps or an international postal coupon). The Call contains current information about the theme (it may change) and how to submit your art and writing (with exact specifications).

Step 2: Fill in the accompanying Contributor's License, giving all the requested information and return it with your art/writing as specified by the due date. *No work will be accepted without it!*

Step 3: Think ahead! Be sure to get your submission in by Fall Equinox (Sept. 22, 2003) to assure your work will be considered.

Now accepting contributions for
WE'MOON '05: SACRED TRADITIONS

Call for Contributions: Sent by June 21, 2003
Due Date for all art and writing: September 22, 2003
Note: It is too late to contribute to
We'Moon '04: Power (due date: Sept. 2002)
but it's not too late to order!

ACKNOWLEDGEMENTS

I'm sitting here on one of my last days as We'Moonager, grateful for the amazing opportunity I've had working on this sacred endeavor. **We'Moon** is a blessing and I'm honored to have helped with her growth over the last eleven years. Thank you, musawa, for your vision and for co-parenting **We'Moon** with me into her next stage of development—she's a beauty!

I have worked with a great staff this last change-filled year. Meghan, I deeply appreciate all the initiative you take and all your fabulous ideas. Sevrance, I'm a tough act to follow and I see that you can do it. It's been a pleasure training you. Amy, thanks for your reliability and the way you take responsibility. Cherie, your laughter and presence bring joy to work. Eagle, thanks for your industriousness and assistance. Grace, you have filled in the cracks and taken up the slack, thanks. Gratitude to the wonderful and gifted literati of S. Oregon **We'Moon** staff diaspora—Bethroot and Ní Aodígaín. Gisela and Rosemarie do a great job translating and distributing the German edition of **We'Moon**.

To the many supporters of **We'Moon** who have generously contributed time, energy and money to help us rebuild after we lost our house/office—thank you, thank you, thank you!

© Beth Freewomon 2002

We'Moon will never be the same without our Beth. She came to us at 25 and is leaving at 36. As the first full-fledged "We'Moonager" (business manager for Mother Tongue Ink), she presided over a power-packed period in our (as well as her) growth. Mother Tongue Ink has benefitted greatly from her "True Capricorn" efficiency, organizational/systems skills, her cheerful multi-tasking, her contagious enthusiasm and her dedication as a priestess of the **We'Moon** Matrix and Creatrix. Is she indispensable? It is a tribute to her that the business she is leaving behind shows strong vital signs of continuing to grow and flourish. Thank you, Bether, for a job well done. Much appreciation and great blessings as you move on into the next cycle of your life. *© musawa 2002*

WE'MOON ANCESTORS PAGE

We honor we'moon who have gone between the worlds of life and death recently, beloved contributors to we'moon culture who continue to bless us from the other side. We appreciate receiving notice of their passing.

Alicia Arrow Troll Carpenter: Troll took her own life August 11, 2001, in Albuquerque, NM. She was a sparky, dynamic dyke who cared about her friends and justice and equality. She loved and was protected by her faithful dog, Roshi, as she left this world. We remember her life, and we are left with many challenging questions about her choice. We send her our love.

Anita Louise (May 27, 1938–April 4, 2001) Anita Louise, a truly eclectic Gemini, left behind a loving family and many friends. An artist, teacher, Web site designer and former Director of Religious Education at First Universalist Church, Houston, Texas, Anita involved herself in an amazing array of circles. Anita created and managed an enterprise known as Sacred Journeys, exploring ancient Goddess worship sites where her travelers found their spiritual lives enlarged. Anita's art appeared in **We'Moon '99**.

Connie Panzarino (Nov. 26, 1947–July 4, 2001) Connie was an author, artist and psychotherapist. An activist with spinal muscular atrophy type II, Connie advocated for the rights of lesbians and others with disabilities. Years ago at the Michigan Womyn's Music Festival she worked on the needs of women with disabilities and helped pave the paths for women with disabilities in the DART Area. Her art was published in **We'Moon '97**: the Communities issue. We have lost one of our warriors.

Teresa Shanks (February 25, 1971–January 6, 2000) Our beloved Teresa Shanks, from Canada, her ocean-blue eyes like crystal saucers, touched so many people, so many children with her love and kindness. Her endless flow of magikal artwork, her gift of bridging gaps with people, her voice and her music remain with us in our hearts. While walking to a new moon sister circle, she was hit by a logging truck. She flew, singing, right into the spirit world, instantly.

© COPYRIGHTS ¤ AND CONTACTING CONTRIBUTORS

CONTRIBUTOR BYLINES AND INDEX*

Each page number at the end of a byline indicates on which page you will find the contributor's work. E-mail and web site addresses are underlined; if it appears that there is a blank space it is really an underscore (_).

Annie Ocean (Roseburg, OR) lives on lesbian lands in So. Oregon for 22 years. Naturalist—Goddess worshiper—12 stepper—Herbalist—Love Love. p. 123

Antonia Matthew (Bloomington, IN): Currently a Cella student with RCG-I. p. 61

Barbara Mor (Siver City, NM)   pp. 34, 49

Beth Budesheim (Kansas City, MO) is an artist/bodyworker who expresses through her art the beauty, depth and core spiritual essences of being human and our interconnection to all that is around us. Contact her at 816-305-4670 or Kiva_b@yahoo.com or http://home.kc.rr.com/kiva.   p. 145

Beth Freewomon (Intransition, Mama Earth): I am a whole-hearted power-house-of-a-womon in recovery from PWSD (post-we'moonager stress disorder). I am embracing the unknown, excited to soar through sound & spirit, and divine union—using my new light blue wings!   pp. 13, 22, 195

Bethroot Gwynn (Myrtle Creek, OR) has been living on wimmin's land for 27 years, growing food, art, ritual. Loves working with **We'Moon**! FFI about spiritual gatherings, working visits or possible residency on the land, send SASE to Fly Away Home, PO Box 593, Myrtle Creek, OR 97457.   pp. 37, 85, 162–163

Carolyn Gage (Portland, ME) is a radical feminist, lesbian playwright living in Maine. Information about her performances and plays is online at: http://www.javanet.com/~cgage.   p. 187

Carolyn Lee Boyd (Concord, MA) is a gardener who grows herbs, a son, an occasional poem, and stories of the Divine Feminine that are of essence for women of today, the women who are rebirthing the Goddess from their minds, spirits and bodies. She can be reached at: GoddessAveA@aol.com.   p. 166

Cathryn Tinker (Powys, Wales, UK): I am learning to carve wood and plan to carve totem poles soon. I live in the beautiful Dyfi Valley in Wales where, at last, I have found peace within myself and my heart is opening.   p. 40

Chandra Passero (Columbus, OH): I am forever amazed and delighted and moved to see the presence of the goddess around me. I am grateful to be alive, in this body, on the earth. I am blessed.   p. 174

Charlotte Tall Mountain (Oakland, CA): I am an eco-feminist who paints, writes, does astrology and participates in rituals.   p. 6

Chesca Potter (Oxford, UK): I have honored the Goddess in the landscape for 20 years. I am currently writing *Goddess of the Ice Age* about Paleolithic Goddess figurines.   p. 96

Christina Baldwin (Langley, WA) is a writer, teacher, facilitator of councils who lives on Whidbey Island, Washington, USA, with 2 corgis, 1 beloved partner and 20,000 neighbors. Her wider work is explained on her website: www.peerspirit.com.   p. 38

Clare McCall (Carbondale, IL): A seasoned witch and writer, I seek to combine both *crafts* in poems, songs and plays. Works include *Womyn's Rites*, and *The Witching Well*.   p. 119

Colette Gardiner (Portland, OR) is an herbalist and green witch. She offers classes and programs in Portland and throughout the west coast. She has spent over 20 years immersed in bringing the green world into this one.   p. 31

Connee L. Pike (Klamath Falls, OR) is a writer, doula and psychotherapist living in Southern Oregon.   p. 121

Cora Greenhill (Grindleford, Hope Valley, UK): Writes, dances, builds labyrinths, travels, gardens, teaches—what I understand of Goddess ways—lives and works in sacred landscapes in England, Crete, Cyprus. cora@thirteenthmoon.devon.co.uk www.thirteenthmoon.devon.co.uk   pp. 54, 191

Corey Alicks Lie-Nielsen (Cottage Grove, OR) is a mother, a midwife, a writer and photographer. She has five young children, is nursing twins and finds her religion through being involved with birth.   pp. 102, 103, 151

Cosima Hewes (Shelburne Falls, MA) currently lives in western Massachusetts. Her paintings celebrate the Process of Pregnancy and Birth.   p. 94

Dánahy Sharonrose (Portland, OR) is a fairy princess masquerading as a Professional Organizer and Workshop Facilitator. Combining counseling, ceremony, Feng Shui, voluntary simplicity and her love of Mother Earth, she guides others in creating Sacred order in their lives. danahyheals@hotmail.com p. 120

Deborah Koff-Chapin (Langley, WA), her evocative images are created through the simple yet profound process of Touch Drawing. Deborah is creator of *SoulCards 1 and 2* and author of *Drawing Out Your Soul*. She teaches and founded The Center for Touch Drawing. www.soulcards.com   p. 44

Deb-RA Sawers (Sexsmith, AB, Canada) is a Goddess *pioneer* in Northern Alberta where she lives with her Green Man on sacred land, celebrating cycles and seasons and hoping to make a difference. Viva la Vulva!! prairiepriestess@hotmail.com (keynotes, workshops, delicious art)   p. 97

Demetra George (Eugene, OR) author of *Asteroid Goddesses, Astrology for Yourself, Mysteries of the Dark Moon, Finding Our Way through the Dark*. She incorporates mythological archetypes into her work, teaches the history of ancient astrology, leads pilgrimages to ancient sites in Greece. dgeorge@orednet.org pp. 207, 208

Diana Tigerlily (Marion, IL): I hope the US government remembers: Together we eat, feed and need this earth. We need to Care to Cure the Core. Sole Presence is Soul Presence. Together we are this Earth.   p. 164

Donna Henes (Brooklyn, NY) publishes *Always in Season: Living in Sync with the Cycles*, author of *Moonwatcher's Manual; Celestially Auspicious Occasions; Dressing Our Wounds in Warm Clothes* and the CD *Mythology, the Matriarchy and Me*. cityshaman@aol.com www.DonnaHenes.com   pp. 42, 61, 90, 138

Durga Bernhard (Phoenicia, NY), painter, printmaker, illustrator for more than 15 children's books, teacher of West African dance/drum and mother of two children. She's inspired by ancient and tribal cultures from all over the world. durga@netstep.net   pp. 110, 135, 149, 163, back cover

Eileen Bellot (London, UK), self-exploratory mixed media artist using ritual, words, dreaming and art as expression of her spirit and connection with the Great Mother. Nurturing her soul with her art and facilitating awakenings in others. For info, email: eileen46@hotmail.com.   p. 166

Elizabeth Roberts (Nyack, NY), a witchy revolutionary, does anti-racist and anti-imperialist education and organizing with Resistance in Brooklyn and The Brecht Forum. She takes leadership from her cats, Mali and Kito. Her chapbook, *Brave as Planets,* is available at lizard@mail.tco.com.   p. 113

Elizabeth Staber (New York, NY): Currently, I am in the process of getting a

Masters in Education. I love taking photographs of inspirational women of the world—may we live and carry peace within our hearts. p. 136

Ellen Jaffe (Hamilton, ON, Canada) is a writer and therapist. She has recently published *Writing Your Way: Creating a Personal Journal* (Sumach Press), and offers workshops for children and adults. Contact her at ejaffe@attcanada.ca. p. 180

Felix (Dublin, Ireland): Cyber-chick, earth-loving, suburban-dwelling, college-attending, writing, musical, painting poetess, loving the goddess in all her aspects, being 22 and glorious, felixbadanimal@hotmail.com. pp. 71, 131, 155

Fi Benson (Green, Lydbrook, UK): I am a child of Mercury, a lesbian mother, a published UK writer. I'm enjoying my journey as apprentice angel and am happy for the help and companionship of my totems and past lives. p. 115

Fiona Murry McAuliffe (Eugene, OR) is a full-time professional artist and illustrator happily living her dream in western Oregon. p. 165

Frankie Hansbearry (Sacramento, CA): My interest is in cultural mythology, particularly primitive cultures and ancient art. My mediums are watercolor, acrylic, clay and multi-media sculpture and masks. front cover

Genevieve Vaughan (Austin, TX) developed the idea of a gift economy and devoted her resources to the all-women activist Foundation for a Compassionate Society (closed in 1988). She is involved with the Temple of Sekhmet in NV and author of *For-Giving, a Feminist Criticism of Exchange*. p. 126

Ginny Salkowski (Manzanita, OR) is an activist, artist, drummer and radical dianic witch. Come visit her at her shop, *Forces of Nature*, located at 1702 NE 42nd Avenue in Portland, 503-493-2968. www.mysticmoonpdx.com
pp. 56, 75, 93, 112, 130, 149, 165, 184

Gretchen Lawlor (Seattle, WA) A passionate astrologer for 30 years, does consults regarding work, love, health, creativity, spiritual development, current challenges/opportunities in person or by phone. light@whidbey.com or gretchenlawlor@earthlink.net or call 206-391-8681. pp. 22, 24, 27, Moons II–XIII

Heather Roan Robbins (New York, NY) is an astrologer from NM and NYC who is fascinated by how astrology maps relationship strengths and challenges within a natal chart: partnership, family, work situation or cultural. You can reach her at RoanRobbins@aol.com or 914-375-9598. pp. 16, 19, 27

Heidi Marion (Whitehorse, Yukon Territory, Canada) is a social justice activist turning farmer mom in Canada's sub-arctic. She welcomes kindred visitors. p. 122

Hilary Anne Campbell (Hampshire, UK): I am a spiral loving 32 year young therapist, poet, explorer of ideas & places. I share my life with my partner & cat in an ordinary suburb. Currently looking to move and live a more nature-based lifestyle. Ho! Email me at: hcampbell@visionwings.com. pp. 48, 76

Holli Zollinger (Tremonton, UT): I started drawing Mandalas ten years ago. I have always been attracted to the circle and in return it has brought much wisdom to my life. The Mandala is a powerful tool and seed for growth and spiritual understanding. It has triggered an inner desire for unity and wholeness. p. 3, 185

Hrana Janto (Tilson, NY) is an artist long inspired by mythology, history, fantasy and the sacred. Works include, *The Goddess Oracle* (Element/HarperCollins), many Llewellyn book covers and calendars, children's book art & more. For info: www.hranajanto.com. pp. 47, 113

Ildiko Cziglenyi (Trinidad, CA) is artist, dancer and soon-to-be a new mother in

2002. Through each of her visions, she tells a story of Mother Nature's timeless mystery and wisdom. For info on cards and prints: www.isledecoco.com or P.O. Box 1141, Trinidad, CA 95570. 888-235-4132.   p. 104

J. Davis Wilson (Eugene, OR): I am rolling along my Saturn return with apparent grace and harmony. Only my cats and my husband know the true deep shadows of living with diabetes that I endure. Painting, bonsai, performing and teaching all bring me back to center. Speak the truth! jdavis@justdavis.net   p. 158

Jan Wright (Coyote, NM) expresses the beauty and spirit of Mother Earth through intense watercolors of desert landscape, petroglyphs/pictographs, kachina and animal spirits. Order Jan's *Hands of the Ancients* Medicine Cards, greeting cards, or Earth Journeys' Stories at janwright@starband.net.   p. 43

Janah Wickett Breidenbach (Circle Pines, MN) a gentle, loving soul, grateful channel of creative energy, lover of water, trees and the magic that happens with soil and seeds.   pp. 79, 84

Jane Redhawk (York, UK): I have worked as an independent counselor for over 12 years. I enjoy creating workshops on the sacred feminine for women to experience our sacredness and power. I write "Goddess" prose, poetry and songs, and I am an initiated Priestess of Avalon.   p. 185

Janice Iliffe-Lewis (Launceston, Cornwall, UK): Whilst I am on this Earth I aim to bring to others an awareness at nature and her wonderful creative possibilities. I do this by song, dance, art and craft, and revealing more of myself everyday. Nam myoho renge kyo.   p. 133

Janine Canan (Sonoma, CA) is a psychiatrist and author of twelve collections of poetry, including *Changing Woman; Star in My Forehead: Poems by Else Lasker-Schüler (tr.); Rhyme of the Ag-ed Mariness: Last Poems of Lynn Lonidier;* and *She Rises like the Sun: Invocations of the Goddess*. Visit JanineCanan.com.
                                                                     pp. 50, 66, 142

Jennifer Beam (Point Richmond, CA) is an artist, writer and educator joyously embracing her Saturn return with the unconditional love and support of her wife, Amory, and her familiars, Max and Ming.   p. 93

Jennifer Lynn Shifflet (Berkeley, CA) currently lives and works as an artist in Berkeley, California. She is working on her Masters in Fine Arts, studying the interconnected relationships between art, consciousness, the natural world and personal and societal healing.   pp. 39, 117, 177

Jennifer Stratton (Orleans, MA) is an artist whose present medium is watercolor. She uses color, the human figure and other types of imagery to create a magical synthesis of shape and form. She has quite a few exhibits on and off Cape Cod.   p. 184

Jessica North-O'Connell (Lake Cowichan, BC, Canada) has been writing since the age of seven. Currently residing on Vancouver Island, she is happily married and is mother to five children, one of whom died April 2001. "Good journey, Vanessa!"   p. 159

Jill Smith (Glastonbury, Somerset, UK) author of *The Callanish Dance*, (Capall Bann Publishing). Artwork inspired by years spent with ancient sites and sacred landscapes of Britain. Originals, prints, cards available from home/mail order. 20, Monington Rd, Glastonbury, BA6 8HE, UK Tel: 01458 831953.   pp. 20, 168

Joyce Ann Mudd (Buena Park, CA): Dedication to the female figure is a reflection of her struggle to accept her large body. She enjoys commissions requested by women of themselves or by their loved ones.   pp. 97, 167

Joyce Radtke (Arcata, CA): I am living in the grace of the sea and coastal redwoods. I find nurturance in the wild rivers, the rains and the raven's cry. I pray for a healing of this blessed land. I am a devoted ritual maker and worshipper of the Great Mother and will always create in her image.   p. 129

Jules Bubacz (Creswell, OR): I honor and celebrate Mother Earth. In nature, I witness (and am part of) her birthings, her creations, her fertility, her art.
                                                                        pp. 65, 132, 157

Julianne Skai Arbor, M.A., M.S. (Santa Rosa, CA) is an environmental artist activist and environmental arts educator. This series of photographs focuses on her sacred connection to ancient trees. She teaches an interdisciplinary curriculum at New College of California, Santa Rosa. skaiarbor@aol.com   p. 75

Julie Weber (Ashland, OR) is a writer and social worker in Ashland, Oregon. She can be reached at jewelz@mind.net.   p. 45

Kara Hunter Moon (Eugene, OR) is a writer, painter, and belly dancer weaving a way through the web of life. She has worked with Latin American survivors of political torture as part of a non-profit healing community. huntermoon13@hotmail.com   p. 171

Karen Bell (Sebastopol, CA) is a Sonoma County, CA folk artist and musician and has been creating art for the empowerment of women since 1987 through her batiks, watercolors, graphics and tee shirts.   p. 160

Karen Russo (Elmira, OR): My art is a woven tapestry of color, texture and form. The threads, ancestral and personal. Nature, the Feminine and the sacred are my inspiration. As are my beautiful family and lovely sisters.   p. 127

Kate Gardner (S. Euclid, OH): I am a womyn identified spirit seeking artist and teacher. I spend as much time as I can doing my art, being in the world with my two canine companions, and enjoying the company of friends.   p. 10

Katherine E. Schoelkopf (Ft. Wayne, IN): My prayer for this work is to speak for our unity with the Wild. May we restore the Wild Earth, Gaia, Her exquisite creatures, our home. Katherine Schoelkopf, Animystic Studio of Sacred Arts. Ph: 219-432-8232, email: earthdream@msn.com.   p. 83

Katheryn M. Trenshaw (MI & Devon, England) is a workshop facilitator integrating creativity, transformation and magic. She brings the sacred back into the mundane and living until we die. She is completing her book, *Breaking the Silence.* Her artwork is available at: www.ktrenshaw.com.   p. 67

Katrina A. Klemens (Walnut Creek, CA): I am a Peace Corps Volunteer in Bolivia, South America. I am blessed to garden with the "sinchi warmis" (strong Quechua women) in our small community, learning about their culture and dedication to Pachamama, Mother Earth.   p. 33

Kimberly Beyer-Nelson (Lincoln, NE) holds a master's degree in comparative religion and a graduate certificate in holistic health care. She is co-owner of the Mandala Yoga Studio in Lincoln, NE.   p. 191

Kirsten D'Andrea Hollander (Mt. Airy, MD): The film still, *Mother of all the Living,* is from the documentary *Eve's Fire. Eve's Fire* shows what happens when contemporary women "meet the snake," as Eve did, and experience the awakening of kundalini energy.   p. 171

Kit Skeoch (Berkeley, CA) is a woman who "walks fire strong" living in Berkeley with her partner Alex, 2 cats and sexy Sadie the snake. pp. 118, 175, 189

Krista Lynn Brown (Sebastopol, CA) mate, mother, painter of visions, budding shamaness, weaving intuitive magic, deep dreamer, earth devotee, daughter of water and believer in the healing power of invocative art. www.devaluna.com p. 77

L.A. Hecht (Ithaca, NY): As a painter, I am passionate to portray bewitching beauty and tradition. This is the essence of my work. p. 101

La Tigresa AKA Dona Nieto (Redway, CA) gained international attention for saving redwood trees with bare breasted recitals of her Goddess poetry before loggers. Her CD and the film about her are available at www.earthfilms.org or PO Box 2198, Redway, CA 95560. serenaallgood@yahoo.com p. 80

Leah Jeannesdaughter (Birdsboro, PA) is approaching her first Saturn return, surrendering to an unfolding vision that includes living the cycles of learning and teaching, creating sacred space through focalizing Moon Circles, and exploring the mysteries of sexuality and menstruation. leah@serve.com p. 192

Lieve Snellings (Wilsele, Belgium) is a social worker and photographer, activist for equal rights for all. Her work and her documentary photos reflect her social engagement; in her "nature" images she searches to visualize the inner world of creatures. p. 114

Lilian de Mello (Kapaa, HI): Nowadays, mostly working with b & w, infrared, transfers and multi-layered photocollages on imagery that contributes to Soul and Planetary Healing. Looking for emotions and the soul/goddess aspect of women and nature. Contact me: lomohoto@gte.net. p. 119

Linda Sweatt (Cundiyo, NM): I am an artist painting life-size nudes of women on silk as well as designing and painting clothes for modern-day Goddesses. My biggest joy is raising my two wonderful children! p. 25

Lisa Robinson (Aspendale, VIC, Australia): Lover of moon cycles. Enjoy playing my drum and chanting. Mother to David and Aben, along with ♀ dog, Buddah. Montessori School teacher, nanny, potter, artist. Involved with wonderful inspiring Wiccan women. Seer of light geometry. p. 30

Lorye Keats Hopper (Glastonbury, Somerset, UK) works with creative healing arts and has been teaching and facilitating women's wisdom groups and healing retreats for the past ten years. She has also worked with young people in schools, youth clubs and conferences in England and America. p. 70

Lynda Healy (Sonora, CA): artist, poet, needleworker. Inspired by visions and dreams. Living in gratitude in the California Sierra Foothills. pp. 81, 106

Lynn Dewart (San Diego, CA): Artist, guide, teacher. I honor the cycles, rhythms and stories of the inner and outer worlds and the human experience. My sculptures serve as icon, avenue, totem, fetish, trophy, mirror and vessel. pp. 53, 172

Mara Friedman (Lorane, OR): Changes, waves of emotion, uncertainty … remember to focus on the Love Light Within. Painting the Sacred Feminine and connecting with the land are my ways of remembrance and prayer. For a free catalog: PO Box 23, Lorane, OR 97451, mara@newmoonvisions.com. pp. 139, 181

Margot Foxfire (Deming, WA): I am a becoming-elder living in community at River Farm. I feel art is a form of prayer—a bridge between the seen and unseen, the known and unknown. p. 14

Mari Susan Selby (Santa Fe, NM) is a poet of the Earth, a Dakini of strong laughter and an astrologer of individual and planetary evolution. Soon to be published *Dancing with Dakinis*, Freedom Oracle with images by Jennet Inglis. 505-992-8072 POB 23823, Santa Fe, NM 87502   p. 28

Marie LoParco, MFA (Cortland, NY) is an artist and teacher. She began as a printmaker and, began painting in 1986. She now interweaves both texture and color together to create multi-media works.   pp. 59, 105

Megaera (Daylesford, Victoria, Australia) is an Australian artist who speaks publicly about child abuse. She lives with her dog Maeve and loves walking and gardening. Cards and prints are available from PO Box 232, Daylesford, Victoria 3460 Australia and www.megaerart.com.   pp. 69, 125, 143, 186

Melissa VanTil (Grand Rapids, MI): I live in the non-existent mountains of Grand Rapids, MI with my beautiful wife and six familiars. I am an artist who has recently learned the art of tattoo.   pp. 91, 99

Michelle Waters (Santa Cruz, CA): I am an eco-activist, artist and pagan. Art is my spiritual path; mama Gaia is my inspiration. Prints and cards featuring my art are available through my website: www.sasquatch.com~michelle or by contacting me at cougargrrl@lycos.com.   p. 64

Monica Sjöö (Bristol, UK): Swedish-born artist and writer and ecofeminist activist. Co-author with Barbara Mor of *The Great Cosmic Mother* and sole author of *Return of the Dark/Light Mother or New Age Armageddon* and *The Norse Goddess*. She is rediscovering ancient Sweden.   pp. 8, 34, 49, 51

musawa (Estacada, OR & Tesuque, NM): 59-year-old founder of *We'Moon*, currently migrating annually between two lovely womyn's lands. Looking for handy hardy we'moon spirits for rustic house share. You get the best deal: Winters in NM, Summers in OR! musawa@wemoon.ws   pp. 10, 13, 20, 22, 32, 37, 195

Myra Dutton (Idyllwild, CA): I pray to wild ones with their ears to the wind, to petals laid in full surrender, and rest my spirit in the beauty of creation. I have collaborated with Trish Tuley on a book of poetry and photography called *Healing Ground* and am looking for a publisher.   p. 108

Nadine Butterfield (Mt. Vernon, NY): My work emanates from a desire to express, to connect with the world of the invisible, a tribute to the angelic realm of guides, beings, ancestors who help us through this journey, whispering their wisdom, giving us hope, and a reason to walk on.   pp. 17, 62

Nancy Blair (Melbourne Beach, FL) is a visionary artist and the author of *Amulets of the Goddess, Goddesses for Every Season* and her latest book, *Goddess Days*, which includes a guidebook and sculpture.   p. 178

Nell Stone Wagenaar (Portland, OR) is about ready to reclaim her time and space by quitting her job in patriarchy and advancing to art, poetry and music with her partner and 7-year-old daughter.   p. 32

Nicolle Morris (Orleans, CA): I live rurally in Northern California while raising my beautiful daughter and seeking sources of inspiration. Would love to be in contact with other sisters, writers, mothers (especially young ones!). blackberrybramble@hotmail.com   pp. 107, 133

Nirav Sumati (Goleta, CA): Fledging poet, mother of Kyra Kestrel, world traveler, Osho Sannyassan, breathing coach, ecologist, lover.   p.148

Pesha Joyce Gertler (Seattle, WA) is recovering from brain surgery, a healing journey filled with terror and illumination. She is grateful for her life, the Divine Mother and the Gang of Angels who sustain her.   p. 99

Raven Hunter (Silver City, NM): Dreamer, singer, songwriter, drummer, artist, Priestess of Gaia dancing, swimming and worshipping the Earth in the Gila Wilderness in my homeland, New Mexico.   p. 104

Rebecca Rajswasser (Rego Park, NY) after a rocky start to 2002, Rebecca has been gifted a silver lining. She lives in Queens with the dictionary definition of adorable giggles, her sweet puddin' surprise; and runs an after-school program in the South Bronx where she is blessed with the wisdom of children.   pp. 74, 147

Rosa Davis (Stroud, Gloucestershire, UK): I dream my dreams, make my images and run creativity workshops.   p. 37

Rose Flint (Bath, Somerset, UK) is a poet, artist and art therapist. As a Priestess of Avalon she celebrates the Goddess in Glastonbury every Lammas with ceremonies, rituals, workshops and the hundreds of other wild women from around the world who attend the yearly Goddess Conference.   pp. 83, 179

S. L. Wilde (Pender Island, BC, Canada): A painter/writer/mother/lover of Ojibwe/Celtic heritage. Grateful for my grandparents, my children, my mate, my dog, seals and ravens, trees and weeds, sanity, peacefulness and love.   pp. 140, 146

Sandra Pastorius (Ashland, OR): I am a crone-wise, heavenly body on a mission now for 23 years as an Astrologer and writer. My birthchart readings and transit updates are lovingly offered by phone or in person. You can contact me at 541-512-1851 or Laughinggiraffe2001@yahoo.com.   p. 28

Sandra Stanton (Farmington, ME): Inspired by a great love of Mother Earth, I have been painting the goddess and her creatures for many years. My work can be seen on the web at www.goddessmyths.com. Prints are available at 180 Main Street-Suite 336, Farmington, ME 04938.   p. 193

Sara Baker (Maryville, TN) lives with her husband and cat in the foothills of the Great Smoky Mountains in East Tennessee. She is an activist for peace and equality and loves reading, organic gardening, and traveling. She has a thing for moon goddesses and faeries. artemisathena@hotmail.com   p. 63

Saya Wolf (Santa Fe, NM) is an artist and healer living in the mountains, canyons, and skies of New Mexico. A conscious daughter of the Great Mother for over 30 years, she is currently writing a book of inspirational herstory.   pp. 41, 58, 153

Selina Di Girolamo (Chilterns, Bucks, UK) is a feminist artist, a writer and a witch, celebrating the dark goddess in her work and play, following the blood lines that lead to her ancestors in India and Civitella, Abruzzo, Italy. selinawitch@darkmother.co.uk.   p. 89

Sue Silvermarie (Ontario, WI): My new collection, *Guatemala Is A Poem,* is based on my experiences as a human rights Accompanier in a Mayan refugee village. It is available by contacting me at: ssilvermarie@yahoo.com.   pp. 46, 95, 156

Susan H. Methvin (Anniston, AL): I'm continually learning about and trying to nurture the feminine in my own life and the world, through writing, teaching and attending our local P.F.L.A.G. Group. I'm straight but not narrow and live in Anniston, Alabama with my husband. p. 145

Susan Levitt (San Francisco, CA) is a witch and author of *Taoist Astrology, Taoist Feng Shui, Teen Feng Shui*, and *Introduction to Tarot*. Susan maintains a web site at www.susanlevitt.com and her phone number is 415-642-8019. pp. 21, 22, 29

Susan Trudeau (Champaign, IL) writes poetry and fiction inspired by her daughter, trees, her menagerie of pets and the Goddess Herself. She gathers with friends Melinda, Kathi and Sarah to celebrate creativity and beauty. p. 152

Susy Cremers Dolloff (West Cork, Ireland) Mother, flying dolphin, lover, moonlodge sister, horse friend, follower of energy, rider of waves, vision holder, creative maker, strider whose goal is to stroll, grateful for all that is. p. 183

Tami Kent (Portland, OR) is a poet mama who is finding her wings and discovering the many faces of the Great Mother. p. 123

Tatiana Bourdillon De Blanco (Anahola, HI) lives with her husband welcoming guests from around the world to their "Island Enchantment" home. www.islandenchantment.com She publishes, records & performs her poetry. tatianab@aloha.net. pp. 134, 189

Timothi Jane Graham (New York City, NY) lives with 1 dog, 1 bird, 4 cats, an open heart and an active imagination. p. 94

Toni Truesdale (Pecos, NM):I desire to build understanding by the use of universal symbols, history and mythology. I like to find those visual symbols that cross centuries, oceans, and language. p. 153

Trisia Eddy (Edmonton, Alberta, Canada): I live and work at home in Edmonton, Canada where I continue to be impressed and inspired by my children and their connection with Spirit. pp. 57, 141

True (Anahula, HI): At the core of self is "True"—unencumbered, free spirit who laughs and plays on the mystical island of Kauai. Artist-writer-muso seeker who revels in the magic of the between and the beyond. Learning (every day) to just be. p.4

Wendy Page (Victoria, B.C., Canada): I try to reflect in my work what I see and believe of the world, "our connectedness," a vital unit, where each entity survives with the love and assistance of the next. p. 112

Witchhazel Wildwood (Oxford, UK): I am a lesbian witch and moving towards sustainability and integration in my life. Working with trees, creativity and music inspire me. Email me: witchhazel@hotmail.com. pp. 55, 109

Yoruba Ze-Ti (London, UK) is an artist, healer and visionary. She seeks to heal herself and the universe through sacred art. p. 56

Zana (Berkeley, CA): Originally from Australia, Zana has created personal healing mandalas for people and organizations worldwide. She currently teaches in the United States and is working on a book for children based on sacred mandala art. www.zandalacreations.com p. 144

Zariah (Paia, HI): Dancing singing artist tantrika of Life, purely, deeply devoted to Divine Love. Honored to share gifts for sacred healing—Light, restoration of Heaven embodied in Earth. May all beings be free!!! p. 159

ASTEROIDS

The asteroids, a belt of planetary bodies orbiting in the solar system mostly between Mars and Jupiter, were discovered in the early 1800's. Since the sighting of new planets in the solar system corresponds to the activation of new centers of consciousness in the human psyche, the discovery of these planetary bodies, carrying the names of hundreds of goddesses, points to an awakening of a feminine-defined principle.

Because traditional astrology uses a ten-planet system (and only two of these symbols, the Moon and Venus, represent feminine archetypes), it has, by default, not had a set of symbols by which to describe other avenues of feminine expression. It has tried to fit all other women's experiences into masculine-defined archetypes.

The asteroids signify new archetypal symbols in the astrological language and they specifically address the current psychological and social issues that are arising in today's world due to the activation of the feminine principle. Synchronistic with the publication of the asteroid goddess ephemeris, the forefront of the women's movement emerged into society. At this time new aspects of feminine expression began to enter into human consciousness. Women became imbued with the possibilities of feminine creativity and intelligence that expanded and transcended the traditional roles of wife and mother (Venus and the Moon). This also marked a time of the rediscovery of women's ancient history, the growth of women's culture and sexuality independent of men and the rebirth of the Goddess in women's spirituality.

The mandala of asteroid goddesses, on the following page, can help us to better understand the meanings of Ceres, Pallas, Juno and Vesta (the first four asteroids discovered). The large circle in the mandala represents the Moon, which is the foundation of the feminine principle and contains potential expressions of the feminine nature. Behind the Moon resides the Sun. The union of these two energies gives rise to what mystics define as "oneness." In the center of the mandala resides Venus, the core essence of the feminine nature in her activated form, who embodies the well-spring of feminine creative, magnetic, sexual, reproductive vital life force. Venus is surrounded by Ceres, Pallas, Vesta and Juno who represent the primary relationships of a woman's life—that of mother, daughter, sister and partner, respectively. Each asteroid utilizes the creative sexual energy of Venus at the center of the circle in her own unique way, as she expresses various functions and activities of the feminine principle. They are placed at the four cardinal directions of the mandala. In the horoscope this four-fold division is designated by the four angles: the Ascendent and Descendent, which define the line of the horizon, and the Midheaven and Nadir, which mark the meridian line.

Ceres, as the Great Mother and Goddess of agriculture, gives birth to the world of physical form; she births children and provides food for their survival. As the Nadir (IC) she represents a point of foundation, roots, and family.

Pallas Athene, as the daughter and the Goddess of Wisdom, generates mental and artistic creations from her mind. At the Midheaven (MC), where visible and socially useful accomplishments are realized, she represents the principle of creative intelligence.

Vesta, as the Sister, is the Temple Priestess and is a virgin in the original sense of being whole and complete in oneself. As the Ascendant (ASC.), Vesta corresponds to the Self. She signifies the principle of spiritual focus and devotion to following one's calling.

Juno, as the Goddess of Partnership, fosters and sustains union with a partner. Placed at the Descendant (DESC.), the point of one-to-one relationships, Juno symbolizes the principle of relatedness and commitment to the other.

© *Demetra George 1996 excerpted and reprinted from* Asteroid Goddesses Natal Report

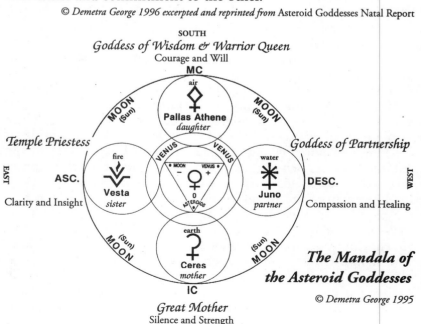

SOUTH
Goddess of Wisdom & Warrior Queen
Courage and Will

MC
air
Pallas Athene
daughter

Temple Priestess

EAST

ASC.
fire
Vesta
sister
Clarity and Insight

MOON (Sun)
MOON (Sun)
VENUS
VENUS
● MOON   VENUS ●
0 ASTEROIDS

water
Juno
partner
DESC.

WEST

Goddess of Partnership
Compassion and Healing

earth
Ceres
mother
IC

The Mandala of the Asteroid Goddesses

© *Demetra George 1995*

Great Mother
Silence and Strength
NORTH

2003 ASTEROID EPHEMERIS

Date 2003	Ceres 1	Pallas 2	Juno 3	Vesta 4
Jan 1	08♈00.6	25≈08.3	10♏18.8	06≏30.3
11	10 15.3	28 05.2	12 51.9	08 54.4
21	12 51.2	01♓09.7	15 07.9	10 47.0
31	15 44.9	04 20.5	17 04.2	12 02.3
Feb 10	18 53.7	07 36.0	18 37.3	12 34.5
20	22 15.0	10 55.1	19 44.2	12♏R19.5
Mar 2	25 46.6	14 16.6	20 21.7	11 16.2
12	29 26.8	17 39.5	20♏R26.7	09 28.6
22	03♉13.9	21 02.7	19 57.8	07 09.0
Apr 1	07 06.7	24 25.5	18 55.1	04 35.4
11	11 04.0	27 46.7	17 21.4	02 09.9
21	15 04.6	01♈05.5	15 23.5	00 13.0
May 1	19 07.9	04 21.0	13 10.8	28♍57.9
11	23 12.9	07 31.9	10 55.2	28 31.7
21	27 18.9	10 37.1	08 49.2	28♍54.6
31	01♊25.3	13 35.4	07 03.1	00≏03.0
Jun 10	05 31.4	16 25.1	05 44.5	01 52.0
20	09 36.5	19 04.2	04 57.4	04 15.8
30	13 39.9	21 30.8	04♏D42.6	07 09.1
Jul 10	17 40.8	23 41.9	04 59.4	10 27.5
20	21 38.5	25 34.5	05 45.2	14 06.8
30	25 32.1	27 04.7	06 57.1	18 03.8
Aug 9	29 20.4	28 08.1	08 32.1	22 16.0
19	03♋02.2	28 40.1	10 27.1	26 40.6
29	06 36.0	28♈R35.5	12 39.5	01♏16.2
Sep 8	10 00.0	27 50.2	15 06.8	06 01.1
18	13 12.0	26 22.4	17 46.9	10 53.8
28	16 09.5	24 13.8	20 37.9	15 53.3
Oct 8	18 49.3	21 32.4	23 38.2	20 58.6
18	21 07.8	18 32.9	26 46.2	26 08.7
28	23 00.8	15 34.0	00♐00.7	01♐23.0
Nov 7	24 23.6	12 56.2	03 20.3	06 40.5
17	25 11.5	10 55.6	06 44.0	12 00.5
27	25♋R20.2	09 41.9	10 10.6	17 22.5
Dec 7	24 47.0	09♓D19.1	13 39.1	22 45.7
17	23 32.8	09 45.9	17 08.4	28 09.4
27	21 42.8	10 58.6	20 37.4	03♐33.2
Jan 6	19♋28.8	12♈52.3	24♐04.9	08♑56.0

Date 2003	Sappho 80	Amor 1221	Pandora 55	Icarus 1566
Jan 1	07♏06.5	05♈42.6	18≏33.1	00♈51.1
11	10 13.4	07 43.9	20 21.8	18♈29.7
21	13 05.0	10 08.2	21 45.7	11♓32.0
31	15 38.3	12 52.1	22 41.3	16 16.8
Feb 10	17 49.4	15 52.5	23 05.2	21 40.2
20	19 34.3	19 06.9	22♏R55.1	26 42.1
Mar 2	20 48.7	22 33.2	22 10.1	01♈17.1
12	21 27.5	26 09.7	20 52.0	05 25.6
22	21♏R26.8	29 55.0	19 06.2	09 08.5
Apr 1	20 43.8	03♉47.9	17 01.3	12 25.9
11	19 18.6	07 47.7	14 49.4	15 15.8
21	17 16.7	11 53.4	12 43.6	17 35.2
May 1	14 48.2	16 04.7	10 55.3	19 19.5
11	12 09.1	20 21.2	09 33.6	20 21.1
21	09 37.8	24 42.5	08 43.8	20♉R30.7
31	07 30.7	29 08.5	08♏D27.3	19 35.5
Jun 10	06 00.4	03♊39.1	08 43.9	17 20.4
20	05 13.1	08 14.4	09 31.1	13 31.9
30	05 02.0	12 54.6	10 45.8	08 04.1
Jul 10	05 50.0	17 39.8	12 25.1	01 11.4
20	07 08.7	22 30.3	14 25.6	23♉37.3
30	09 02.0	27 26.6	16 44.5	16 21.7
Aug 9	11 25.7	02♋29.1	19 19.3	10 17.7
19	14 15.6	07 38.5	22 07.7	05 50.5
29	17 28.5	12 55.6	25 07.9	03 00.8
Sep 8	21 01.6	18 21.1	28 18.2	01 37.2
18	24 52.2	23 56.2	01♏36.9	01♊D24.0
28	28 58.5	29 42.5	05 03.1	02 07.6
Oct 8	03♐18.9	05♋41.3	08 35.4	03 37.1
18	07 51.6	11 54.9	12 12.6	05 43.9
28	12 35.9	18 25.7	15 54.1	08 22.1
Nov 7	17 30.5	25 16.6	19 38.7	11 27.8
17	22 34.4	02♍31.4	23 25.4	14 57.9
27	27 47.2	10 14.2	27 13.5	18 51.6
Dec 7	03♑07.8	18 29.5	01♐01.8	23 08.6
17	08 35.6	27 22.5	04 49.5	27 50.1
27	14 10.2	06≏56.9	08 35.5	02♈59.4
Jan 6	19♑50.7	17≏14.0	12♐18.6	08≈41.3

Date 2003	Psyche 16	Eros 433	Lilith 1181	Toro 1685
Jan 1	12♏49.2	01♈36.0	27♐05.5	04≈03.8
11	15 28.2	08 03.4	00♑44.6	14 01.9
21	17 53.1	15 00.4	04 21.5	24 46.4
31	20 01.3	22 23.5	07 55.2	06♓18.3
Feb 10	21 49.8	00♉10.6	11 24.5	18 34.8
20	23 15.6	08 18.5	14 47.8	01♈28.0
Mar 2	24 15.5	16 44.8	18 04.1	14 46.4
12	24 46.4	25 27.3	21 11.3	28 15.7
22	24♏R46.1	04♊23.0	24 07.7	11♉39.7
Apr 1	24 13.3	13 29.3	26 51.3	24 43.5
11	23 09.0	22 43.9	29 19.4	07♊14.1
21	21 37.3	02♋03.4	01≈29.3	19 01.7
May 1	19 45.0	11 25.1	03 18.0	00♋01.9
11	17 42.2	20 46.4	04 41.8	10 14.4
21	15 40.7	00♍04.0	05 37.1	19 41.4
31	13 51.7	09 15.4	06 00.3	28 27.7
Jun 10	12 24.9	18 18.6	05♈R48.5	06♌38.4
20	11 26.5	27 11.1	05 00.8	14 18.3
30	10 59.6	05♍51.5	03 38.4	21 32.4
Jul 10	11♏D05.0	14 19.1	01 46.8	28 24.7
20	11 41.2	22 33.0	29♑35.9	04♍58.6
30	12 45.8	00≏33.3	27 18.7	11 17.3
Aug 9	14 16.1	08 20.3	25 10.2	17 23.3
19	16 09.0	15 54.4	23 24.1	23 18.5
29	18 21.8	23 16.6	22 09.9	29 04.9
Sep 8	20 52.1	00♏27.8	21 33.9	04≏43.9
18	23 37.2	07 28.6	21♑D37.4	10 16.5
28	26 35.4	14 20.3	22 19.3	15 43.9
Oct 8	29 44.9	21 03.9	23 37.2	21 06.9
18	03♐04.0	27 40.0	25 27.2	26 26.0
28	06 31.3	04♐09.7	27 45.6	01♏42.1
Nov 7	10 05.6	10 33.6	00≈29.1	06 55.3
17	13 45.7	16 52.3	03 34.2	12 06.0
27	17 30.5	23 06.8	06 58.1	17 14.7
Dec 7	21 19.0	29 17.2	10 38.5	22 21.3
17	25 10.1	05♑24.1	14 32.9	27 26.1
27	29 03.0	11 28.1	18 39.7	02♐29.2
Jan 6	02♐56.5	17♑29.3	22≈57.1	07♐30.5

Date 2003	Diana 78	Hidalgo 944	Urania 30	Chiron 2060
Jan 1	24♏10.5	04≈57.6	12♐19.8	10♑45.3
11	26 02.8	07 15.5	16 31.7	11 45.7
21	27 09.6	09 37.9	20 39.3	12 44.9
31	27♏R26.1	12 03.5	24 41.8	13 41.8
Feb 10	26 50.1	14 30.9	28 37.6	14 35.6
20	25 25.6	16 58.5	02♑25.2	15 25.1
Mar 2	23 23.3	19 25.1	06 03.0	16 09.5
12	21 01.3	21 49.1	09 28.9	16 47.8
22	18 42.6	24 08.9	12 40.5	17 19.4
Apr 1	16 47.4	26 23.3	15 35.1	17 43.6
11	15 30.9	28 30.3	18 09.4	17 59.9
21	15 00.2	00♓28.2	20 19.7	18 07.9
May 1	15♏D15.6	02 15.1	22 01.8	18♑R07.7
11	16 14.3	03 48.6	23 10.8	17 59.3
21	17 50.6	05 06.6	23 42.4	17 43.4
31	19 58.8	06 06.3	23♐R32.9	17 20.5
Jun 10	22 33.8	06 44.9	22 40.4	16 51.8
20	25 30.5	07 00.0	21 07.7	16 18.7
30	28 45.0	06♓R49.0	19 01.9	15 42.6
Jul 10	02♐14.2	06 10.1	16 36.8	15 05.2
20	05 55.0	05 03.3	14 10.2	14 28.4
30	09 45.5	03 30.0	12 00.2	13 53.7
Aug 9	13 43.7	01 34.4	10 22.4	13 23.0
19	17 48.0	29≈23.7	09♐D15.8	12 57.4
29	21 57.3	27 06.9	09♑D15.8	12 38.2
Sep 8	26 10.4	24 54.7	09 50.5	12 26.3
18	00♏26.4	22 57.1	11 07.1	12 22.1
28	04 44.5	21 22.1	13 01.1	12D25.9
Oct 8	09 03.9	20 15.5	15 28.2	12 37.8
18	13 23.8	19 39.7	18 23.6	12 57.5
28	17 43.7	19♓D35.2	21 43.5	13 24.5
Nov 7	22 02.8	20 00.9	25 24.4	13 58.3
17	26 20.3	20 54.4	29 23.3	14 38.2
27	00♐35.6	22 12.9	03♑37.8	15 23.2
Dec 7	04 47.8	23 53.8	08 05.6	16 12.5
17	08 56.1	25 54.0	12 44.9	17 05.2
27	12 59.7	28 11.2	17 34.2	18 00.3
Jan 6	16♐57.4	00♓42.9	22♑32.0	18♑56.0

Giving the positions of asteroids every
ten days in LONGITUDE at 00:00 GMT

NOON PLANETARY EPHEMERIS: GMT* JANUARY 2003

Day	Sid.Time	☉	0 hr ☽	Noon ☽	True ☊	☿	♀	♂	♃	♄	♅	♆	♇
1 W	18 42 54	10♑38 45	16♐ 1 31	23♐ 6 47	8♊28.0	28♑18.9	24♏ 8.4	19♏53.4	16♌50.8	24♊24.4	26♒17.1	9♒34.9	18♐17.8
2 Th	18 46 51	11 39 56	0♑ 9 38	7♑ 9 32	8R 25.4	28R 27.4	25 5.3	20 32.1	16R 45.4	24R 19.8	26 19.7	9 36.9	18 19.9
3 F	18 50 47	12 41 7	14 5 55	20 58 21	8 21.1	28 24.6	26 2.6	21 10.8	16 40.0	24 15.2	26 22.5	9 39.0	18 22.1
4 Sa	18 54 44	13 42 18	27 46 25	4♒29 46	8 15.4	28 10.3	27 0.5	21 49.5	16 34.4	24 10.7	26 25.2	9 41.1	18 24.2
5 Su	18 58 40	14 43 29	11♒ 8 10	17 41 30	8 8.9	27 44.1	27 58.9	22 28.1	16 28.6	24 6.2	26 28.0	9 43.2	18 26.3
6 M	19 2 37	15 44 39	24 9 43	0♓32 54	8 2.4	27 6.1	28 57.8	23 6.8	16 22.7	24 1.8	26 30.8	9 45.3	18 28.4
7 Tu	19 6 34	16 45 50	6♓51 12	13 4 55	7 56.6	26 17.0	29 57.2	23 45.5	16 16.6	23 57.4	26 33.6	9 47.4	18 30.5
8 W	19 10 30	17 46 59	19 14 23	25 20 3	7 52.2	25 17.8	0♐57.0	24 24.2	16 10.4	23 53.1	26 36.5	9 49.6	18 32.6
9 Th	19 14 27	18 48 9	1♈22 22	7♈21 56	7 49.6	24 10.1	1 57.2	25 2.9	16 4.1	23 48.8	26 39.3	9 51.7	18 34.6
10 F	19 18 23	19 49 18	13 19 17	19 15 5	7D 48.7	22 56.0	2 57.8	25 41.5	15 57.7	23 44.6	26 42.3	9 53.9	18 36.7
11 Sa	19 22 20	20 50 26	25 9 58	1♉ 4 35	7 49.3	21 37.7	3 58.9	26 20.2	15 51.1	23 40.5	26 45.2	9 56.1	18 38.7
12 Su	19 26 16	21 51 34	6♉59 35	12 55 39	7 50.8	20 17.8	5 0.3	26 58.9	15 44.4	23 36.4	26 48.2	9 58.2	18 40.7
13 M	19 30 13	22 52 41	18 53 23	24 53 25	7 52.3	18 58.9	6 2.1	27 37.6	15 37.6	23 32.4	26 51.2	10 0.4	18 42.7
14 Tu	19 34 9	23 53 48	0♊56 19	7♊ 2 37	7R 53.0	17 43.4	7 4.3	28 16.2	15 30.7	23 28.5	26 54.2	10 2.6	18 44.7
15 W	19 38 6	24 54 54	13 12 48	19 27 14	7 52.3	16 33.2	8 6.8	28 54.9	15 23.6	23 24.7	26 57.2	10 4.8	18 46.6
16 Th	19 42 3	25 56 0	25 46 17	2♋10 10	7 49.4	15 30.0	9 9.7	29 33.6	15 16.5	23 20.9	27 0.3	10 7.1	18 48.6
17 F	19 45 59	26 57 5	8♋39 2	15 12 54	7 44.3	14 35.1	10 12.9	0♐12.3	15 9.3	23 17.2	27 3.4	10 9.3	18 50.5
18 Sa	19 49 56	27 58 9	21 51 43	28 35 17	7 37.1	13 49.2	11 16.4	0 50.9	15 2.0	23 13.6	27 6.5	10 11.5	18 52.4
19 Su	19 53 52	28 59 13	5♌23 21	12♌15 31	7 28.4	13 12.6	12 20.2	1 29.6	14 54.6	23 10.1	27 9.7	10 13.8	18 54.2
20 M	19 57 49	0♒ 0 16	19 11 19	26 10 17	7 19.2	12 45.6	13 24.3	2 8.3	14 47.1	23 6.6	27 12.8	10 16.0	18 56.1
21 Tu	20 1 45	1 1 19	3♍11 49	10♍15 21	7 10.5	12 27.8	14 28.7	2 47.0	14 39.6	23 3.2	27 16.0	10 18.3	18 57.9
22 W	20 5 42	2 2 21	17 20 20	24 26 14	7 3.4	12 19.0	15 33.4	3 25.6	14 32.0	22 60.0	27 19.2	10 20.5	18 59.7
23 Th	20 9 38	3 3 23	1♎32 32	8♎38 50	6 58.4	12D 18.5	16 38.4	4 4.3	14 24.3	22 56.8	27 22.4	10 22.8	19 1.5
24 F	20 13 35	4 4 24	15 44 44	22 49 58	6 55.8	12 26.0	17 43.6	4 43.0	14 16.5	22 53.7	27 25.7	10 25.1	19 3.3
25 Sa	20 17 32	5 5 25	29 54 18	6♏57 33	6D 55.2	12 40.8	18 49.1	5 21.7	14 8.7	22 50.6	27 28.9	10 27.3	19 5.0
26 Su	20 21 28	6 6 26	13♏59 37	21 0 24	6 55.8	13 2.3	19 54.8	6 0.3	14 0.9	22 47.7	27 32.2	10 29.6	19 6.8
27 M	20 25 25	7 7 26	27 59 49	4♐57 49	6R 56.4	13 29.9	21 0.8	6 39.0	13 53.0	22 44.9	27 35.5	10 31.9	19 8.5
28 Tu	20 29 21	8 8 25	11♐54 18	18 49 11	6 55.8	14 3.1	22 7.0	7 17.7	13 45.1	22 42.2	27 38.8	10 34.2	19 10.1
29 W	20 33 18	9 9 24	25 42 19	2♑33 33	6 53.0	14 41.4	23 13.4	7 56.3	13 37.1	22 39.5	27 42.1	10 36.4	19 11.8
30 Th	20 37 14	10 10 22	9♑22 40	16 9 26	6 47.4	15 24.3	24 20.0	8 35.0	13 29.2	22 37.0	27 45.4	10 38.7	19 13.4
31 F	20 41 11	11 11 19	22 53 36	29 34 53	6 39.0	16 11.5	25 26.8	9 13.6	13 21.2	22 34.6	27 48.8	10 40.9	19 15.0

LONGITUDE FEBRUARY 2003

Day	Sid.Time	☉	0 hr ☽	Noon ☽	True ☊	☿	♀	♂	♃	♄	♅	♆	♇
1 Sa	20 45 8	12♒12 15	6♒13 2	12♒47 48	6♊28.2	17♑ 2.4	26♐33.8	9♐52.3	13♌13.2	22♊32.2	27♒52.2	10♒43.3	19♐16.6
2 Su	20 49 4	13 13 10	19 18 56	25 46 17	6R 15.9	17 56.8	27 41.0	10 30.9	13R 5.2	22R 30.0	27 55.5	10 45.6	19 18.2
3 M	20 53 1	14 14 4	2♓ 9 44	8♓29 13	6 3.3	18 54.4	28 48.3	11 9.5	12 57.2	22 27.9	27 58.9	10 47.8	19 19.7
4 Tu	20 56 57	15 14 57	14 44 47	20 56 31	5 51.6	19 54.8	29 55.9	11 48.1	12 49.2	22 25.8	28 2.3	10 50.1	19 21.2
5 W	21 0 54	16 15 48	27 4 37	3♈ 9 21	5 41.8	20 57.9	1♑ 3.6	12 26.7	12 41.2	22 23.9	28 5.7	10 52.4	19 22.6
6 Th	21 4 50	17 16 38	9♈11 4	15 10 11	5 34.5	22 3.4	2 11.4	13 5.3	12 33.2	22 22.1	28 9.1	10 54.7	19 24.1
7 F	21 8 47	18 17 27	21 7 10	27 2 33	5 29.9	23 11.1	3 19.4	13 43.9	12 25.3	22 20.4	28 12.5	10 56.9	19 25.5
8 Sa	21 12 43	19 18 14	2♉56 57	8♉50 59	5 27.7	24 20.9	4 27.6	14 22.5	12 17.4	22 18.8	28 16.0	10 59.2	19 26.9
9 Su	21 16 40	20 18 59	14 45 18	20 40 35	5D 27.2	25 32.6	5 35.9	15 1.1	12 9.5	22 17.3	28 19.4	11 1.4	19 28.2
10 M	21 20 36	21 19 43	26 37 33	2♊36 54	5R 27.4	26 46.0	6 44.4	15 39.6	12 1.7	22 16.0	28 22.9	11 3.7	19 29.6
11 Tu	21 24 33	22 20 26	8♊39 18	14 45 27	5 27.1	28 1.1	7 52.9	16 18.2	11 53.9	22 14.7	28 26.3	11 5.9	19 30.9
12 W	21 28 30	23 21 7	20 55 57	27 11 24	5 25.3	29 17.8	9 1.7	16 56.7	11 46.2	22 13.5	28 29.8	11 8.2	19 32.2
13 Th	21 32 26	24 21 46	3♋32 18	9♋59 3	5 21.1	0♒35.9	10 10.5	17 35.2	11 38.5	22 12.5	28 33.2	11 10.4	19 33.4
14 F	21 36 23	25 22 24	16 31 59	23 11 15	5 14.1	1 55.4	11 19.5	18 13.8	11 30.9	22 11.6	28 36.7	11 12.7	19 34.6
15 Sa	21 40 19	26 23 0	29 56 53	6♌48 46	5 4.5	3 16.3	12 28.6	18 52.3	11 23.4	22 10.7	28 40.1	11 14.9	19 35.8
16 Su	21 44 16	27 23 35	13♌46 37	20 49 57	4 53.0	4 38.4	13 37.8	19 30.8	11 16.0	22 10.0	28 43.6	11 17.1	19 37.0
17 M	21 48 12	28 24 8	27 58 10	5♍10 31	4 40.7	6 1.7	14 47.2	20 9.3	11 8.6	22 9.4	28 47.1	11 19.3	19 38.1
18 Tu	21 52 9	29 24 39	12♍26 8	19 44 6	4 28.9	7 26.2	15 56.6	20 47.7	11 1.3	22 8.9	28 50.5	11 21.5	19 39.2
19 W	21 56 5	0♓25 9	27 3 27	4♎23 13	4 18.8	8 51.9	17 6.2	21 26.2	10 54.1	22 8.6	28 54.0	11 23.7	19 40.2
20 Th	22 0 2	1 25 38	11♎42 33	19 0 36	4 11.4	10 18.6	18 15.9	22 4.7	10 47.0	22 8.3	28 57.4	11 25.9	19 41.3
21 F	22 3 59	2 26 5	26 16 41	3♏30 15	4 7.0	11 46.4	19 25.7	22 43.1	10 40.1	22 8.2	29 0.9	11 28.0	19 42.3
22 Sa	22 7 55	3 26 31	10♏40 51	17 48 11	4 5.0	13 15.3	20 35.6	23 21.6	10 33.2	22D 8.1	29 4.4	11 30.2	19 43.2
23 Su	22 11 52	4 26 56	24 52 3	1♐52 25	4 4.6	14 45.3	21 45.6	24 0.0	10 26.4	22 8.2	29 7.8	11 32.3	19 44.2
24 M	22 15 48	5 27 19	8♐49 15	15 42 37	4 4.5	16 16.3	22 55.6	24 38.4	10 19.7	22 8.4	29 11.3	11 34.4	19 45.1
25 Tu	22 19 45	6 27 42	22 32 39	29 19 28	4 3.2	17 48.3	24 5.8	25 16.8	10 13.2	22 8.7	29 14.7	11 36.6	19 46.0
26 W	22 23 41	7 28 2	6♑ 3 11	12♑43 56	3 59.8	19 21.4	25 16.1	25 55.2	10 6.8	22 9.1	29 18.2	11 38.7	19 46.8
27 Th	22 27 38	8 28 22	19 21 49	25 56 54	3 53.3	20 55.4	26 26.5	26 33.6	10 0.5	22 9.6	29 21.6	11 40.8	19 47.6
28 F	22 31 34	9 28 39	2♒29 14	8♒58 50	3 43.9	22 30.5	27 36.9	27 12.0	9 54.3	22 10.3	29 25.0	11 42.8	19 48.4

Ephemeris reprinted with permission from Astro Communications Services, Inc.
Each planet's retrograde period is shaded gray.

*Giving the positions of planets daily at noon, in LONGITUDE Greenwich Mean Time

Noon Ephemeris: GMT*

March 2003

Day	Sid.Time	☉	0 hr ☽	Noon ☽	True ☊	☿	♀	♂	♃	♄	♅	♆	♇
1 Sa	22 35 31	10♓28 55	15♒25 41	21♒49 44	3♊31.9	24♒ 6.7	28♑47.4	27♐50.3	9♌48.3	22♊11.0	29♒28.5	11♒44.9	19♐49.1
2 Su	22 39 28	11 29 10	28 10 58	4♓29 20	3R 18.2	25 43.8	29 58.0	28 28.6	9R 42.4	22 11.9	29 31.9	11 47.0	19 49.8
3 M	22 43 24	12 29 22	10♓44 48	16 57 22	3 4.1	27 22.0	1♒ 8.7	29 6.9	9 36.7	22 12.9	29 35.3	11 49.0	19 50.5
4 Tu	22 47 21	13 29 33	23 7 3	29 13 55	2 50.7	29 1.3	2 19.4	29 45.2	9 31.1	22 14.0	29 38.7	11 51.0	19 51.2
5 W	22 51 17	14 29 41	5♈18 5	11♈19 44	2 39.3	0♓41.6	3 30.2	0♑23.4	9 25.6	22 15.2	29 42.0	11 53.0	19 51.8
6 Th	22 55 14	15 29 48	17 19 4	23 16 24	2 30.5	2 22.9	4 41.0	1 1.6	9 20.4	22 16.5	29 45.4	11 55.0	19 52.3
7 F	22 59 10	16 29 53	29 12 4	5♉ 6 29	2 24.6	4 5.4	5 52.0	1 39.8	9 15.2	22 17.9	29 48.8	11 57.0	19 52.9
8 Sa	23 3 7	17 29 56	11♉ 0 7	16 53 28	2 21.4	5 49.0	7 2.9	2 18.0	9 10.3	22 19.5	29 52.1	11 58.9	19 53.4
9 Su	23 7 3	18 29 56	22 47 8	28 41 42	2D 20.3	7 33.6	8 14.0	2 56.2	9 5.5	22 21.1	29 55.5	12 0.8	19 53.9
10 M	23 11 0	19 29 55	4♊37 49	10♊36 9	2 20.4	9 19.4	9 25.1	3 34.3	9 0.8	22 22.9	29 58.8	12 2.7	19 54.3
11 Tu	23 14 57	20 29 51	16 37 25	22 42 16	2R 20.6	11 6.3	10 36.2	4 12.4	8 56.4	22 24.7	0♓ 2.1	12 4.6	19 54.7
12 W	23 18 53	21 29 46	28 51 26	5♋ 5 33	2 19.7	12 54.4	11 47.4	4 50.5	8 52.1	22 26.7	0 5.4	12 6.5	19 55.1
13 Th	23 22 50	22 29 38	11♋25 14	17 51 4	2 16.9	14 43.6	12 58.7	5 28.5	8 47.9	22 28.8	0 8.6	12 8.4	19 55.4
14 F	23 26 46	23 29 28	24 23 30	1♌ 2 54	2 11.7	16 34.0	14 10.0	6 6.5	8 44.0	22 31.0	0 11.9	12 10.2	19 55.7
15 Sa	23 30 43	24 29 15	7♌49 28	14 43 18	2 4.1	18 25.6	15 21.3	6 44.5	8 40.2	22 33.3	0 15.1	12 12.0	19 56.0
16 Su	23 34 39	25 29 1	21 44 14	28 51 59	1 54.7	20 18.3	16 32.7	7 22.5	8 36.6	22 35.7	0 18.4	12 13.8	19 56.3
17 M	23 38 36	26 28 44	6♍ 6 0	13♍25 33	1 44.4	22 12.2	17 44.2	8 0.4	8 33.2	22 38.2	0 21.6	12 15.6	19 56.5
18 Tu	23 42 32	27 28 25	20 49 45	28 17 32	1 34.3	24 7.1	18 55.7	8 38.4	8 30.0	22 40.8	0 24.7	12 17.3	19 56.6
19 W	23 46 29	28 28 4	5♎47 45	13♎19 10	1 25.8	26 3.3	20 7.3	9 16.3	8 26.9	22 43.5	0 27.9	12 19.0	19 56.8
20 Th	23 50 26	29 27 41	20 50 36	28 20 51	1 19.5	28 0.4	21 18.8	9 54.1	8 24.1	22 46.3	0 31.0	12 20.8	19 56.9
21 F	23 54 22	0♈27 16	5♏48 53	13♏13 46	1 15.9	29 58.6	22 30.5	10 32.0	8 21.4	22 49.2	0 34.2	12 22.4	19 56.9
22 Sa	23 58 19	1 26 50	20 34 45	27 51 13	1D 14.6	1♈57.8	23 42.2	11 9.8	8 18.9	22 52.2	0 37.3	12 24.1	19 57.0
23 Su	0 2 15	2 26 22	5♐ 2 47	12♐ 9 9	1 14.8	3 57.8	24 53.9	11 47.5	8 16.6	22 55.3	0 40.3	12 25.7	19R 57.0
24 M	0 6 12	3 25 52	19 10 15	26 6 4	1 15.6	5 58.5	26 5.7	12 25.3	8 14.5	22 58.5	0 43.4	12 27.3	19 57.0
25 Tu	0 10 8	4 25 21	2♑56 42	9♑42 22	1R 15.6	7 59.9	27 17.5	13 3.0	8 12.5	23 1.9	0 46.4	12 28.9	19 56.9
26 W	0 14 5	5 24 48	16 23 17	22 59 43	1 14.1	10 1.7	28 29.4	13 40.7	8 10.8	23 5.3	0 49.4	12 30.5	19 56.8
27 Th	0 18 1	6 24 13	29 31 57	6♒ 0 17	1 10.3	12 3.8	29 41.3	14 18.3	8 9.2	23 8.8	0 52.4	12 32.0	19 56.7
28 F	0 21 58	7 23 36	12♒24 58	18 46 16	1 4.1	14 5.9	0♓53.2	14 55.9	8 7.9	23 12.4	0 55.4	12 33.5	19 56.5
29 Sa	0 25 55	8 22 57	25 4 26	1♓19 40	0 56.0	16 7.8	2 5.2	15 33.4	8 6.7	23 16.1	0 58.3	12 35.0	19 56.3
30 Su	0 29 51	9 22 16	7♓32 10	13 42 6	0 46.5	18 9.2	3 17.2	16 10.9	8 5.7	23 19.8	1 1.2	12 36.5	19 56.1
31 M	0 33 48	10 21 34	19 49 38	25 54 53	0 36.6	20 9.8	4 29.2	16 48.4	8 4.9	23 23.7	1 4.1	12 37.9	19 55.8

Longitude

April 2003

Day	Sid.Time	☉	0 hr ☽	Noon ☽	True ☊	☿	♀	♂	♃	♄	♅	♆	♇
1 Tu	0 37 44	11♈20 49	1♈58 2	7♈59 12	0♊27.2	22♈ 9.2	5♓41.2	17♑25.8	8♌ 4.3	23♊27.7	1♓ 6.9	12♒39.3	19♐55.6
2 W	0 41 41	12 20 3	13 58 34	19 56 19	0R 19.3	24 7.1	6 53.3	18 3.2	8R 3.9	23 31.7	1 9.7	12 40.7	19R 55.2
3 Th	0 45 37	13 19 14	25 52 37	1♉47 45	0 13.3	26 3.1	8 5.4	18 40.5	8 3.7	23 35.9	1 12.5	12 42.0	19 54.9
4 F	0 49 34	14 18 23	7♉41 57	13 35 32	0 9.5	27 56.9	9 17.6	19 17.7	8D 3.7	23 40.1	1 15.3	12 43.4	19 54.5
5 Sa	0 53 30	15 17 30	19 28 51	25 22 17	0D 7.9	29 48.0	10 29.7	19 54.9	8 3.8	23 44.5	1 18.0	12 44.6	19 54.1
6 Su	0 57 27	16 16 35	1♊16 17	7♊11 19	0 8.0	1♉36.0	11 41.9	20 32.1	8 4.2	23 48.9	1 20.7	12 45.9	19 53.6
7 M	1 1 23	17 15 38	13 7 54	19 6 35	0 9.2	3 20.6	12 54.1	21 9.2	8 4.7	23 53.4	1 23.4	12 47.2	19 53.1
8 Tu	1 5 20	18 14 38	25 7 56	1♋12 34	0 10.7	5 1.5	14 6.3	21 46.2	8 5.5	23 58.0	1 26.0	12 48.4	19 52.6
9 W	1 9 17	19 13 37	7♋21 5	13 34 6	0R 11.8	6 38.3	15 18.6	22 23.2	8 6.4	24 2.6	1 28.6	12 49.5	19 52.1
10 Th	1 13 13	20 12 32	19 52 14	26 16 2	0 11.8	8 10.7	16 30.8	23 0.1	8 7.5	24 7.4	1 31.2	12 50.7	19 51.5
11 F	1 17 10	21 11 26	2♌46 2	9♌22 41	0 10.2	9 38.4	17 43.1	23 37.0	8 8.8	24 12.2	1 33.7	12 51.8	19 50.9
12 Sa	1 21 6	22 10 17	16 6 19	22 57 11	0 7.0	11 1.3	18 55.4	24 13.8	8 10.3	24 17.1	1 36.2	12 52.9	19 50.3
13 Su	1 25 3	23 9 6	29 55 21	7♍ 0 43	0 2.5	12 19.1	20 7.7	24 50.5	8 12.0	24 22.1	1 38.7	12 54.0	19 49.6
14 M	1 28 59	24 7 53	14♍13 0	21 31 41	29♉57.3	13 31.7	21 20.1	25 27.2	8 13.8	24 27.2	1 41.1	12 55.0	19 48.9
15 Tu	1 32 56	25 6 37	28 56 7	6♎25 23	29 52.0	14 38.7	22 32.4	26 3.8	8 15.9	24 32.3	1 43.5	12 56.0	19 48.2
16 W	1 36 52	26 5 20	13♎58 26	21 34 6	29 47.6	15 40.3	23 44.8	26 40.4	8 18.1	24 37.6	1 45.8	12 57.0	19 47.4
17 Th	1 40 49	27 4 0	29 11 6	6♏48 9	29 44.4	16 36.1	24 57.2	27 16.9	8 20.5	24 42.9	1 48.2	12 57.9	19 46.7
18 F	1 44 46	28 2 39	14♏23 59	21 57 24	29 42.9	17 26.1	26 9.6	27 53.3	8 23.1	24 48.2	1 50.4	12 58.8	19 45.9
19 Sa	1 48 42	29 1 15	29 27 20	6♐52 53	29D 42.9	18 10.3	27 22.0	28 29.7	8 25.8	24 53.7	1 52.7	12 59.7	19 45.0
20 Su	1 52 39	29 59 51	14♐13 17	21 27 59	29 43.9	18 48.5	28 34.5	29 6.0	8 28.7	24 59.2	1 54.9	13 0.5	19 44.2
21 M	1 56 35	0♉58 24	28 36 35	5♑38 53	29 45.4	19 20.8	29 47.0	29 42.2	8 31.8	25 4.8	1 57.1	13 1.4	19 43.3
22 Tu	2 0 32	1 56 56	12♑34 49	19 24 26	29 46.7	19 47.1	0♈59.5	0♒18.3	8 35.1	25 10.4	1 59.2	13 2.1	19 42.4
23 W	2 4 28	2 55 26	26 7 56	2♒45 34	29R 47.2	20 7.4	2 12.0	0 54.4	8 38.6	25 16.1	2 1.3	13 2.9	19 41.5
24 Th	2 8 25	3 53 55	9♒17 39	15 44 33	29 46.6	20 21.8	3 24.5	1 30.4	8 42.2	25 21.9	2 3.4	13 3.6	19 40.5
25 F	2 12 22	4 52 22	22 6 42	28 24 28	29 44.9	20 30.4	4 37.1	2 6.3	8 46.0	25 27.8	2 5.4	13 4.3	19 39.5
26 Sa	2 16 18	5 50 47	4♓38 18	10♓48 35	29 42.1	20R 33.2	5 49.6	2 42.1	8 49.9	25 33.7	2 7.3	13 5.0	19 38.5
27 Su	2 20 15	6 49 11	16 55 45	23 0 9	29 38.7	20 30.5	7 2.2	3 17.8	8 54.1	25 39.7	2 9.3	13 5.6	19 37.4
28 M	2 24 11	7 47 33	29 2 9	5♈ 2 5	29 35.0	20 22.4	8 14.8	3 53.4	8 58.3	25 45.7	2 11.1	13 6.2	19 36.4
29 Tu	2 28 8	8 45 53	11♈ 0 18	16 57 4	29 31.5	20 9.2	9 27.4	4 28.9	9 2.8	25 51.8	2 13.0	13 6.7	19 35.3
30 W	2 32 4	9 44 12	22 52 41	28 47 25	29 28.6	19 51.3	10 40.0	5 4.3	9 7.4	25 58.0	2 14.8	13 7.2	19 34.2

*Giving the positions of planets daily at noon, in LONGITUDE Greenwich Mean Time

NOON EPHEMERIS: GMT* MAY 2003

Day	Sid.Time	☉	0 hr ☽	Noon☽	True☊	☿	♀	♂	♃	♄	♅	♆	♇
1 Th	2 36 1	10♉42 28	4♉41 33	10♉35 19	29♉26.6	19♉29.0	11♈52.6	5♒39.6	9♌12.2	26♊ 4.2	2♓16.6	13♒ 7.7	19♐33.0
2 F	2 39 57	11 40 44	16 29 1	22 22 55	29R 25.6	19R 2.8	13 5.3	6 14.7	9 17.1	26 10.5	2 18.3	13 8.2	19R 31.9
3 Sa	2 43 54	12 38 57	28 17 16	4♊12 25	29D 25.5	18 33.3	14 17.9	6 49.8	9 22.2	26 16.9	2 19.9	13 8.6	19 30.7
4 Su	2 47 50	13 37 9	10♊ 8 38	16 6 17	29 26.2	18 0.9	15 30.6	7 24.8	9 27.5	26 23.3	2 21.6	13 9.0	19 29.5
5 M	2 51 47	14 35 18	22 5 44	28 7 22	29 27.3	17 26.3	16 43.2	7 59.6	9 32.9	26 29.7	2 23.2	13 9.4	19 28.3
6 Tu	2 55 44	15 33 26	4♋11 34	10♋18 47	29 28.6	16 50.2	17 55.9	8 34.3	9 38.5	26 36.2	2 24.7	13 9.7	19 27.1
7 W	2 59 40	16 31 32	16 29 28	22 44 4	29 29.8	16 13.1	19 8.6	9 8.9	9 44.2	26 42.8	2 26.2	13 10.0	19 25.8
8 Th	3 3 37	17 29 37	29 3 2	5♌26 49	29 30.5	15 35.8	20 21.3	9 43.4	9 50.1	26 49.4	2 27.7	13 10.3	19 24.5
9 F	3 7 33	18 27 39	11♌55 52	18 30 34	29R 30.8	14 58.9	21 34.0	10 17.8	9 56.1	26 56.1	2 29.1	13 10.5	19 23.2
10 Sa	3 11 30	19 25 39	25 11 15	1♍58 11	29 30.5	14 23.0	22 46.7	10 52.0	10 2.3	27 2.8	2 30.4	13 10.7	19 21.9
11 Su	3 15 26	20 23 37	8♍51 33	15 51 23	29 29.9	13 48.8	23 59.4	11 26.1	10 8.6	27 9.5	2 31.7	13 10.9	19 20.6
12 M	3 19 23	21 21 34	22 57 38	0♎10 2	29 29.0	13 16.7	25 12.1	12 0.0	10 15.0	27 16.3	2 33.0	13 11.0	19 19.2
13 Tu	3 23 19	22 19 28	7♎28 12	14 51 33	29 28.2	12 47.4	26 24.8	12 33.8	10 21.6	27 23.2	2 34.2	13 11.1	19 17.9
14 W	3 27 16	23 17 21	22 19 23	29 50 46	29 27.5	12 21.3	27 37.6	13 7.5	10 28.3	27 30.1	2 35.4	13 11.1	19 16.5
15 Th	3 31 13	24 15 12	7♏24 42	15♏ 0 3	29 27.1	11 58.7	28 50.3	13 41.0	10 35.2	27 37.0	2 36.5	13 11.2	19 15.1
16 F	3 35 9	25 13 2	22 35 39	0♐10 17	29D 27.0	11 39.9	0♉ 3.1	14 14.4	10 42.2	27 44.0	2 37.6	13R 11.2	19 13.7
17 Sa	3 39 6	26 10 51	7♐42 48	15 12 7	29 27.1	11 25.2	1 15.8	14 47.6	10 49.3	27 51.0	2 38.6	13 11.1	19 12.2
18 Su	3 43 2	27 8 38	22 37 14	29 57 19	29 27.3	11 14.9	2 28.6	15 20.7	10 56.6	27 58.1	2 39.6	13 11.1	19 10.8
19 M	3 46 59	28 6 24	7♑11 41	14♑19 50	29 27.5	11 8.9	3 41.4	15 53.6	11 4.0	28 5.2	2 40.6	13 11.0	19 9.4
20 Tu	3 50 55	29 4 8	21 21 24	28 16 15	29R 27.6	11D 7.5	4 54.2	16 26.4	11 11.5	28 12.3	2 41.5	13 10.9	19 7.9
21 W	3 54 52	0♊ 1 52	5♒ 4 20	11♒45 46	29 27.6	11 10.6	6 7.1	16 59.0	11 19.1	28 19.5	2 42.3	13 10.7	19 6.4
22 Th	3 58 49	0 59 34	18 20 47	24 49 42	29 27.5	11 18.3	7 19.9	17 31.4	11 26.9	28 26.7	2 43.1	13 10.5	19 4.9
23 F	4 2 45	1 57 16	1♓12 55	7♓30 53	29D 27.5	11 30.5	8 32.7	18 3.6	11 34.8	28 34.0	2 43.9	13 10.3	19 3.4
24 Sa	4 6 42	2 54 56	13 44 7	19 53 7	29 27.7	11 47.2	9 45.6	18 35.6	11 42.8	28 41.3	2 44.6	13 10.0	19 1.9
25 Su	4 10 38	3 52 35	25 58 24	2♈ 0 32	29 28.0	12 8.2	10 58.5	19 7.4	11 51.0	28 48.6	2 45.2	13 9.7	19 0.4
26 M	4 14 35	4 50 14	8♈ 0 1	13 57 22	29 28.5	12 33.6	12 11.3	19 39.0	11 59.2	28 55.9	2 45.8	13 9.4	18 58.8
27 Tu	4 18 31	5 47 51	19 53 5	25 47 37	29 29.1	13 3.2	13 24.2	20 10.4	12 7.6	29 3.3	2 46.4	13 9.1	18 57.3
28 W	4 22 28	6 45 27	1♉41 25	7♉34 54	29 29.8	13 37.0	14 37.1	20 41.6	12 16.1	29 10.7	2 46.9	13 8.7	18 55.8
29 Th	4 26 24	7 43 2	13 28 27	19 22 25	29 30.3	14 14.7	15 50.0	21 12.6	12 24.7	29 18.1	2 47.3	13 8.3	18 54.2
30 F	4 30 21	8 40 37	25 17 7	1♊12 54	29R 30.4	14 56.3	17 3.0	21 43.3	12 33.4	29 25.6	2 47.7	13 7.8	18 52.6
31 Sa	4 34 18	9 38 10	7♊10 1	13 8 44	29 30.1	15 41.7	18 15.9	22 13.8	12 42.2	29 33.1	2 48.1	13 7.3	18 51.1

LONGITUDE JUNE 2003

Day	Sid.Time	☉	0 hr ☽	Noon☽	True☊	☿	♀	♂	♃	♄	♅	♆	♇
1 Su	4 38 14	10♊35 42	19♊ 9 19	25♊12 0	29♉29.3	16♉30.8	19♉28.8	22♒44.0	12♌51.2	29♊40.6	2♓48.4	13♒ 6.8	18♐49.5
2 M	4 42 11	11 33 13	1♋17 1	7♋24 36	29R 27.9	17 23.5	20 41.8	23 14.0	13 0.2	29 48.2	2 48.7	13R 6.3	18R 47.9
3 Tu	4 46 7	12 30 43	13 34 57	19 48 20	29 26.1	18 19.7	21 54.8	23 43.8	13 9.4	29 55.7	2 48.9	13 5.7	18 46.3
4 W	4 50 4	13 28 12	26 4 57	2♌25 2	29 24.3	19 19.3	23 7.7	24 13.3	13 18.7	0♋ 3.3	2 49.0	13 5.1	18 44.7
5 Th	4 54 0	14 25 40	8♌48 50	15 16 34	29 22.5	20 22.2	24 20.7	24 42.5	13 28.0	0 10.9	2 49.1	13 4.5	18 43.1
6 F	4 57 57	15 23 6	21 48 28	28 24 46	29 21.2	21 28.4	25 33.7	25 11.5	13 37.5	0 18.6	2 49.2	13 3.8	18 41.5
7 Sa	5 1 53	16 20 31	5♍ 5 38	11♍51 16	29D 20.5	22 37.7	26 46.7	25 40.1	13 47.1	0 26.2	2R 49.2	13 3.2	18 39.9
8 Su	5 5 50	17 17 55	18 41 46	25 37 13	29 20.7	23 50.3	27 59.7	26 8.5	13 56.7	0 33.9	2 49.2	13 2.4	18 38.3
9 M	5 9 47	18 15 18	2♎37 37	9♎42 53	29 21.4	25 5.9	29 12.7	26 36.6	14 6.5	0 41.6	2 49.1	13 1.7	18 36.7
10 Tu	5 13 43	19 12 40	16 52 51	24 7 13	29 22.7	26 24.5	0♊25.7	27 4.4	14 16.3	0 49.2	2 49.0	13 0.9	18 35.1
11 W	5 17 40	20 10 0	1♏25 33	8♏47 21	29 23.9	27 46.2	1 38.7	27 31.9	14 26.2	0 57.0	2 48.8	13 0.1	18 33.5
12 Th	5 21 36	21 7 20	16 11 56	23 38 32	29R 24.6	29 10.8	2 51.8	27 59.1	14 36.3	1 4.7	2 48.6	12 59.3	18 31.9
13 F	5 25 33	22 4 39	1♐ 6 17	8♐34 14	29 24.5	0♊38.4	4 4.8	28 26.0	14 46.4	1 12.4	2 48.3	12 58.5	18 30.3
14 Sa	5 29 29	23 1 57	16 1 24	23 26 47	29 23.3	2 8.9	5 17.9	28 52.5	14 56.6	1 20.2	2 48.0	12 57.6	18 28.8
15 Su	5 33 26	23 59 15	0♑49 23	8♑ 8 17	29 20.9	3 42.4	6 31.0	29 18.7	15 6.9	1 27.9	2 47.6	12 56.7	18 27.2
16 M	5 37 22	24 56 32	15 22 40	22 31 50	29 17.6	5 18.7	7 44.1	29 44.6	15 17.3	1 35.7	2 47.2	12 55.7	18 25.6
17 Tu	5 41 19	25 53 48	29 35 12	6♒32 22	29 13.9	6 57.9	8 57.2	0♓10.1	15 27.7	1 43.5	2 46.7	12 54.8	18 24.0
18 W	5 45 16	26 51 4	13♒23 4	20 7 12	29 10.2	8 39.9	10 10.3	0 35.3	15 38.3	1 51.2	2 46.2	12 53.8	18 22.4
19 Th	5 49 12	27 48 20	26 44 49	3♓16 5	29 7.2	10 24.8	11 23.5	1 0.0	15 48.9	1 59.0	2 45.7	12 52.8	18 20.8
20 F	5 53 9	28 45 35	9♓41 18	16 0 50	29 5.2	12 12.4	12 36.6	1 24.4	15 59.6	2 6.8	2 45.1	12 51.8	18 19.3
21 Sa	5 57 5	29 42 51	22 15 10	28 24 48	29D 4.5	14 2.7	13 49.8	1 48.4	16 10.4	2 14.6	2 44.4	12 50.7	18 17.7
22 Su	6 1 2	0♋40 6	4♈30 19	10♈32 20	29 4.9	15 55.6	15 3.0	2 11.9	16 21.2	2 22.4	2 43.7	12 49.6	18 16.1
23 M	6 4 58	1 37 20	16 31 26	22 28 15	29 6.2	17 51.1	16 16.2	2 35.1	16 32.2	2 30.2	2 43.0	12 48.5	18 14.6
24 Tu	6 8 55	2 34 35	28 23 24	4♉17 29	29 7.9	19 49.0	17 29.5	2 57.8	16 43.2	2 38.0	2 42.2	12 47.4	18 13.1
25 W	6 12 51	3 31 50	10♉11 5	16 4 44	29 9.4	21 49.1	18 42.7	3 20.0	16 54.3	2 45.8	2 41.4	12 46.2	18 11.5
26 Th	6 16 48	4 29 4	21 59 0	27 54 19	29R 10.1	23 51.4	19 56.0	3 41.8	17 5.4	2 53.6	2 40.5	12 45.1	18 10.0
27 F	6 20 45	5 26 19	3♊51 9	9♊49 54	29 9.5	25 55.7	21 9.3	4 3.1	17 16.6	3 1.5	2 39.6	12 43.9	18 8.5
28 Sa	6 24 41	6 23 33	15 50 54	21 54 28	29 7.3	28 1.6	22 22.6	4 23.9	17 27.9	3 9.3	2 38.6	12 42.7	18 7.0
29 Su	6 28 38	7 20 47	28 0 50	4♋10 14	29 3.3	0♋ 9.1	23 35.9	4 44.3	17 39.3	3 17.1	2 37.6	12 41.4	18 5.5
30 M	6 32 34	8 18 2	10♋22 48	16 38 39	28 57.8	2 17.7	24 49.2	5 4.1	17 50.7	3 24.9	2 36.5	12 40.2	18 4.0

*Giving the positions of planets daily at noon, in LONGITUDE Greenwich Mean Time

Noon Ephemeris: GMT* July 2003

Day	Sid.Time	☉	0 hr ☽	Noon ☽	True ☊	☿	♀	♂	♃	♄	♅	♆	♇
1 Tu	6 36 31	9♋15 15	22♋57 51	29♋20 27	28♉51.2	4♋27.3	26♊ 2.6	5♓23.4	18♌ 2.2	3♋32.6	2♓35.4	12♒38.9	18♐ 2.6
2 W	6 40 27	10 12 29	5♌46 28	12♌15 51	28R 44.3	6 37.5	27 15.9	5 42.1	18 13.7	3 40.4	2R 34.3	12R 37.6	18R 1.1
3 Th	6 44 24	11 9 42	18 48 36	25 24 40	28 37.7	8 48.1	28 29.3	6 0.4	18 25.4	3 48.2	2 33.1	12 36.3	17 59.7
4 F	6 48 21	12 6 55	2♍ 4 1	8♍46 35	28 32.3	10 58.7	29 42.7	6 18.1	18 37.0	3 56.0	2 31.9	12 35.0	17 58.2
5 Sa	6 52 17	13 4 8	15 32 20	22 21 15	28 28.6	13 9.1	0♋56.1	6 35.2	18 48.8	4 3.7	2 30.6	12 33.6	17 56.8
6 Su	6 56 14	14 1 20	29 13 17	6♎ 8 24	28 26.8	15 19.1	2 9.5	6 51.7	19 0.5	4 11.4	2 29.3	12 32.2	17 55.4
7 M	7 0 10	14 58 32	13♎ 6 33	20 7 41	28D 26.6	17 28.4	3 22.9	7 7.7	19 12.4	4 19.2	2 28.0	12 30.8	17 54.0
8 Tu	7 4 7	15 55 44	27 11 41	4♏18 25	28 27.5	19 36.7	4 36.4	7 23.0	19 24.3	4 26.9	2 26.6	12 29.4	17 52.7
9 W	7 8 3	16 52 56	11♏27 42	18 39 17	28 28.5	21 44.0	5 49.9	7 37.8	19 36.2	4 34.6	2 25.2	12 28.0	17 51.3
10 Th	7 12 0	17 50 8	25 52 47	3♐ 7 49	28R 28.7	23 50.0	7 3.3	7 52.0	19 48.2	4 42.3	2 23.7	12 26.6	17 50.0
11 F	7 15 56	18 47 20	10♐23 51	17 40 17	28 27.3	25 54.6	8 16.8	8 5.5	20 0.3	4 49.9	2 22.2	12 25.1	17 48.7
12 Sa	7 19 53	19 44 31	24 56 28	2♑11 40	28 23.7	27 57.6	9 30.4	8 18.4	20 12.4	4 57.6	2 20.7	12 23.7	17 47.4
13 Su	7 23 50	20 41 43	9♑25 7	16 36 3	28 17.9	29 59.1	10 43.9	8 30.7	20 24.5	5 5.2	2 19.1	12 22.2	17 46.1
14 M	7 27 46	21 38 55	23 43 43	0♒47 26	28 10.3	1♌58.9	11 57.5	8 42.2	20 36.7	5 12.8	2 17.5	12 20.7	17 44.8
15 Tu	7 31 43	22 36 8	7♒46 35	14 40 40	28 1.6	3 57.0	13 11.0	8 53.1	20 48.9	5 20.4	2 15.9	12 19.2	17 43.6
16 W	7 35 39	23 33 20	21 29 15	28 12 7	27 52.8	5 53.3	14 24.6	9 3.4	21 1.2	5 28.0	2 14.2	12 17.7	17 42.4
17 Th	7 39 36	24 30 34	4♓49 6	11♓20 14	27 45.0	7 47.8	15 38.2	9 12.9	21 13.5	5 35.5	2 12.5	12 16.2	17 41.2
18 F	7 43 32	25 27 47	17 45 38	24 5 34	27 38.8	9 40.5	16 51.9	9 21.7	21 25.9	5 43.0	2 10.8	12 14.6	17 40.0
19 Sa	7 47 29	26 25 2	0♈20 21	6♈30 28	27 34.6	11 31.4	18 5.5	9 29.7	21 38.3	5 50.5	2 9.0	12 13.1	17 38.8
20 Su	7 51 25	27 22 17	12 36 24	18 38 44	27 32.5	13 20.5	19 19.2	9 37.1	21 50.8	5 58.0	2 7.2	12 11.5	17 37.7
21 M	7 55 22	28 19 33	24 38 4	0♉35 4	27D 32.1	15 7.8	20 32.9	9 43.6	22 3.2	6 5.4	2 5.4	12 10.0	17 36.6
22 Tu	7 59 19	29 16 49	6♉30 24	12 24 43	27 32.7	16 53.2	21 46.6	9 49.4	22 15.8	6 12.8	2 3.5	12 8.4	17 35.5
23 W	8 3 15	0♌14 7	18 18 42	24 13 0	27R 33.2	18 36.9	23 0.4	9 54.5	22 28.3	6 20.2	2 1.6	12 6.8	17 34.4
24 Th	8 7 12	1 11 25	0♊ 8 16	6♊ 5 5	27 32.9	20 18.7	24 14.1	9 58.7	22 40.9	6 27.6	1 59.7	12 5.2	17 33.4
25 F	8 11 8	2 8 45	12 4 2	18 5 37	27 30.9	21 58.8	25 27.9	10 2.2	22 53.5	6 34.9	1 57.7	12 3.6	17 32.3
26 Sa	8 15 5	3 6 5	24 10 19	0♋18 31	27 26.5	23 37.0	26 41.7	10 4.8	23 6.2	6 42.2	1 55.7	12 2.0	17 31.3
27 Su	8 19 1	4 3 26	6♋30 32	12 46 37	27 19.6	25 13.5	27 55.6	10 6.7	23 18.9	6 49.5	1 53.7	12 0.4	17 30.4
28 M	8 22 58	5 0 47	19 6 57	25 31 35	27 10.4	26 48.2	29 9.4	10 7.8	23 31.6	6 56.7	1 51.7	11 58.8	17 29.4
29 Tu	8 26 54	5 58 10	2♌ 0 31	8♌33 40	26 59.7	28 21.0	0♌23.3	10R 8.0	23 44.4	7 3.9	1 49.6	11 57.2	17 28.5
30 W	8 30 51	6 55 33	15 10 53	21 51 54	26 48.3	29 52.1	1 37.2	10 7.5	23 57.2	7 11.1	1 47.5	11 55.6	17 27.6
31 Th	8 34 48	7 52 57	28 36 28	5♍24 14	26 37.4	1♍21.3	2 51.1	10 6.1	24 10.0	7 18.2	1 45.4	11 53.9	17 26.7

Longitude August 2003

Day	Sid.Time	☉	0 hr ☽	Noon ☽	True ☊	☿	♀	♂	♃	♄	♅	♆	♇
1 F	8 38 44	8♌50 21	12♍14 52	19♍ 8 1	26♉28.2	2♍48.8	4♌ 5.0	10♓ 4.0	24♌22.8	7♋25.2	1♓43.3	11♒52.3	17♐25.9
2 Sa	8 42 41	9 47 47	26 3 20	3♎ 0 30	26R 21.3	4 14.3	5 18.9	10R 1.0	24 35.7	7 32.3	1R 41.1	11R 50.7	17R 25.1
3 Su	8 46 37	10 45 12	9♎59 14	16 59 17	26 17.1	5 38.0	6 32.9	9 57.3	24 48.5	7 39.3	1 39.0	11 49.0	17 24.3
4 M	8 50 34	11 42 39	24 0 26	1♏ 2 31	26 15.2	6 59.8	7 46.9	9 52.8	25 1.4	7 46.2	1 36.8	11 47.4	17 23.5
5 Tu	8 54 30	12 40 6	8♏ 5 24	15 8 58	26D 14.9	8 19.6	9 0.8	9 47.6	25 14.4	7 53.1	1 34.6	11 45.8	17 22.8
6 W	8 58 27	13 37 34	22 13 5	29 17 38	26R 15.0	9 37.4	10 14.8	9 41.6	25 27.3	8 0.0	1 32.3	11 44.1	17 22.1
7 Th	9 2 23	14 35 2	6♐22 28	13♐27 25	26 14.2	10 53.2	11 28.9	9 34.9	25 40.2	8 6.8	1 30.1	11 42.5	17 21.4
8 F	9 6 20	15 32 31	20 32 14	27 36 39	26 11.4	12 6.8	12 42.9	9 27.5	25 53.2	8 13.6	1 27.8	11 40.9	17 20.7
9 Sa	9 10 17	16 30 2	4♑40 20	11♑42 51	26 5.9	13 18.3	13 57.0	9 19.3	26 6.2	8 20.3	1 25.6	11 39.3	17 20.1
10 Su	9 14 13	17 27 33	18 43 47	25 42 39	25 57.7	14 27.6	15 11.0	9 10.5	26 19.2	8 27.0	1 23.3	11 37.6	17 19.5
11 M	9 18 10	18 25 5	2♒38 57	9♒32 11	25 47.1	15 34.5	16 25.1	9 1.0	26 32.2	8 33.6	1 21.0	11 36.0	17 19.0
12 Tu	9 22 6	19 22 38	16 21 54	23 7 38	25 35.1	16 39.0	17 39.2	8 50.9	26 45.3	8 40.2	1 18.6	11 34.4	17 18.4
13 W	9 26 3	20 20 12	29 49 3	6♓25 52	25 22.9	17 41.0	18 53.3	8 40.1	26 58.3	8 46.7	1 16.3	11 32.8	17 17.9
14 Th	9 29 59	21 17 47	12♓57 53	19 25 2	25 11.6	18 40.4	20 7.5	8 28.8	27 11.3	8 53.2	1 14.0	11 31.2	17 17.4
15 F	9 33 56	22 15 24	25 47 19	2♈ 4 53	25 2.2	19 37.0	21 21.6	8 16.9	27 24.4	8 59.6	1 11.6	11 29.6	17 17.0
16 Sa	9 37 52	23 13 2	8♈17 55	14 26 46	24 55.3	20 30.6	22 35.8	8 4.4	27 37.5	9 6.0	1 9.3	11 28.0	17 16.6
17 Su	9 41 49	24 10 42	20 31 49	26 33 33	24 51.0	21 21.2	23 50.0	7 51.4	27 50.5	9 12.3	1 6.9	11 26.4	17 16.2
18 M	9 45 46	25 8 23	2♉32 30	8♉29 14	24 48.9	22 8.6	25 4.2	7 37.9	28 3.6	9 18.6	1 4.5	11 24.8	17 15.8
19 Tu	9 49 42	26 6 5	14 24 25	20 18 40	24 48.4	22 52.6	26 18.4	7 24.0	28 16.7	9 24.8	1 2.1	11 23.2	17 15.5
20 W	9 53 39	27 3 50	26 12 42	2♊ 7 11	24 48.3	23 33.0	27 32.7	7 9.6	28 29.8	9 30.9	0 59.8	11 21.7	17 15.2
21 Th	9 57 35	28 1 36	8♊ 2 50	14 0 18	24 47.7	24 9.6	28 46.9	6 54.9	28 42.9	9 37.0	0 57.4	11 20.1	17 15.0
22 F	10 1 32	28 59 24	20 0 16	26 3 20	24 45.5	24 42.2	0♍ 1.2	6 39.9	28 55.9	9 43.0	0 55.0	11 18.6	17 14.7
23 Sa	10 5 28	29 57 13	2♋10 6	8♋21 5	24 41.0	25 10.5	1 15.5	6 24.5	29 9.0	9 49.0	0 52.6	11 17.1	17 14.5
24 Su	10 9 25	0♍55 4	14 36 43	20 57 22	24 33.8	25 34.3	2 29.8	6 9.0	29 22.1	9 54.9	0 50.2	11 15.5	17 14.4
25 M	10 13 21	1 52 57	27 23 18	3♌54 40	24 24.3	25 53.4	3 44.2	5 53.2	29 35.2	10 0.7	0 47.8	11 14.0	17 14.3
26 Tu	10 17 18	2 50 51	10♌31 28	17 13 39	24 12.9	26 7.4	4 58.5	5 37.3	29 48.3	10 6.5	0 45.4	11 12.5	17 14.2
27 W	10 21 15	3 48 47	24 0 58	0♍53 5	24 0.8	26 16.2	6 12.9	5 21.3	0♍ 1.4	10 12.1	0 43.0	11 11.1	17 14.1
28 Th	10 25 11	4 46 44	7♍49 33	14 49 50	23 49.2	26R 19.4	7 27.2	5 5.2	0 14.5	10 17.8	0 40.6	11 9.6	17 14.0
29 F	10 29 8	5 44 43	21 53 19	28 59 21	23 39.3	26 16.9	8 41.6	4 49.2	0 27.5	10 23.3	0 38.2	11 8.1	17D 14.0
30 Sa	10 33 4	6 42 43	6♎ 7 17	13♎16 27	23 31.9	26 8.5	9 56.0	4 33.2	0 40.6	10 28.8	0 35.8	11 6.7	17 14.1
31 Su	10 37 1	7 40 45	20 26 16	27 36 9	23 27.3	25 53.9	11 10.4	4 17.4	0 53.6	10 34.2	0 33.5	11 5.3	17 14.1

*Giving the positions of planets daily at noon, in LONGITUDE Greenwich Mean Time

NOON EPHEMERIS: GMT* — SEPTEMBER 2003

Day	Sid.Time	☉	0 hr ☽	Noon ☽	True ☊	☿	♀	♂	♃	♄	♅	♆	♇
1 M	10 40 57	8♍38 48	4♏45 39	11♏54 20	23♉25.2	25♍33.2	12♍24.9	4♓ 1.7	1♍ 6.7	10♋39.6	0♓31.1	11♒ 3.9	17♐14.2
2 Tu	10 44 54	9 36 53	19 1 55	26 8 7	23D 24.9	25R 6.4	13 39.3	3R 46.2	1 19.7	10 44.8	0R 28.7	11R 2.5	17 14.4
3 W	10 48 50	10 34 59	3♐12 47	10♐15 47	23R 25.0	24 33.4	14 53.7	3 30.9	1 32.7	10 50.0	0 26.4	11 1.1	17 14.5
4 Th	10 52 47	11 33 6	17 17 1	24 16 25	23 24.5	23 54.6	16 8.2	3 16.0	1 45.7	10 55.2	0 24.1	10 59.7	17 14.7
5 F	10 56 44	12 31 15	1♑13 55	8♑ 9 27	23 22.1	23 10.3	17 22.6	3 1.4	1 58.7	11 0.2	0 21.7	10 58.4	17 14.9
6 Sa	11 0 40	13 29 25	15 2 56	21 54 14	23 17.2	22 21.1	18 37.1	2 47.2	2 11.6	11 5.2	0 19.4	10 57.1	17 15.2
7 Su	11 4 37	14 27 36	28 43 12	5♒29 42	23 9.8	21 27.6	19 51.6	2 33.4	2 24.6	11 10.1	0 17.1	10 55.8	17 15.5
8 M	11 8 33	15 25 50	12♒13 31	18 54 27	23 0.1	20 30.7	21 6.0	2 20.1	2 37.5	11 14.9	0 14.8	10 54.5	17 15.8
9 Tu	11 12 30	16 24 4	25 32 18	2♓ 6 50	22 49.0	19 31.6	22 20.5	2 7.2	2 50.4	11 19.6	0 12.6	10 53.3	17 16.2
10 W	11 16 26	17 22 21	8♓37 54	15 5 20	22 37.6	18 31.3	23 35.0	1 54.9	3 3.3	11 24.2	0 10.3	10 52.0	17 16.6
11 Th	11 20 23	18 20 39	21 29 2	27 48 57	22 27.1	17 31.3	24 49.5	1 43.1	3 16.1	11 28.8	0 8.1	10 50.8	17 17.0
12 F	11 24 19	19 18 59	4♈ 5 4	10♈17 30	22 18.3	16 32.8	26 4.0	1 31.9	3 29.0	11 33.3	0 5.8	10 49.6	17 17.4
13 Sa	11 28 16	20 17 21	16 26 22	22 31 54	22 11.9	15 37.4	27 18.6	1 21.3	3 41.8	11 37.7	0 3.6	10 48.4	17 17.9
14 Su	11 32 12	21 15 44	28 34 23	4♉34 9	22 7.9	14 46.3	28 33.1	1 11.3	3 54.5	11 42.0	0 1.4	10 47.3	17 18.4
15 M	11 36 9	22 14 10	10♉31 39	16 27 20	22D 6.2	14 0.8	29 47.6	1 2.0	4 7.3	11 46.2	29♒59.3	10 46.1	17 19.0
16 Tu	11 40 6	23 12 39	22 21 43	28 15 24	22 6.2	13 22.2	1♎ 2.2	0 53.3	4 20.0	11 50.3	29 57.1	10 45.0	17 19.6
17 W	11 44 2	24 11 9	4♊ 8 58	10♊ 3 4	22 7.0	12 51.3	2 16.7	0 45.3	4 32.7	11 54.4	29 55.0	10 44.0	17 20.2
18 Th	11 47 59	25 9 41	15 58 21	21 55 30	22R 7.7	12 29.0	3 31.3	0 38.1	4 45.4	11 58.4	29 52.9	10 42.9	17 20.8
19 F	11 51 55	26 8 16	27 55 10	3♋58 3	22 7.4	12 15.9	4 45.9	0 31.6	4 58.0	12 2.2	29 50.8	10 41.9	17 21.5
20 Sa	11 55 52	27 6 53	10♋ 4 46	16 15 57	22 5.4	12D 12.3	6 0.5	0 25.8	5 10.6	12 6.0	29 48.8	10 40.9	17 22.2
21 Su	11 59 48	28 5 32	22 32 9	28 53 51	22 1.4	12 18.5	7 15.1	0 20.8	5 23.2	12 9.7	29 46.7	10 39.9	17 23.0
22 M	12 3 45	29 4 13	5♌21 28	11♌55 18	21 55.3	12 34.3	8 29.7	0 16.5	5 35.7	12 13.3	29 44.7	10 38.9	17 23.7
23 Tu	12 7 41	0♎ 2 56	18 35 32	25 22 10	21 47.6	12 59.8	9 44.3	0 13.0	5 48.2	12 16.8	29 42.8	10 38.0	17 24.5
24 W	12 11 38	1 1 42	2♍15 8	9♍14 8	21 39.2	13 34.5	10 58.9	0 10.4	6 0.6	12 20.2	29 40.8	10 37.1	17 25.4
25 Th	12 15 35	2 0 29	16 18 45	23 28 24	21 31.0	14 18.0	12 13.5	0 8.5	6 13.0	12 23.5	29 38.9	10 36.2	17 26.3
26 F	12 19 31	2 59 19	0♎42 22	7♎59 51	21 24.1	15 9.8	13 28.1	0 7.4	6 25.4	12 26.7	29 37.0	10 35.4	17 27.2
27 Sa	12 23 28	3 58 10	15 19 56	22 41 41	21 19.0	16 9.4	14 42.7	0D 7.1	6 37.7	12 29.8	29 35.2	10 34.5	17 28.1
28 Su	12 27 24	4 57 4	0♏ 4 12	7♏26 33	21 16.2	17 16.0	15 57.4	0 7.7	6 50.0	12 32.8	29 33.3	10 33.8	17 29.0
29 M	12 31 21	5 55 59	14 47 55	22 7 33	21D 15.4	18 29.0	17 12.0	0 9.0	7 2.2	12 35.7	29 31.6	10 33.0	17 30.0
30 Tu	12 35 17	6 54 56	29 24 49	6♐39 12	21 16.1	19 47.7	18 26.7	0 11.2	7 14.4	12 38.6	29 29.8	10 32.3	17 31.1

LONGITUDE — OCTOBER 2003

Day	Sid.Time	☉	0 hr ☽	Noon ☽	True ☊	☿	♀	♂	♃	♄	♅	♆	♇
1 W	12 39 14	7♎53 55	13♐50 19	20♐57 50	21♉17.3	21♍11.4	19♎41.3	0♓14.2	7♍26.5	12♋41.3	29♒28.1	10♒31.6	17♐32.1
2 Th	12 43 10	8 52 56	28 1 36	5♑ 1 28	21R 18.2	22 39.4	20 55.9	0 18.0	7 38.6	12 43.9	29R 26.4	10R 30.9	17 33.2
3 F	12 47 7	9 51 58	11♑57 25	18 49 29	21 17.9	24 11.2	22 10.6	0 22.6	7 50.6	12 46.4	29 24.8	10 30.2	17 34.3
4 Sa	12 51 4	10 51 2	25 37 40	2♒22 6	21 15.9	25 46.1	23 25.2	0 27.9	8 2.6	12 48.8	29 23.1	10 29.6	17 35.5
5 Su	12 55 0	11 50 8	9♒ 2 50	15 39 58	21 12.1	27 23.6	24 39.9	0 34.0	8 14.5	12 51.1	29 21.6	10 29.0	17 36.6
6 M	12 58 57	12 49 15	22 13 37	28 43 52	21 6.7	29 3.2	25 54.5	0 40.9	8 26.3	12 53.3	29 20.0	10 28.5	17 37.8
7 Tu	13 2 53	13 48 25	5♓10 46	11♓34 26	21 0.4	0♎44.6	27 9.1	0 48.6	8 38.1	12 55.4	29 18.5	10 28.0	17 39.1
8 W	13 6 50	14 47 36	17 54 54	24 12 17	20 53.9	2 27.2	28 23.8	0 57.0	8 49.9	12 57.3	29 17.1	10 27.5	17 40.3
9 Th	13 10 46	15 46 49	0♈26 38	6♈38 3	20 47.8	4 10.8	29 38.4	1 6.1	9 1.6	12 59.2	29 15.6	10 27.0	17 41.6
10 F	13 14 43	16 46 4	12 46 38	18 52 32	20 42.9	5 55.1	0♏53.0	1 15.9	9 13.2	13 1.0	29 14.2	10 26.6	17 42.9
11 Sa	13 18 39	17 45 21	24 55 55	0♉56 57	20 39.4	7 39.8	2 7.6	1 26.5	9 24.7	13 2.6	29 12.9	10 26.2	17 44.3
12 Su	13 22 36	18 44 41	6♉55 52	12 52 57	20 37.7	9 24.8	3 22.3	1 37.7	9 36.2	13 4.2	29 11.6	10 25.8	17 45.6
13 M	13 26 33	19 44 2	18 48 30	24 42 52	20D 37.4	11 9.8	4 36.9	1 49.6	9 47.6	13 5.6	29 10.3	10 25.5	17 47.0
14 Tu	13 30 29	20 43 26	0♊36 27	6♊29 41	20 38.4	12 54.7	5 51.6	2 2.2	9 59.0	13 7.0	29 9.1	10 25.2	17 48.4
15 W	13 34 26	21 42 52	12 23 2	18 17 0	20 40.1	14 39.5	7 6.2	2 15.4	10 10.2	13 8.2	29 7.9	10 24.9	17 49.9
16 Th	13 38 22	22 42 20	24 12 9	0♋ 9 2	20 41.9	16 23.9	8 20.8	2 29.3	10 21.5	13 9.3	29 6.8	10 24.7	17 51.4
17 F	13 42 19	23 41 51	6♋ 8 16	12 10 25	20 43.3	18 8.0	9 35.5	2 43.8	10 32.6	13 10.3	29 5.7	10 24.5	17 52.9
18 Sa	13 46 15	24 41 23	18 16 8	24 26 0	20R 43.9	19 51.7	10 50.1	2 58.9	10 43.7	13 11.2	29 4.7	10 24.3	17 54.4
19 Su	13 50 12	25 40 59	0♌40 37	7♌ 0 32	20 43.3	21 34.9	12 4.8	3 14.6	10 54.6	13 12.0	29 3.7	10 24.2	17 56.0
20 M	13 54 8	26 40 36	13 26 16	19 58 15	20 41.7	23 17.5	13 19.4	3 31.0	11 5.5	13 12.7	29 2.7	10 24.1	17 57.5
21 Tu	13 58 5	27 40 15	26 36 48	3♍22 12	20 39.1	24 59.7	14 34.1	3 47.9	11 16.4	13 13.3	29 1.8	10 24.0	17 59.1
22 W	14 2 2	28 39 57	10♍14 31	17 13 42	20 36.0	26 41.2	15 48.7	4 5.4	11 27.1	13 13.7	29 0.9	10 24.0	18 0.8
23 Th	14 5 58	29 39 41	24 19 34	1♎31 41	20 33.0	28 22.3	17 3.4	4 23.5	11 37.8	13 14.1	29 0.1	10D 24.0	18 2.4
24 F	14 9 55	0♏39 27	8♎49 31	16 12 20	20 30.3	0♏ 2.7	18 18.0	4 42.1	11 48.4	13 14.3	28 59.4	10 24.0	18 4.1
25 Sa	14 13 51	1 39 15	23 39 13	1♏ 9 12	20 28.6	1 42.6	19 32.7	5 1.2	11 58.9	13R 14.4	28 58.6	10 24.1	18 5.8
26 Su	14 17 48	2 39 6	8♏41 9	16 13 57	20D 27.8	3 21.9	20 47.3	5 21.0	12 9.3	13 14.4	28 58.0	10 24.2	18 7.5
27 M	14 21 44	3 38 58	23 46 27	1♐17 34	20 28.0	5 0.7	22 2.0	5 41.2	12 19.6	13 14.3	28 57.3	10 24.3	18 9.2
28 Tu	14 25 41	4 38 52	8♐46 16	16 11 39	20 28.9	6 39.0	23 16.6	6 2.0	12 29.8	13 14.0	28 56.8	10 24.5	18 11.0
29 W	14 29 37	5 38 48	23 32 57	0♑49 32	20 30.0	8 16.7	24 31.3	6 23.2	12 39.9	13 13.7	28 56.2	10 24.7	18 12.8
30 Th	14 33 34	6 38 45	8♑ 0 57	15 6 51	20 31.1	9 53.9	25 45.9	6 45.0	12 50.0	13 13.3	28 55.8	10 24.9	18 14.6
31 F	14 37 31	7 38 44	22 7 5	29 1 34	20 31.8	11 30.6	27 0.5	7 7.2	12 59.9	13 12.7	28 55.3	10 25.2	18 16.4

*Giving the positions of planets daily at noon, in LONGITUDE Greenwich Mean Time

Noon Ephemeris: GMT*

November 2003

Day	Sid.Time	☉	0 hr ☽	Noon ☽	True ☊	☿	♀	♂	♃	♄	♅	♆	♇
1 Sa	14 41 27	8♏38 44	5♒50 23	12♒33 39	20♉31.9	13♏ 6.8	28♏15.2	7♓29.9	13♍ 9.7	13♋12.0	28♒55.0	10♒25.5	18♐18.3
2 Su	14 45 24	9 38 47	19 11 35	25 44 27	20R 31.4	14 42.6	29 29.8	7 53.0	13 19.5	13R 11.2	28R 54.6	10 25.9	18 20.1
3 M	14 49 20	10 38 50	2♓12 33	8♓36 13	20 30.5	16 17.9	0♐44.4	8 16.6	13 29.1	13 10.3	28 54.3	10 26.2	18 22.0
4 Tu	14 53 17	11 38 55	14 55 47	21 11 35	20 29.3	17 52.7	1 59.0	8 40.6	13 38.6	13 9.3	28 54.1	10 26.6	18 23.9
5 W	14 57 13	12 39 2	27 23 58	3♈33 14	20 28.1	19 27.2	3 13.6	9 5.0	13 48.1	13 8.2	28 53.9	10 27.1	18 25.9
6 Th	15 1 10	13 39 10	9♈39 43	15 43 43	20 27.1	21 1.2	4 28.2	9 29.8	13 57.4	13 7.0	28 53.8	10 27.6	18 27.8
7 F	15 5 6	14 39 20	21 45 31	27 45 23	20 26.4	22 34.9	5 42.8	9 55.0	14 6.6	13 5.7	28 53.7	10 28.1	18 29.8
8 Sa	15 9 3	15 39 32	3♉43 35	9♉40 24	20 26.0	24 8.1	6 57.4	10 20.6	14 15.7	13 4.2	28D 53.7	10 28.6	18 31.7
9 Su	15 13 0	16 39 46	15 36 3	21 30 49	20D 25.9	25 41.1	8 12.0	10 46.5	14 24.7	13 2.7	28 53.7	10 29.2	18 33.7
10 M	15 16 56	17 40 1	27 24 57	3♊18 44	20 26.0	27 13.7	9 26.5	11 12.8	14 33.5	13 1.0	28 53.8	10 29.8	18 35.7
11 Tu	15 20 53	18 40 19	9♊12 27	15 6 24	20 26.2	28 45.9	10 41.1	11 39.5	14 42.3	12 59.2	28 53.9	10 30.4	18 37.8
12 W	15 24 49	19 40 38	21 0 55	26 56 21	20 26.3	0♐17.8	11 55.7	12 6.5	14 50.9	12 57.4	28 54.1	10 31.1	18 39.8
13 Th	15 28 46	20 40 59	2♋53 4	8♋51 28	20R 26.4	1 49.4	13 10.3	12 33.8	14 59.5	12 55.4	28 54.3	10 31.8	18 41.9
14 F	15 32 42	21 41 21	14 51 59	20 55 3	20 26.3	3 20.7	14 24.8	13 1.5	15 7.9	12 53.3	28 54.6	10 32.6	18 43.9
15 Sa	15 36 39	22 41 46	27 1 10	3♌10 47	20 26.1	4 51.7	15 39.4	13 29.4	15 16.1	12 51.2	28 55.0	10 33.3	18 46.0
16 Su	15 40 35	23 42 13	9♌24 25	15 42 34	20 26.0	6 22.4	16 53.9	13 57.7	15 24.3	12 48.9	28 55.3	10 34.1	18 48.1
17 M	15 44 32	24 42 41	22 5 42	28 34 16	20D 25.9	7 52.7	18 8.5	14 26.3	15 32.3	12 46.5	28 55.8	10 35.0	18 50.2
18 Tu	15 48 29	25 43 11	5♍ 8 43	11♍49 22	20 26.1	9 22.8	19 23.0	14 55.2	15 40.2	12 44.0	28 56.3	10 35.9	18 52.4
19 W	15 52 25	26 43 43	18 36 32	25 30 23	20 26.6	10 52.5	20 37.6	15 24.3	15 48.0	12 41.4	28 56.8	10 36.8	18 54.5
20 Th	15 56 22	27 44 17	2♎30 58	9♎38 11	20 27.2	12 21.8	21 52.1	15 53.8	15 55.6	12 38.7	28 57.4	10 37.7	18 56.7
21 F	16 0 18	28 44 52	16 51 49	24 11 25	20 27.9	13 50.8	23 6.6	16 23.5	16 3.1	12 36.0	28 58.0	10 38.7	18 58.8
22 Sa	16 4 15	29 45 30	1♏36 24	9♏ 5 58	20 28.4	15 19.3	24 21.1	16 53.5	16 10.5	12 33.1	28 58.7	10 39.7	19 1.0
23 Su	16 8 11	0♐46 9	16 39 10	24 14 56	20R 28.6	16 47.4	25 35.7	17 23.7	16 17.7	12 30.1	28 59.4	10 40.7	19 3.2
24 M	16 12 8	1 46 49	1♐52 3	9♐29 18	20 28.1	18 15.0	26 50.2	17 54.3	16 24.8	12 27.1	29 0.2	10 41.8	19 5.4
25 Tu	16 16 4	2 47 31	17 5 24	24 39 7	20 27.1	19 42.1	28 4.7	18 25.0	16 31.7	12 23.9	29 1.1	10 42.9	19 7.6
26 W	16 20 1	3 48 14	2♑ 9 20	9♑35 1	20 25.5	21 8.5	29 19.2	18 56.1	16 38.5	12 20.7	29 2.0	10 44.0	19 9.8
27 Th	16 23 58	4 48 58	16 55 19	24 9 35	20 23.7	22 34.2	0♑33.7	19 27.3	16 45.2	12 17.3	29 2.9	10 45.1	19 12.0
28 F	16 27 54	5 49 44	1♒17 18	8♒18 11	20 21.9	23 59.2	1 48.2	19 58.8	16 51.7	12 13.9	29 3.9	10 46.3	19 14.2
29 Sa	16 31 51	6 50 30	15 12 7	21 59 8	20 20.6	25 23.2	3 2.7	20 30.5	16 58.0	12 10.4	29 5.0	10 47.6	19 16.5
30 Su	16 35 47	7 51 17	28 39 24	5♓13 12	20D 20.0	26 46.2	4 17.1	21 2.5	17 4.2	12 6.9	29 6.0	10 48.8	19 18.7

Longitude

December 2003

Day	Sid.Time	☉	0 hr ☽	Noon ☽	True ☊	☿	♀	♂	♃	♄	♅	♆	♇
1 M	16 39 44	8♐52 5	11♓40 57	18♓ 3 3	20♉20.3	28♐ 7.9	5♑31.5	21♓34.6	17♍10.3	12♋ 3.2	29♒ 7.2	10♒50.1	19♐21.0
2 Tu	16 43 40	9 52 54	24 20 3	0♈32 26	20 21.3	29 28.3	6 46.0	22 7.0	17 16.2	11R 59.5	29 8.4	10 51.4	19 23.2
3 W	16 47 37	10 53 43	6♈40 46	12 45 34	20 22.8	0♑47.1	8 0.4	22 39.5	17 21.9	11 55.6	29 9.6	10 52.7	19 25.5
4 Th	16 51 33	11 54 34	18 47 24	24 46 44	20 24.5	2 4.1	9 14.8	23 12.2	17 27.5	11 51.8	29 10.9	10 54.1	19 27.7
5 F	16 55 30	12 55 26	0♉44 6	6♉39 55	20 26.0	3 18.9	10 29.2	23 45.2	17 32.9	11 47.8	29 12.2	10 55.5	19 30.0
6 Sa	16 59 27	13 56 18	12 34 39	18 28 41	20R 26.7	4 31.3	11 43.5	24 18.3	17 38.2	11 43.8	29 13.6	10 56.9	19 32.3
7 Su	17 3 23	14 57 12	24 22 22	0♊16 3	20 26.3	5 40.9	12 57.9	24 51.5	17 43.3	11 39.7	29 15.1	10 58.3	19 34.5
8 M	17 7 20	15 58 6	6♊10 1	12 4 34	20 24.5	6 47.2	14 12.2	25 25.0	17 48.2	11 35.5	29 16.5	10 59.8	19 36.8
9 Tu	17 11 16	16 59 2	17 59 56	23 56 21	20 21.4	7 49.7	15 26.5	25 58.6	17 53.0	11 31.3	29 18.1	11 1.3	19 39.1
10 W	17 15 13	17 59 58	29 54 4	5♋53 16	20 17.1	8 47.9	16 40.8	26 32.3	17 57.6	11 27.0	29 19.6	11 2.8	19 41.4
11 Th	17 19 9	19 0 56	11♋54 12	17 57 3	20 12.0	9 41.2	17 55.1	27 6.2	18 2.0	11 22.7	29 21.3	11 4.4	19 43.6
12 F	17 23 6	20 1 54	24 2 4	0♌ 9 29	20 6.6	10 28.8	19 9.3	27 40.3	18 6.3	11 18.3	29 22.9	11 5.9	19 45.9
13 Sa	17 27 3	21 2 54	6♌19 33	12 32 33	20 1.5	11 10.0	20 23.6	28 14.5	18 10.4	11 13.9	29 24.6	11 7.5	19 48.2
14 Su	17 30 59	22 3 54	18 48 45	25 8 30	19 57.4	11 43.9	21 37.8	28 48.8	18 14.3	11 9.4	29 26.4	11 9.2	19 50.5
15 M	17 34 56	23 4 56	1♍32 6	7♍59 53	19 54.7	12 9.8	22 52.0	29 23.3	18 18.1	11 4.8	29 28.2	11 10.8	19 52.8
16 Tu	17 38 52	24 5 58	14 32 13	21 9 23	19D 53.6	12 26.6	24 6.2	29 58.0	18 21.6	11 0.2	29 30.0	11 12.5	19 55.0
17 W	17 42 49	25 7 1	27 51 43	4♎39 29	19 53.9	12R 33.6	25 20.3	0♈32.7	18 25.0	10 55.6	29 31.9	11 14.2	19 57.3
18 Th	17 46 45	26 8 6	11♎32 53	18 32 3	19 55.2	12 30.0	26 34.5	1 7.6	18 28.2	10 50.9	29 33.9	11 15.9	19 59.6
19 F	17 50 42	27 9 11	25 36 59	2♏47 37	19 56.7	12 15.1	27 48.6	1 42.6	18 31.3	10 46.2	29 35.8	11 17.6	20 1.8
20 Sa	17 54 38	28 10 17	10♏ 3 41	17 24 47	19R 57.6	11 48.5	29 2.7	2 17.7	18 34.1	10 41.4	29 37.8	11 19.4	20 4.1
21 Su	17 58 35	29 11 24	24 50 21	2♐19 37	19 57.0	11 10.3	0♒16.8	2 53.0	18 36.8	10 36.6	29 39.9	11 21.2	20 6.4
22 M	18 2 32	0♑12 32	9♐51 40	17 25 27	19 54.5	10 20.8	1 30.9	3 28.4	18 39.3	10 31.8	29 42.0	11 23.0	20 8.6
23 Tu	18 6 28	1 13 40	24 59 47	2♑33 26	19 50.0	9 21.0	2 44.9	4 3.9	18 41.5	10 27.0	29 44.2	11 24.8	20 10.9
24 W	18 10 25	2 14 49	10♑ 5 10	17 33 45	19 43.7	8 12.1	3 58.9	4 39.5	18 43.7	10 22.1	29 46.3	11 26.7	20 13.1
25 Th	18 14 21	3 15 58	24 58 5	2♒17 11	19 36.6	6 56.3	5 12.9	5 15.3	18 45.6	10 17.2	29 48.6	11 28.6	20 15.4
26 F	18 18 18	4 17 7	9♒30 14	16 36 37	19 29.5	5 36.0	6 26.8	5 51.1	18 47.3	10 12.3	29 50.8	11 30.5	20 17.6
27 Sa	18 22 14	5 18 16	23 35 56	0♓27 57	19 23.3	4 13.7	7 40.8	6 27.0	18 48.8	10 7.4	29 53.1	11 32.4	20 19.8
28 Su	18 26 11	6 19 26	7♓12 40	13 50 14	19 18.8	2 52.3	8 54.6	7 3.1	18 50.2	10 2.5	29 55.5	11 34.3	20 22.0
29 M	18 30 7	7 20 35	20 20 56	26 45 10	19 16.2	1 34.3	10 8.5	7 39.2	18 51.3	9 57.5	29 57.9	11 36.3	20 24.2
30 Tu	18 34 4	8 21 44	3♈ 3 27	9♈16 22	19D 15.5	0 22.1	11 22.3	8 15.4	18 52.3	9 52.6	0♓ 0.3	11 38.2	20 26.4
31 W	18 38 1	9 22 53	15 24 33	21 28 37	19 16.2	29♐17.6	12 36.0	8 51.8	18 53.0	9 47.6	0 2.7	11 40.2	20 28.6

*Giving the positions of planets daily at noon, in LONGITUDE Greenwich Mean Time

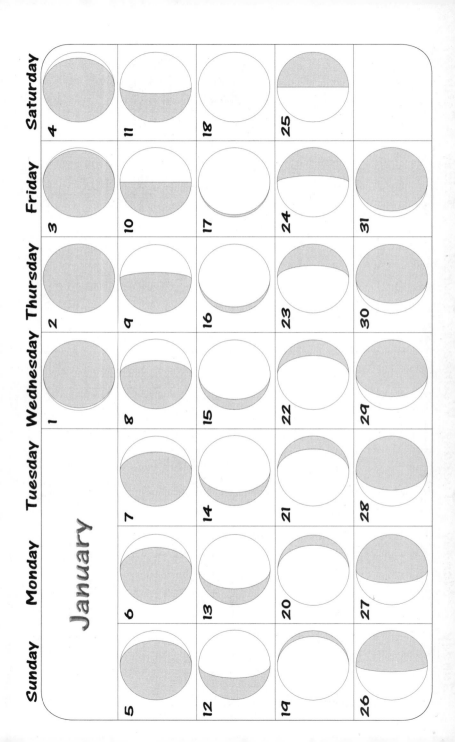

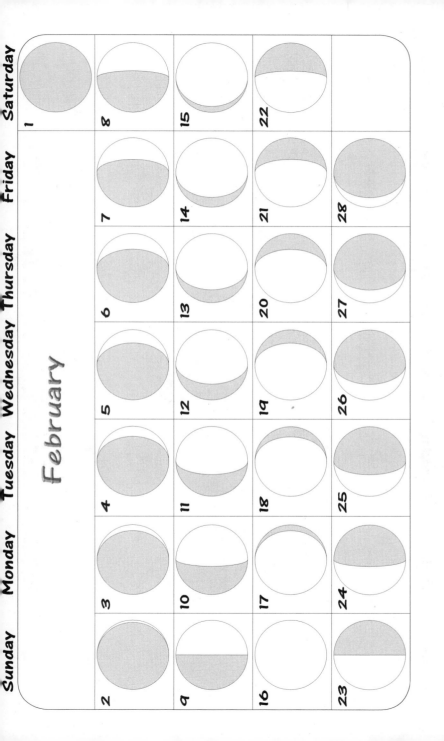

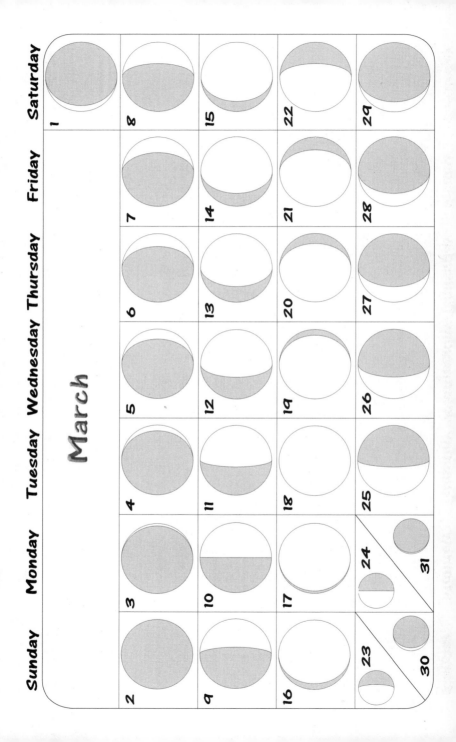

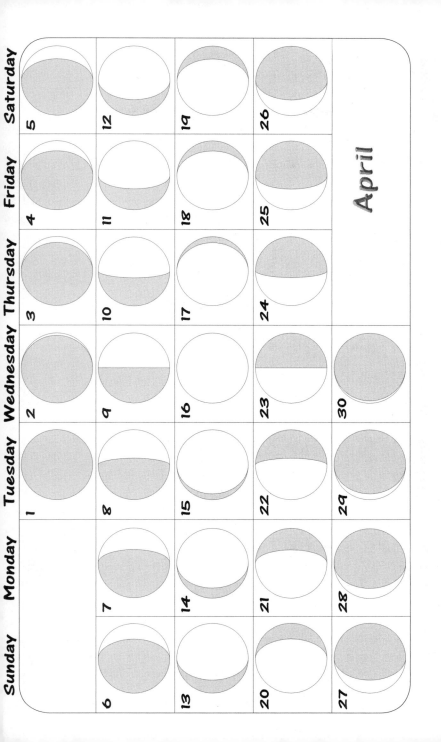

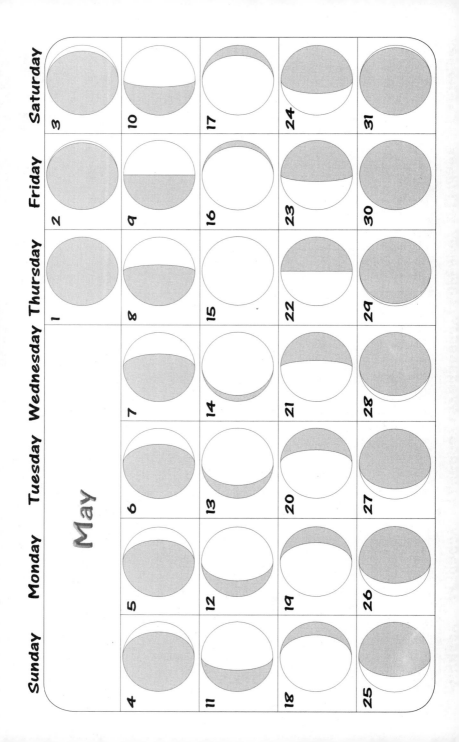

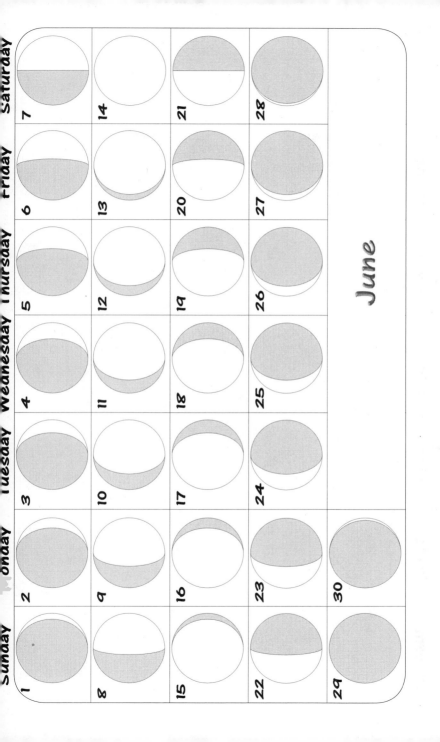

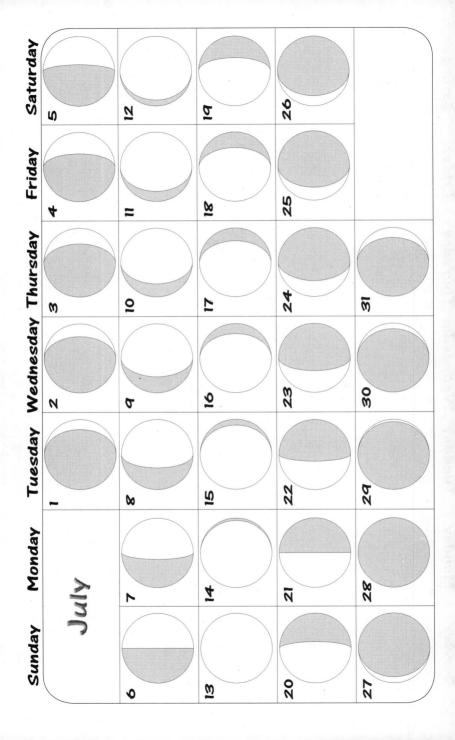

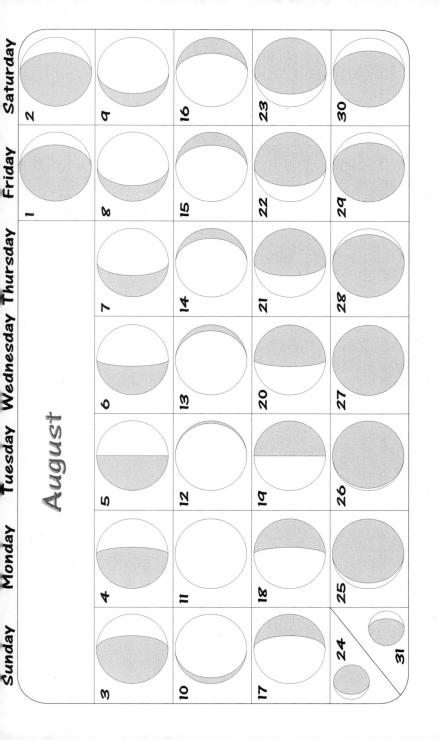

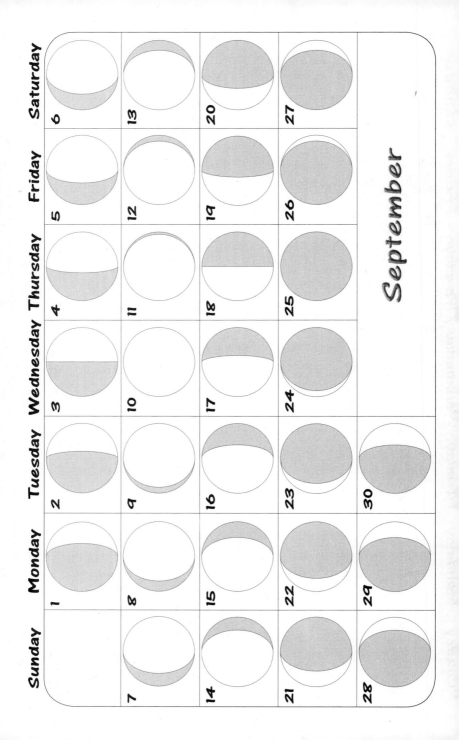

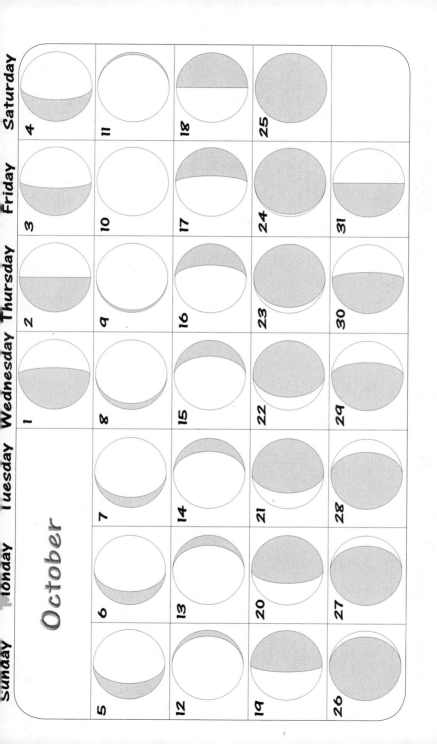

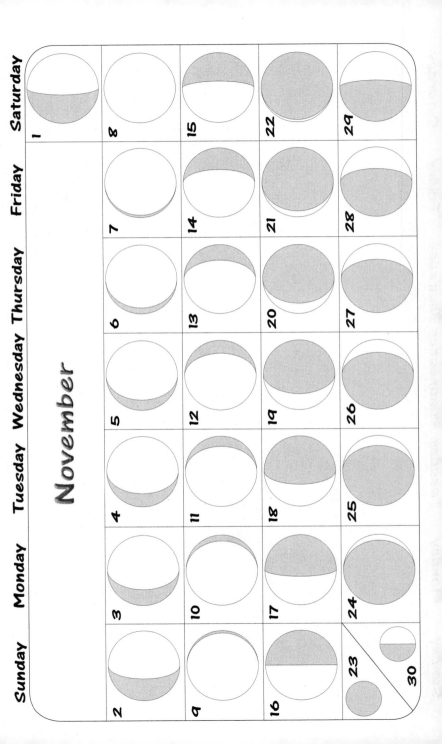

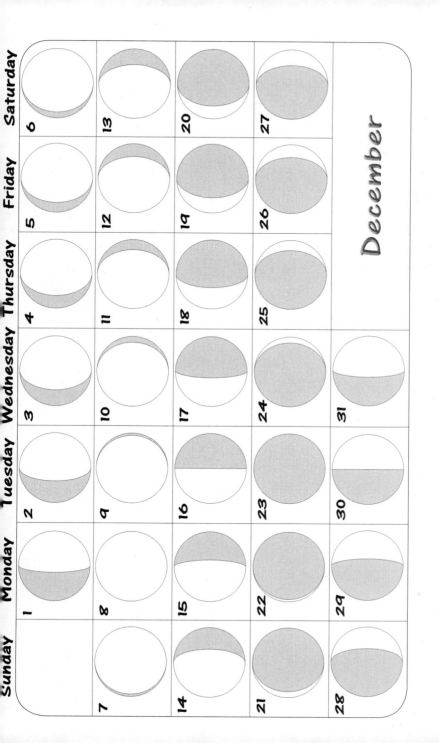

December

Sunday	Monday	Tuesday	Wednesday	Thursday	Friday	Saturday
	1	2	3	4	5	6
7	8	9	10	11	12	13
14	15	16	17	18	19	20
21	22	23	24	25	26	27
28	29	30	31			

FGHIJ

KLMNO

PQRST

UVWXYZ

WORLD TIME ZONES

ID LW	NT BT	CA HT	YST	PST	MST	CST	EST	AST	BST	AT	WAT	GMT	CET	EET	BT	USSR Z3	USSR Z4	USSR Z5	SST	CCT	JST	GST	USSR Z10	ID LE
-12	-11	-10	-9	-8	-7	-6	-5	-4	-3	-2	-1	0	+1	+2	+3	+4	+5	+6	+7	+8	+9	+10	+11	+12
-4	-3	-2	-1	0	+1	+2	+3	+4	+5	+6	+7	+8	+9	+10	+11	+12	+13	+14	+15	+16	+17	+18	+19	+20

STANDARD TIME ZONES FROM WEST TO EAST CALCULATED FROM PST AS ZERO POINT:

IDLW:	International Date Line West	-4
NT/BT:	Nome Time/Bering Time	-3
CA/HT:	Central Alaska & Hawaiian Time	-2
YST:	Yukon Standard Time	-1
PST:	Pacific Standard Time	0
MST:	Mountain Standard Time	+1
CST:	Central Standard Time	+2
EST:	Eastern Standard Time	+3
AST:	Atlantic Standard Time	+4
NFT:	Newfoundland Time	+4 1/2
BST:	Brazil Standard Time	+5
AT:	Azores Time	+6
WAT:	West African Time	+7
GMT:	Greenwich Mean Time	+8
WET:	Western European Time (England)	+8
CET:	Central European Time	+9
EET:	Eastern European Time	+10
BT:	Bagdhad Time	+11
IT:	Iran Time	+11 1/2
USSR	Zone 3	+12
USSR	Zone 4	+13
IST:	Indian Standard Time	+13 1/2
USSR	Zone 5	+14
NST:	North Sumatra Time	+14 1/2
SST:	South Sumatra Time & USSR Zone 6	+15
JT:	Java Time	+15 1/2
CCT:	China Coast Time	+16
MT:	Moluccas Time	+16 1/2
JST:	Japanese Standard Time	+17
SAST:	South Australian Standard Time	+17 1/2
GST:	Guam Standard Time	+18
USSR	Zone 10	+19
IDLE:	International Date Line East	+20

HOW TO CALCULATE TIME ZONE CORRECTIONS IN YOUR AREA:

ADD to the listed times if you are **east** of PST (Pacific Standard Time); SUBTRACT if you are **west** of PST on this map (see right-hand column of chart above).

All times in this calendar are calculated from the West Coast of North America where it is made. Pacific Standard Time (PST Zone 8) is zero point for this calendar except during Daylight Savings Time (April 6–October 26, 2003 during which times are given for PDT Zone 7). If your time zone does not use Daylight Savings Time, add one hour to the standard correction during this time. At the bottom of each page EST/EDT (Eastern Standard or Daylight Time) and GMT (Greenwich Mean Time) times are also given. For all other time zones, calculate your time zone correction(s) from this map and write it on the inside cover for easy reference.

SIGNS AND SYMBOLS AT A GLANCE

PLANETS

Personal Planets are closest to Earth.

⊙ **Sun**: self radiating outward, character, ego
☽ **Moon**: inward sense of self, emotions, psyche
☿ **Mercury**: communication, travel, thought
♀ **Venus**: relationship, love, sense of beauty, empathy
♂ **Mars**: will to act, initiative, ambition

Asteroids are between Mars and Jupiter and reflect the awakening of feminine-defined energy centers in human consciousness. See "Asteroids" (p.199).

Social Planets are between personal and outer planets.

♃ **Jupiter**: expansion, opportunities, leadership
♄ **Saturn**: limits, structure, discipline
Note: the seven days of the week are named after the above seven heavenly bodies.

⚷ **Chiron**: is a small planetary body between Saturn and Uranus representing the wounded healer.

Transpersonal Planets are the outer planets.

♅ **Uranus**: cosmic consciousness, revolutionary change
♆ **Neptune**: spiritual awakening, cosmic love, all one
♇ **Pluto**: death and rebirth, deep, total change

ZODIAC SIGNS

♈	Aries
♉	Taurus
♊	Gemini
♋	Cancer
♌	Leo
♍	Virgo
♎	Libra
♏	Scorpio
♐	Sagittarius
♑	Capricorn
♒	Aquarius
♓	Pisces

ASPECTS

Aspects show the angle between planets; this informs how the planets influence each other and us. **We'Moon** lists only significant aspects:

♂ CONJUNCTION (planets are 0–5° apart)
   linked together, energy of aspected planets is mutually enhancing
✶ SEXTILE (planets are 60° apart)
   cooperative, energies of this aspect blend well
□ SQUARE (planets are 90° apart)
   challenging, energies of this aspect are different from each other
△ TRINE (planets are 120° apart)
   harmonizing, energies of this aspect are in the same element
☍ OPPOSITION (planets are 180° apart)
   polarizing or complementing, energies are diametrically opposite
⚻ QUINCUNX (planets are 150° apart)
   variable, energies of this aspect combine contrary elements

OTHER SYMBOLS

☽ **v/c**: Moon is void of course from last lunar aspect till it enters new sign.
ApG–Apogee: Point in the orbit of a planet that's farthest from Earth.
PrG–Perigee: Point in the orbit of a planet that's nearest to Earth.
D or R–Direct or Retrograde: Describes when a planet moves forward (D) through the zodiac or appears to move backward (R).